Introduction to Media Studies

Eckart Voigts-Virchow

Ernst Klett Sprachen
Barcelona · Belgrad · Budapest · Ljubljana · London
Posen · Prag · Sofia · Stuttgart · Zagreb

Bibliographische Information der Deutschen Bibliothek.
Die Deutsche Bibliothek verzeichnet diese Publikation in der
Deutschen Nationalbibliographie; detaillierte bibliographische
Daten sind im Internet über http://dnb.ddb.de abrufbar.

1. Auflage 1 $^{5\,4\,3\,2\,1}$ | 2008 2007 2006 2005
© Ernst Klett Sprachen GmbH, Stuttgart 2005. Alle Rechte vorbehalten.
Das Werk und seine Teile sind urheberrechtlich geschützt.
Jede Nutzung in anderen als den gesetzlichen Fällen bedarf der vorherigen schrift-
lichen Einwilligung des Verlages. Hinweis zu § 52 a UrhG: Weder das Werk noch
seine Teile dürfen ohne eine solche Einwilligung eingescannt und in ein Netzwerk
eingestellt werden. Dies gilt auch für Intranets von Schulen und sonstigen
Bildungseinrichtungen.
Internetadresse | http://www.klett.de
Bildnachweis | Corbis/Bettmann, Düsseldorf
Redaktion | Natalie Voss
Satz | media office gmbh, Kornwestheim
Druck | Ludwig Auer GmbH, Donauwörth. Printed in Germany.
ISBN 3-12-939612-8

Contents

Acknowledgements

I am grateful to the series editor, Ansgar Nünning, for his encouragement, his unflinching support of the project, and his generous editorial advice. I am also indebted to Sean Nowak for invaluable editorial comment on early drafts of this book. Further thanks are due to Nadja Majid for compiling data on media courses in German *Anglistik*, and to the students in my classes at the Universities of Giessen and Vienna. Finally, the book would not have been possible without the commitment of the Klett Verlag and, in particular, my supportive and patient liaison there, Natalie Voss.

A basic outline of media studies

CHAPTER

1 Preface – Why media studies?

The great thing about writing on the media is that it means writing on everything: religion, music, literature, politics, sex, money, art, technology, business, food and gardening. JAMES PONIEWOZIK (1999)

This book must start from stating the obvious, which in fact, ASKEW (2002: 1) has called "a truism-*cum*-platitude". We live in a thoroughly 'mediatized' world, a social and cultural environment which is permeated by the media, and, more specifically, electronic media. More than one key text in media studies starts from this premise: "Whatever we know about our society or the world in which we live, we know it from the mass media" is NIKLAS LUHMANN's first sentence in *Die Realität der Massenmedien* (1996: 9), and JAN & ALEIDA ASSMANN (1990: 2) echo: "Everything that can be known, thought, and said about the world, is knowable, thinkable and sayable only in relation to the media that communicate this knowledge" (my translations). If this is indeed so, then media studies belong in the very core of any curriculum.

The world as media world

The media penetrate our business as well as our leisure activities; they pervade politics as well as art. One might declare that the media determine how we think, that they control what appears to us as 'real'. The media are powerful, because they shape our opinions and because they are a huge global industry. We regularly communicate beyond the conditions of bodily presence. One might say that the media organize absence, expanding and manipulating the continuum of space and time. Books put us in touch with the thoughts of PLATO and ARISTOTLE; via mobile phone we talk to a friend in Australia while we ride a train; at our office computers we write essays or fake identities in chats with strangers; we go for a walk, listening to music on the MP3 player; we watch the Olympic Games and the fall of the Twin Towers on TV; we listen to the traffic news on the radio; we write e-mails to colleagues and tutors; we meet in a café or in 'blogosphere' (blog = web log, a list of chronological entries on a given topic) to talk about the movie we have just watched in the multiplex.

Mediatized society

Media studies are driven by the dynamics in media usage and media technologies; there is an in-built, automatic obsolescence. The media survey by FAULSTICH, for instance, had to change dramatically from the first (1994) to the fifth edition, which addresses chats, intranet, WWW, cell-phones, e-mail etc. (2004). This, how-

Dynamic media usage

ever, may be an institutional advantage; permanent media change requires the permanent change of media studies. In fact, it might be useful to pause for a moment and consider your own current media usage: What do you read? How and when do you read? How do you use your computer and the Internet? What films have you seen recently? Do you use VCR (video-cassette recorder) or DVD (digital video or versatile disk)? Do you use cable or satellite or terrestrial TV? When do you tune in to the radio and which are your favourite channels? What kind of telephone do you use and how do you listen to music? How much time do you spend on these media – and how much money? Then pause another second to think about how your fellow students from the US, Iran, India, China or Poland use their media (synchronic comparison), or for that matter, your parents and grandparents used theirs (diachronic comparison). In an instant, it will become clear that, under the conditions of perpetual media accessibility, human existence has changed dramatically, tapping into new potentials, but also creating permanent instability.

2 The expansion of media studies

By giving us the opinions of the uneducated, [journalism] keeps us in touch with the ignorance of the community OSCAR WILDE

Size matters: Expansion

Small wonder, then, that in view of the intensified media awareness the subject of media studies is *en vogue*: In the USA, enrolment in "communication studies" has been growing exponentially since the 1960s, particularly at undergraduate level. According to the US Digest of Education Statistics, almost 60,000 students took a B.A. and 5,800 an M.A. in communication studies in 2002 – a significant increase all through the 1990s. According to the US National Communication Association (NCA), nearly 1,250 institutions offer programmes in "communications" (about 70 in Germany and the UK). Many rivalling media-studies associations and competing media-studies journals people the English-speaking academic world. In Britain, enrolment in media studies went up by 40% between 1994/95 and 1998/99 according to the *Media Guardian*. Nearly 40,000 students took a media degree at GCSE level and 23,000 at A-level in 2004 (only about 6,000 took German), yet another substantial rise from the 9.5% increase in 2003 (CURTIS 2003, WARD 2004, MCLEOD 2005). In comparison to Britain and the US, communication and media studies have not made enough headway into German schools and universities. CURTIS (2003), however, also reports on the closure of the renowned communications and cultural-studies department at Birmingham in

2002 and the imminent shutdown of the media-studies department at Leicester.

The language of global media is English, and the USA (and, to a smaller extent, Britain) shape the cultural practice of the global media, for better or for worse. Even a haphazard list of recent German media careers testifies to the dominance of English: "Screen-Designer", "Online-Producer", "New Media Consultant", "Film- und Video-Producer", "Informationsbroker", "Storyliner", "Consultant", "Scout" (for these career opportunities, see NAUMANN 1999; an up-to-date study guide in German journalism, communication and media studies is GAVIN-KRAMER 2003). It follows that a combination of English and American Studies and media studies seems an excellent career move for German students. While there is a consensus, however, that media studies are relevant, they are also perilously heterogeneous and there is little agreement as to what should be the prime object of media studies or its preferred method. Emerging media-studies departments in Britain and the USA have been founded on the premise that the increasing economic importance of the media industries will continue to provide attractive communication and media-related careers – and therefore there is strong pressure on departments in these areas to move towards practical skills and empirical work and away from abstraction and critical theory.

> **Media careers**

The fact that the dominant global media corporations are based in the English-speaking west, the US and – to a lesser extent – in Britain goes some way to explain the fundamental distinction between (vocational, empiricist) Anglo-American and (hermeneutical, idealist) European media studies. Vocational training seeks to prepare students specifically for media careers, often in non-academic professions. Traditionally, there has been a rift between hermeneutical, text-orientated (qualitative) approaches and statistical (quantitative) approaches. Do we need to read and criticize texts (hermeneutics) or should we teach skills and gather data (statistics)? In the programme of the 2003 conference of the Media, Communications, and Cultural Studies Association (MeCCSA), CHRISTINE GERAGHTY paints a bleak picture:

> **Vocational training**

As a relatively new discipline which runs across the creative arts/humanities/social sciences boundaries we sometimes feel more buffeted than most. One example of this is the functionalist drive in the government which seems to lean towards a crude vocationalism in higher education.

GERAGHTY deplores "*a narrow definition of graduate skills*" and a 'dumbing down' in the academic book market with an emphasis on textbooks and a reluctance to publish original research. A new version of the "*ritual attack*" (G. TURNER 2003: 73) on Amer-

> **Communication vs. media studies**

ican communication studies can be found in GAUNTLETT / HORSLEY (2004). In his introduction, DAVID GAUNTLETT polemically complains about *"pointlessly contrived 'readings' of media texts, an inability to identify the real impact of the media, and a black hole left by the total failure of vacuous US-style 'communications science' quantitative research, which remained unfilled due to a corresponding absence of much imaginative qualitative research."* Often the dividing line is in the name; there is research in journalism, sociology, psychology, linguistics and business that designates itself communication studies on the one hand – and there is interest in aesthetics, poetics, cultures, textual readings and representation that prefers the term media studies on the other hand.

'Dumbing down'

Both methodological anarchy and the conflation of popular culture and media culture have probably contributed to earning the subject the infamous reputation of awarding 'Mickey Mouse' degrees for analysing the phatic communication (i.e., chit-chat) of 'mere' images and media babble (see STANITZEK 2001). 70% of British media teachers think that their colleagues hold the subject in low esteem, while 92% maintain that it is highly regarded by students (McLEOD 2005). The media were equated with mass culture. The influence of communication studies in the US, empiricist traditions, the semiotic expansion of the scope for interpretation and narrative analysis, the revaluation of working-class culture in British cultural studies and the rapid integration of media studies into schools at A and AS levels in Britain have fostered the idea that media studies often address the commonplace, pedestrian, mundane and banal. In this situation, a vocational approach promises jobs, whereas the concentration on digital *avant-garde* art avoids mass phenomena, and rigorous empiricism pre-empts accusations of relativism. Without a doubt, however, one can (and must) read computer games or reality TV – currently the low ends in the cultural hierarchy of media products, but nevertheless crucial and important media practices – in a sophisticated manner.

Media studies in Germany

In this respect, cultural-studies approaches with an exclusive focus on new media technologies and popular culture may profit from indigenous German experience (in spite of their appeal and success). Media studies have become part of the curricula at German universities; they are, however, still located somewhat uneasily at the crossroads of communication studies, journalism, social sciences, psychology, linguistics, literary studies, performance studies, and art. It is interesting to note that the institutional development of media studies in Germany has led to structures that are to some extent reminiscent of the precarious status of the field in the English-language world. At the risk of oversimplification, one may see four strands:

CHAPTER **1** A basic outline of media studies

(1) Sociology and communication studies have been largely inspired by the post-war communication studies in the US (McQUAIL 2000) which have had a global impact.

(2) With some delay, German media studies have been stimulated by British cultural studies, beginning in the 1950s as part of the cultural and semiotic turn in British Studies by RICHARD HOGGART (*1918) and STUART HALL (*1932). These complemented approaches from the so-called Frankfurt School, the Critical Theory of WALTER BENJAMIN (1892–1940), THEODOR W. ADORNO (1903–1969), MAX HORKHEIMER (1895–1973).

(3) There is an indigenous European tradition of media studies embedded within the field of Humanities. In Germany, media studies are situated either at German-studies or theatre-studies institutes ("Theater-, Film- und Fernsehwissenschaft" or "Drama, Theater, Medien"). Inspired by H. MARSHALL MCLUHAN (1911–1980), this approach has spread on the European mainland through the work of VILÉM FLUSSER (1920–1991), PAUL VIRILIO (*1932), FRIEDRICH KITTLER (*1943), and RÉGIS DEBRAY (*1940), who called his hybrid mix of philosophy, technology, culture and media studies "médiologie" (DEBRAY 2003, HARTMANN 2003). Since the 1980s, concerns of art and art history have merged with cultural studies in the field of visual culture (W. J. T. MITCHELL, NICHOLAS MIRZOEFF, HANS BELTING, GOTTFRIED BÖHM).

(4) Finally, systems theory in the vein of NIKLAS LUHMANN (1927–1998) has inspired a new approach to media studies in the 1990s for which SIEGFRIED J. SCHMIDT (2003: 353) has coined the term *Medienkulturwissenschaft*. It seeks to overcome boundaries between the study of individual media or media genres or cultural phenomena. SCHMIDT seeks to integrate seemingly incompatible approaches such as communication studies and media theory. For SCHMIDT, culture is a meaning-making programme that models reality, and the media generate and shape the public spheres for these cultures.

A number of recent research training groups ("Graduiertenkollegs") and special centres of research ("Sonderforschungsbereiche") at German universities offer the chance to foster the co-operation of English studies with media studies, German studies and other disciplines:

- "Literature and Anthropology" (Constance), with ALEIDA ASSMANN's project on writing, the body and media anthropology, and JOACHIM PAECH's work on media and cultural identity
- "Performativity and Culture" (Berlin, ERIKA FISCHER-LICHTE), with SYBILLE KRÄMER's research team on media and MANFRED PFISTER's project on theatre and media in early modern England

Trans-disciplinary research

- "Media Upheavals" (Siegen), guided by RALF SCHNELL, PETER GENDOLLA and others, which examines sea changes and breakthroughs with a focus on 21st-century digital media
- "Media and Cultural Communication" (Cologne, LUDWIG JÄGER, networking with Aachen, Bonn, and Bochum), with various projects on mediality, gender, new media and film by IRMELA SCHNEIDER, WOLFGANG BEILENHOFF, WILHELM VOSSKAMP, JÜRGEN FOHRMANN and others
- "The Experience of War" (Tübingen), with BARBARA KORTE and RALF SCHNEIDER's work on the mediatization of war in Britain
- "Knowledge Acquisition and Knowledge Exchange with New Media" (a virtual PhD programme)
- "Aesthetic Perception and the Experience of Time" (Frankfurt/Main), headed by HANS-THIES LEHMANN
- "Image, Body, Medium" in the context of the *Hochschule für Gestaltung* which addresses visual studies, led by HANS BELTING and BEAT WYSS (Karlsruhe) – the Centre for Art and Media (ZKM, PETER WEIBEL) which spearheaded investigations of new media art is also located in Karlsruhe
- "Media Changes and the Encoding of Violence" (Berlin, KLAUS R. SCHERPE, THOMAS MACHO)
- "Cultural Hermeneutics of Difference and Transdifference", with contributions from English studies (DORIS FELDMANN), Canadian studies (DIETER MEINDL) and American studies (HELMBRECHT BREINIG and KLAUS LÖSCH)
- "Cultures of Mendacity", which has obviously to do with the media (Regensburg, JOCHEN MECKE)
- "Transnational Media Events"/"Centre for Media and Interactivity" (ZMI, CLAUS LEGGEWIE) both located at Giessen and teaming up with other related projects ("Cultures of Memory", "Graduate Centre for Cultural Studies", ANSGAR NÜNNING)
- "Media Historiographies" at the Bauhaus University, Weimar (JOSEPH VOGL)
- "Centre for Interdisciplinary Media Studies" (ZIM, HELMUT KORTE, Göttingen)

Modular English studies and media studies in Germany

This is the first introduction to media studies that directly addresses the context of German *Anglistik*. In the face of the blatant Anglo-American domination of the global media, it is long overdue. It is also overdue because the redefinition of German studies in the 1970s and 1980s achieved by HELMUT KREUZER, HELMUT SCHANZE, KNUT HICKETHIER, FRIEDRICH KNILLI, SIEGFRIED J. SCHMIDT, KARL PRÜMM and others (see VIEHOFF 2002, SCHMIDT 2003, SCHNELL 2003) was only half-heartedly embraced by German *Anglistik*. When media studies emerged in the 1970s, it ploughed a field which was already taken care of by journalism and sociology. It was only when the field was redefined under the influence of cultural studies in the late 1980s, however, that media studies fully arrived in German *Anglistik*, beyond the mere re-labelling as "screen philologies" – a debate between WILHELM VOSSKAMP and SCHMIDT (2003: 252), continued in the contributions collected in SCHNELL (2003).

The scope of this book encompasses at least six of the 'turns' that have been designated as paradigm shifts in the humanities (cultural, communicative, visual, intermedial, performative, digital). Gradually, English studies in Germany are picking up the call for interdisciplinary and intercultural approaches. They expand and redefine themselves towards an integrated study of media cultures (FOLTINEK / LEITGEB 2002, E. KLEIN et al. 2000, NÜNNING / JUCKER 1999: 93–94, see also KORTE / MÜLLER 1995). A brief look at the curricula in English departments in Germany, however, exposes the sad fact that media studies have not been fully absorbed into English studies in Germany. Although the number of media-related courses is rising, they continue to be appendixed with some uneasiness to the modules of literary studies, cultural (area) studies, linguistics and English as a foreign language (EFL). It is my hope that this book will help stimulate a more comprehensive and less blinkered approach to media studies.

Media studies in a modular future

Most of the recent introductions to literary studies used in English departments in Germany have featured chapters on the media or at least on film (SCHNEIDER 2004, NÜNNING / NÜNNING 2001, BÖKER / HOUSWITSCHKA 2000, KLARER 1998). The introduction by NÜNNING / NÜNNING (2001), for instance, has a full chapter on media genres, covering film, TV, and radio plays. HANS-PETER WAGNER's *History of British, Irish and American Literature* (2003) defines literature as an iconotext in which word and image are mutually interdependent. WAGNER provides a wealth of accompanying visual material. A new textbook splits the object of literary studies into oral, written, and audiovisual literature (MEYER 2004: 8–9). In literary media studies (often defined as *Medienkunde*, aiming for media literacy) one finds a clear emphasis on adaptation studies of text transfers, hermeneutic-aesthetic readings or textual and narratological analysis of films, with seemingly innocent conjunctions such as "Literature through Film", "Film from Fiction", "Text and Film" or "Page to Screen" and courses devoted to individual *auteurs* such as DAVID LYNCH or ALFRED HITCHCOCK, to "Performance on Stage and Screen", SHAKESPEARE movies or heritage adaptations from E. M. FORSTER or JANE AUSTEN. Obviously, the discreet 'artworks' of 'authored' film can be integrated relatively smoothly into literary

(1) Literary studies

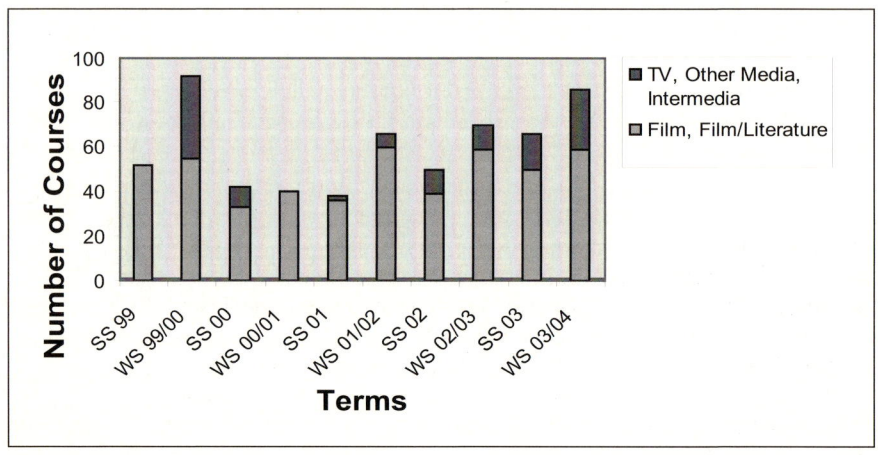

Fig. 1: Media-related courses in English Literary and Cultural Studies
(in Austria, Germany, and Switzerland, according to AREAS)

methodologies (and, unlike TV or radio, find their way into intro-ductions to literary studies, see STERNBERG 2004). In Britain, a recent overview suggests, film studies is *"linked to more established aca-demic subjects such as English literature, and is more like literary study in its approach."* (MCLEOD 2005). This is supported by our survey on media-related courses in English Literary and Cultural Studies in Germany (see fig. 1). One may also note, however, recent forays into TV, audiobooks or hypertext literature. The adaptationist con-cerns seem to merge gradually into a wider approach reflected in the term "intermediality".

Increasing diversi-fication

A number of recent publications mark this departure in Eng-lish/American literature departments at German universities: Beginnings, with a focus on film and literature, may be found in GRABES 1980, STRATMANN et al. 1988, and WEBER/FRIEDL 1988. Since then, the field has diversified: GOETSCH/SCHEUNEMANN 1997, PET-ZOLD 1996, DREXLER 1998, and HELBIG 1999 continue the work on film. Television (and under the influence of cultural studies, spe-cifically, soap opera) has been addressed from various viewpoints by SEITER et al. 1989, FREY-VOR 1991, KREUTZNER 1992, LUDWIG et al. 1992, BORCHERS et al. 1994, VOIGTS-VIRCHOW 1995, and SCHLAEGER 1997. Subsequently, a number of approaches have addressed media hybridity (STERNBERG 1997 on screenplays, GRIEM 1997 on 'screen media', VOIGTS-VIRCHOW 2000 on theatre and media, PFEIFFER 1999 on media anthropology, KREWANI 2001 on TV and film hybridity, NÜNNING/NÜNNING 2002 on media and narrato-logy, WOLF 1999, HELBIG 1998, MOSTHAF 2000, BROSCH 2000, KLARER

2001 on intermediality and text-sound-image relations, KEITEL et al. 1999–2003 on new media). Unlike analyses of (ephemeral) broadcast television or theatre, the emanations of a global entertainment industry spread transnationally, so that the burgeoning field of heritage films and SHAKESPEARE films is readily accessible to German research, for instance, by HABICHT / KLOTZ 1993, DREXLER / GUNTNER 1995, WEISS 1999, SCHMIDT 2001, SUNARA 2004, BRUSBERG-KIERMEIER / HELBIG 2004, VOIGTS-VIRCHOW 2004).

The cultural-studies modules of English and American studies in recent years have comprised courses, for instance, on documentary film, Hollywood cinema, postcolonial, Scottish, Canadian, Irish or Australian film, working-class film, James Bond, and occasionally have even gone beyond film and addressed television soap operas or sitcoms. The scope reflects the expansion of English studies after the cultural turn as it has been charted in BASSNETT (1997), HEPP (1999), TURNER (2003) or SOMMER (2003: 53–63). English studies in Germany have thus come to cover mass media products in the entire Anglosphere or "Terranglia" (HORST PRIESS-NITZ). In view of the fact that cultural studies, media studies and communication studies have been cross-fertilizing each other for some years (for the German situation, see HEPP 1999: 105–107), it is high time that they should be fully absorbed into English and American studies in Germany. Overcoming geographical distance, online media promise ready access to cultural materials for what has been termed "cyberspace ethnography" (BERNARDI 1998: 155).

(2) Cultural and media studies

In linguistics there has been a long tradition of incorporating new media into the curriculum. In Germany, for instance, there are about twenty departments of computational linguistics. Textbooks come on CD-ROM, such as JÜRGEN HANDKE's Interactive Introduction to Linguistics (2001) or as combined media (HANDKE 2000, KORT-MANN / SCHNEIDER 2004). There are several Internet grammars of English (University College London; Chemnitz University, JOSEF SCHMIED). A number of projects are devoted to online language learning (Virtual Linguistics Campus, HANDKE; PortaLingua, SCHMITZ 2004) and the HUMANIST discussion group has been active since 1987. There is an emphasis on analysing speech, natural-dialogue systems, machine translation, text and hypertext analysis. Online access to pronunciations and sound atlases is changing approaches to phonetics. New corpora have been investigated within digital environments (British National Corpus, containing more than 100 million words; International Corpus of English; International Computer Archive of Modern and Medieval English; Oxford English Dictionary). Since the communicative turn in linguistics from the late 1950s to the 1970s (HERBERT

(3) Linguistics

P. GRICE 1913–1988, John L. AUSTIN 1911–1960, JOHN R. SEARLE *1932), fields in applied linguistics such as pragmatics, speech-act theory and discourse analysis have directly inspired communication and media studies.

(4) English language teaching (ELT)

Finally, in the field of language teaching methodology or pedagogy ("Fachdidaktik"), auditive, visual and audiovisual media have long been accepted as routine components into classrooms (for the recent example of MTV, see THALER 1999); pioneers include SCHWERDTFEGER (1973) and WEIAND (1978). This is reflected in all of the new introductions to the field (MÜLLER-HARTMANN / SCHOCKER-VON DITFURTH 2004, BACH / TIMM 2003, WESKAMP 2001). In schools, adult education and English for specific purposes (ESP), technologies have been mined for enrichment and authentification of learning materials, combining texts, images, and sounds. Online media are useful for intercultural linking (e-mail, World Wide Web) and autonomous learning and evaluation. Advances in CALL (Computer Assisted Language Learning) and TELL (Technology Enhanced Language Learning) have been most significant in the development of curricula across the media range as well as in interactive e-learning and teaching. Organizations such as CELA (Center on English Learning and Achievement) and, in Germany, activities by DONATH (1996, 1997, 2000, 2001), LEGUTKE / RÖSLER (2003), LIEBELT (1999), BORRMANN / GERDZEN (1998), RÜSCHOFF / WOLFF (1999), DECKE-CORNHILL / REICHART-WALLRABENSTEIN (2002) and others, have improved ELT media in and beyond classrooms.

English studies and new media culture

New electronic resources, the computer media and, above all, the Internet have changed the nature of English studies to a great extent. Presentations are now prepared using MS PowerPoint or similar software. Instead of being read, academic talks have often turned into multimedia performances. Internet databases provide easy and instant access to literary texts (Project Gutenberg, Project Bartleby, Oxford Text Archive) – and these machine-readable corpora (in conjunction with concordance software) offer new perspectives for textual and intertextual analysis (NEUMANN 2000: 337–341). Students use word processors, create homepages, ask questions via e-mail, they read newspapers and search the British Library, the Library of Congress and countless other libraries to build their bibliographies online – some may even commit plagiarism using Internet content. The Oxford English Dictionary and various encyclopaedia portals (such as Webster, Encyclopaedia Britannica, leo.org or wikipedia) offer online service.

Virtual university

The impact of inexpensive, instant, global and transmedial information services is reflected in a number of publications which seek to introduce students to the new methods, routines, sources and opportunities in English studies (LUDWIG / ROMMEL 2003, NEUMANN

Fig. 2: Screenshot from my Vienna e-learning environment,
winter term 2004/05

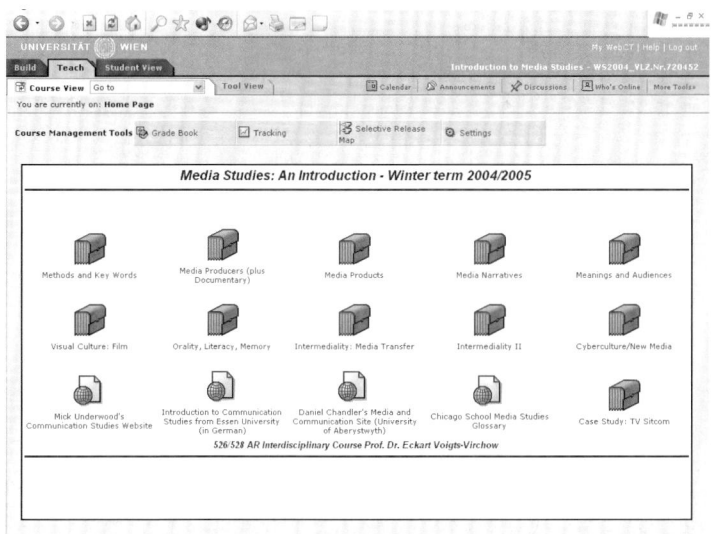

2000, KRANZ / TIEDEMANN 2000, FELDMANN et al. 1997). As FELDMANN
et al. (1997: iii) programmatically declared: *"[...] the Internet and
the new media culture which is rapidly evolving around it actually challenge us to analyse and dissect the new semiotics in the same way as
we have done in dealing with centuries of printed media."* Within the
field of English studies, therefore, it is mandatory to spread computer literacy. In addition, English studies will face the global challenges to universities and university departments, namely of
preventing information poverty, of countering rampant commercialization, and of answering the threat to local structures by the
vision of a globalized, virtual university.

At the risk of over-generalization, one might argue that the vocational, technology-driven media studies in the Anglosphere suffer
from a reflexivity deficit, while the historically orientated mediality research in Germany may be reproached with applicability
deficits. One of the aims of this book is both to aid smooth absorp-
tion of the existing traditions of media studies within the various
curricula as well as to provide an impetus for overcoming the mere
decoration of old approaches with new media products. This book
responds to the eclecticism of media studies and theories in that
it provides a first overview of the field of the media (developed
with Gießen and Vienna students in an Internet-based learning
environment, see fig. 2).

**Reflexivity
deficits *vs.*
applicability
deficits**

English vs. German media studies?	By definition, media studies are transnational. Recently, however, HICKETHIER (in SCHNELL 2003: 134) has warned against a colonization of German media studies by Anglo-American approaches, invoking national differences in the media set-up, and German *Anglistik* should be well equipped to respond to these differences. Unlike many German introductions and anthologies on media studies (HICKETHIER 2003, RUSCH 2003, LESCHKE 2003, FAULSTICH 2002, HELMES/KÖSTER 2002, SCHANZE 2002, KRALLMANN/ZIEMANN 2001, PIAS 1999, LUDES 1998, KLOOCK/SPAHR 1997) this introduction will cater specifically to the increasing number of media components in English-studies curricula at university level. Unlike many current introductions in English (BURTON 2002, BIGNELL 2002, LACEY 1998, 2000, 2002, RAYNER et al. 2001, STEWART et al. 2001, STURKEN/CARTWRIGHT 2001, McQUAIL 2000, WATSON 1998) it will also transcend its immediate medio-cultural climate to pursue more fundamental and historically informed questions, questions rarely asked in English-language textbooks, such as "What is mediality?", "What is intermediality?" or "What is a medium?"

❸ Medium / media – definitions and concepts

If you wish to converse with me, define your terms. VOLTAIRE

Definitions of 'medium'	ERNIE KOVACS is on record to have quipped that television is a medium because it is neither rare nor well done. This witticism suggests the wide spectrum of meanings of the term. In Latin, *medius* simply means 'middle', also in the sense of 'intermediate', 'average', 'middling'. According to the Oxford English Dictionary (OED), a "medium" is "*something which is intermediate between two degrees, amounts, qualities, or classes; a middle state*". This is why steaks are served medium rare and wine is medium dry. In biology and chemistry, a medium is an enveloping substance in which an organism lives, in sociology it is one's environment, conditions of life, or general social setting. In chemistry, the term 'medium' is often used for liquids, and in this sense it is used as a technical term in photography and painting. A medium is also an intervening substance through which a force acts on objects at a distance, or through which impressions are conveyed to the senses. It can also be used with respect to a person or thing which acts as an intermediary, thus we speak of a mediator who resolves social conflicts and of a clairvoyant medium who communicates with the dead. The term 'mixed media' illustrates that a medium is also the material in an artistic or creative activity. Then again, one may conceive of money as a medium of exchange or token of value circulating in trading transactions. Rejecting these 'nomi-

nal' definitions, FAULSTICH (2002: 21) finds fault with more than 20 'media' in MARSHALL MCLUHAN's *Understanding Media*, such as the media 'railway', 'wheel', or 'stone'. For FAULSTICH, an 'operational' definition, that is, one that refers specifically to the 21 individual media he isolates, is equally obsolete because of its limited scope and merely didactic value.

MCLUHAN (1964) famously claimed that "The medium is the message", but whatever we may think of this far-reaching and ambiguous claim, there can be neither message nor meaning without a medium. In very broad terms, a medium is "what transforms experience into knowledge" or what provides "the signs which give *meaning* to the events of everyday life" (INGLIS 1990: 3). This definition embraces the most heterogeneous phenomena: How do we translate paint on a canvas into landscapes; how do we turn sounds into words in a president's speech, a sequence of '0's and '1's into a website or black blobs on paper into writing?

Media and meaning

A narrower definition, on the other hand, distinguishes between mutual communication of individuals and one-way mass media communication (*massa*, Latin 'dough, clay' = a unified body of matter with no specific shape). One may also refer to the distinction of 'push' media that merely offer programmes (TV, newspapers) and 'pull' media that depend on user activity (WWW). After the invention of movable-type print by GUTENBERG in the 1450s, early pamphlets and journals can be characterized as the first mass media. Mass media may be defined as media which operate in the public sphere and communicate 'one to many' (rather than 'one to one' or 'many to many'), to a dispersed, potentially unlimited audience. The definition is based, therefore, on the communicative range. Usage has transformed the plural into a singular noun: "the media", referring to the main areas of mass communication, such as newspapers, radio, television.

Individual medium *vs.* 'the media'

Terms such as 'many to many' or 'one to one' media raise the question of interactivity. One may bracket off interactive media from unidirectional, static or dynamic media, according to their responsiveness or the degree of control a media user has over the process and content of information. The rise of the Internet has challenged traditional mass-media research because (in contrast to, for instance, broadcast TV) it is a multidirectional medium. The question of 'interactivity' has contributed to modifications of the mass communication model. According to the seminal definition by ANDREW LIPPMANN (who developed the interactive hypermedia Aspen Movie Map at the Massachusetts Institute of Technology (MIT) in 1978), interactivity is a "*mutual and simultaneous activity on the part of both participants usually working towards some*

Unidirectional, static, dynamic and multidirectional media

goal but not necessarily" (see BRAND 1988: 46) – a requirement ideally fulfilled in human face-to-face interaction, but not in the online transactions of e-commerce or e-banking.

Media dimensions

The following matrix (see fig. 3) illustrates the manifold dimensions of the term 'medium/media'. The semiotic approach by POSNER shows that the scope of the term 'media' reaches far beyond

Fig. 3: Media dimensions (modified from POSNER 2003: 43)

media dimension	definition	exemplary usage	discipline, field
biological	media as biological set-up	auditive media	biology, physiology
physical	media as physical set-up	acoustic media	physics
technological	media as technical channel	cable, screens, printing press	engineering
sociological	media as social interaction	money, power, love	sociology, psychology
institutional	media according to social institution	press agencies, TV companies	politics, sociology, business studies, law
functional	media according to function	media marketing, didactic media	pedagogy, business studies, journalism, communication studies, psychology
cybernetic	media as data	programming, computer interaction	mathematics, computing, cybernetics, information theory
coded	media as sign transfer	language	semiotics, linguistics
aesthetic	media as artistic means	theatre, painting etc.	arts, music, film, literature
(para-) psychological	media as intermediary agent	divination etc.	occultism, spiritualism

A basic outline of media studies

the term 'mass media'. It follows that media studies should do more than merely addressing media technologies.

A brief look at an individual medium, the telephone, will serve to illustrate how these media dimensions work. On the medium telephone, one may bring to bear physiology (the ear), physics (sound transmission), technology (cell-phones), sociology (impact on communities), institutions (A,T&T), functions (telephone marketing), cybernetics (the mathematical communication model by NORBERT WIENER (1894–1964)), semiotics and linguistics (telephone conversations), and even aesthetics (telephone art) or (para-) psychology (telephony as disembodied – spiritual – speech).

Example: Telephone

Beyond these categories, one may further investigate the telephone's history, the impact of digital technologies or the retarded development of the videophone, the augmentation of its transmission function by storing data on answering machines, or the role of women as telephone communicators or telephone operators. One may intend to cleverly market new telephone services, train employees to talk efficiently on the phone or teach language learners to manage phone calls in foreign languages. One may also want to find out how talking on the phone influences the partners psychologically, or how recent legislation changed the market for telephone companies. The movies *Cellular* (2004, D: DAVID ELLIS) and *Phone Booth* (2002, D: JOEL SCHUMACHER) or NICOLSON BAKER's novel *Vox* (1992, subtitled "A Novel About Telephone Sex") may be analysed as incorporating a media system or apparatus into its form and structure. Finally, one may want to test the hypothesis that the telephone contributed to the media acceleration and "culture of simultaneity" (STEPHEN KERN) in the 20th century. In order to account for these, in part, overlapping interests, media studies must necessarily be transdisciplinary even beyond POSNER's media dimensions.

Trans-disciplinary approaches

Each disciplinary approach to the media has generated its own sets of metaphors which give away its preoccupations. MEYROWITZ (1993) distinguishes between three dominant media metaphors which cast the media as

Channels, languages and environments

- **channels (or conduits)**: (technological approach) interpreting media contents (genres, narratives, ideas, roles)
- **languages**: (humanities approach) understanding media grammar and intermediality (sound and vision, media design etc.)
- **(social) environments**: (social- and cultural-studies approach) mapping the media context (media usage, interactivity, dissemination).

Linguistic approach	A 'linguistic' or 'semiotic' approach looks at the specific processes of signification in various media, their signs, languages, and codes. Linguistic approaches to communication such as pragmatics and speech-act theory have addressed the question of how one may achieve effective communication.
Conversational maxims	H. P. Grice has given a clear answer in that successful communication is based on a cooperative principle. He isolated a number of maxims that are needed for effective communication and that may serve as basic criteria for good communication: (1) The maxim of quantity: Be as informative as necessary, but not over-informative. (2) The maxim of quality: Do not say what you believe to be false or that for which you lack adequate evidence. (3) The maxim of relevance: Say things that are related to the topic of conversation. (4) The maxim of manner: Avoid obscurity and ambiguity; be brief and orderly.
Techno-functional approach	In a technical sense, a medium refers to the physical material for storing or reproducing data, images, or sound (disks, paper). Hans H. Hiebel's techno-functional approach (1997: 9) therefore distinguishes between • input / output media (typewriter, keyboard, camera, microphone, scanner) • reproduction and dissemination media (printing, photography, film) • storage media (book, photography, disk, hard disk, film) • transmission media (mail, telegraphy, telephone, radio, TV, cable, satellite). For Hiebel (1997: 8), media are *"means of material or energetic (electrical, electronical, opto-electronical) data or information storage and transmission"*. There is a tendency for media to accumulate and differentiate functions. With an Internet-connected computer you can not only watch a film, but also store, transmit, reproduce, and modify it.
Primary, secondary, tertiary, quaternary media	From the technological point of view, therefore, one may subdivide the media according to the increasing degree of technological saturation (Pross 1972):

*Fig. 4: Media and technology (*Pross *1972; for quaternary media, see*
Faulstich *2002: 25)*

media and technology			
primary media	secondary media	tertiary media	quaternary media "metamedia"
no technology involved in elementary human contact: language, body language	technology involved in production: writing, images, smoke or flag signals, posters, letters and other print media	technology involved in both production and reception: telegraph, telephone, mass media such as radio and TV, computer media	digital technology involved: computer, multimedia, e-mail, WWW, chats

A technical definition of the media may also distinguish between analogue and digital media. Analogue media are based on the physical conversion or translation of information (e.g., sound, images) into another technical system (a clock with hands, a speedometer, a photograph, a vinyl record). Digital media, on the other hand, are based on encoding information in numbers (especially, sequences of the binary digits 0 and 1). The discreet character of the encoding into digital units or (computer) language is different from the continuity of analogue representation. It offers enhanced potential of storing, disseminating and editing of data or 'content' in digital files.

Analogue media *vs.* digital media

Traditional film is a good example of analogue media. Technically, a film relies on a celluloid strip on a reel which passes through a light-tight chamber. A lens-and-shutter mechanism exposes the light-sensitive strip at a standard rate of 24 frames per second, and the result is a succession of images produced in a chemical process. This will then be edited (in a linear fashion) and copied for projection in the cinema, where it passes again through a lens-and-light mechanism that projects an image on the screen. Arriving on the retina of the viewer the projected succession of images generates the impression of movement. Video (which emerged in the late 1950s and as a consumer product in the 1970s) is also an analogue recording device; it stores sound and images on (re-recordable) magnetic tape, using electronic cameras and editing systems.

Example: Film and video

Digital media: Convergence in film	What has been termed the 'digital revolution' has led to the convergence of traditional media (film, TV, print) into digital formats. Thus, storage of images is switching from (analogue) magnetic tape to (digital) DVD. The music industries have switched from vinyl records to the digital storage of CD and MP3. Film is now recorded by digital cameras that store the image information in files and databases. It is edited in a non-linear way. Analogue photographs are converted back and forth to digital files, thus generating the hybrids of computer-generated imagery (CGI). Celluloid classics such as *Metropolis* are digitally re-edited in order to delete or erase corrupt or deteriorated celluloid frames.
Media convergence and intermediality	This digital revolution has had immense consequences on the production and reception of visual (and auditory) data, which become easier and cheaper to generate and copy as well as easier to manipulate. The media convergence of the 21st century therefore offers potential but also challenges established critical practices. Whereas for a long time researchers concentrated on articulating the specifics of clearly demarcated media, recent approaches have focused on intermediality as artistic process (intermedia art) as well as cultural phenomena of hybridity (THOMSEN 1994, SCHNEIDER/THOMSEN 1997, BOLTER/GRUSIN 1999, KREWANI 2001). STURKEN/CARTWRIGHT (2001: 345) chart the hope that "*this convergence will collapse distances and democratize knowledge. Key to this is the idea that image, text, sound, and objects also converge in the social production of meaning, and can no longer be studied in isolation.*"
Mediality	Consequently, HICKETHIER (2003: 26) distinguishes the field of mediality from media use and media technology. The term 'mediality' is directed against an exclusively technology-orientated focus on the latest 'new' media. Beyond institutions and objects, the term mediality denotes the specific cultural conditions of various media. For instance, rather than address a film as uncinematic (arguing that it does not fulfil a 'natural' potential of the medium) one should locate the film in its specific relation to film's mediality (its culture, not its nature). According to HICKETHIER, there are forms of mediality which cut across individual media (such as orality/literacy, theatricality, audiovisuality, and, one may add, performativity). SYBILLE KRÄMER (2002: 332) argues that mediality transcends intended or controlled meanings; the message is a trace left by the media.
Example: 'Live' performance and the 'performative turn'	One example of mediality across individual media is denoted by the terms 'performance' and 'performativity'. The traditional co-presence of performer and audience in the essentially 'fictional' medium that is theatre has been replaced by innumerable mediatized performances. The virtual co-presence facilitated by transmission media such as television and radio has prompted the term

'live' performance (with its mediatized *ersatz* interactivity of phone-ins and chats). This is distinct from 'recorded' performances in which production and reception have been separated (anything 'canned' and stored on celluloid, magnetic tape or digital files: film, tape, videotape, CD, DVD). In the field of media aesthetics, ERIKA FISCHER-LICHTE (2004: 29) has described the reaction of the arts as a performative turn that replaces the work or object of art as its prime aesthetic aim with the creative process, the action or event.

ERIKA FISCHER-LICHTE seeks to substitute the triad 'production – work – reception' with the process of '*mise-en-scène* – event – aesthetic experience'. Witnessing a performance, we experience the complex results of various transformations: a *mise-en-scène* has been developed which plans, prepares and rehearses the situation and designs a space for the performance. The *mise-en-scène*, therefore, scripts a subsequent performance – an event which inevitably contains unscripted elements. Anthropologically, performativity can be described as the basis of human identity. The term originated in speech-act theory (JOHN AUSTIN). It was used in an influential appropriation in gender studies by JUDITH BUTLER (*1956). BUTLER defined performativity as 'doing one's body' – illustrating the fact that identity (such as, for instance, gender identity) is instable and results from an incessant series of performative acts. These performative acts are in turn determined by their mediality.

Performativity

The approaches to mediality by KRÄMER and others or to performativity by FISCHER-LICHTE and others seek to overcome the technical definition of the media. By arguing that our performances depend to a large extent on their mediality, theses approaches are close to the concept of the media *dispositif* (or apparatus). A term borrowed from cultural theorist MICHEL FOUCAULT (1926–1984) and film theoretician JEAN-LOUIS BAUDRY (*1930), it denotes the social regulation of perception and knowledge building. The media *dispositif* (from Latin *dispositio*, 'arrangement of oration' in ancient rhetoric) refers to the general media apparatus, a network of social and political conventions and connections between their technology, their conditions of production, reception, and form. One may think of oneself as a user reigning supreme, steering the medium as if at the helm of a ship, but theories of the media apparatus hold that the media actually shape and model their users according to their requirements.

Media *dispositif* or apparatus

As a media *dispositif*, therefore, a television set is not just a technical appliance. Just as film, it communicates audiovisually, but its invention changed the way we see. One may sum up some differences between television and cinema (TV's potential for 'live'

Example: Television

transmission, no darkened film theatre, no audience focussed on the screen, a luminous cathode-ray image with a specific resolution, attention dispersal in channel switching, a 'window' rhetoric and illusion, reception in the private home, in living rooms, bedrooms, children's rooms). The private use of this public medium creates its own rituals and redefines structures of space and time. This regulating TV apparatus, therefore, has its share in determining what is considered 'normal' in a given community. It stabilizes social power (by excluding transgressive or incompatible practices) – not because of individual manipulators, but through the force of its apparatus. Even seemingly innocent or insignificant technological innovations (such as remote control) may redefine the entire media *dispositif* 'television' with new media practices. As KREWANI (2001) has shown in the case of film and television, the convergence of TV and film in the audiovisual *dispositif* has to some extent dissolved the media specificity of TV *vs.* film.

'Liveness': Auslander *vs.* Phelan

The television apparatus has obviously influenced other media as well. The increasing mediatization of the audiovisual aesthetic experience has prompted a redefinition of theatrical practice, which sees the physical co-presence of performers and audiences in a performative space as the (unmediatized) essence of theatre: "*To the degree that performance attempts to enter the economy of reproduction, it betrays and lessens the promise of its own ontology*" (PEGGY PHELAN 1993: 146). PHILIP AUSLANDER (1999) challenged this claim, arguing that the clear-cut distinction between 'live' and 'mediatized' performance is untenable because (a) reproductions of performances are everywhere, (b) the intimacy and immediacy of 'live' performance survives (without physical co-presence) on television, (c) live performances emulate mediatized ones and (d) they do not exclude technologies of reproduction.

Media systems

It seems clear now that media are based on sign systems (text composed of alphabetic characters, images, sounds), but that these sign systems are embedded within media systems, in the sense that printed text is different from electronic hypertext and printed books are different from handwritten codices. A precise, if abstract, theoretical definition of the term 'medium' has been suggested by ULRICH SAXER (1998: 54), who sees media as "*complex, institutionalized systems built around organized communication channels with specific potential*" (my translation). This means that they are more than mere communication channels, technologies, or products; they are also sign systems, organizations. They have sub-systems (on macro-, meso-, and micro-levels) from individual to global scale. The billsticker and the advertising agency, the telephone operator and British Telecom, the software programme and Lara Croft, the musician, the membrane and the MP3 file, the teacher as well as the Secretary of Education – all of these are components of various media systems. The systemic approach clearly transcends the scope of traditional research into the mass media.

The constructivist reformulation of media studies (as provided by S. J. SCHMIDT 2003, SCHMIDT / ZURSTIEGE 2000) is based on SAXER's definition. Sharing SAXER's assumption that a medium is much more than a mere channel or a technical mass medium, SCHMIDT argues that media systems consist of four components,

Components of media systems

(1) a semiotic instrument of communication, the prototype being natural oral language,
(2) a media technology; since the development of writing examples of media technologies have included print, film, both kinds of 'notebooks',
(3) a social system, that is, institutions on which technologies are based, such as schools or TV stations,
(4) media products or offerings such as literature or music that provide the opportunity to study aspects like production, distribution, reception, and processing.

Media communication: models, schools, and theories

CHAPTER 2

1 Transmission models: Lasswell and Shannon / Weaver

The single biggest problem in communication is the illusion that it has taken place.
GEORGE BERNARD SHAW

Transmission model

Multidirectional media as well as human face-to-face interaction challenge the foundational models in the study of communication, the transmission models. In its initial phase, the study of media communication was dominated by transmission models, such as the LASSWELL formula of mass communication (1948, see fig. 5). The transition from communication studies to media studies has determined the subsequent modification of these media-communication models. While transmission models seemed to work with reference to telephones, human face-to-face conversation exposed their limits.

Lasswell formula

For any communication process, the political scientist HAROLD D. LASSWELL argues, we must consider five elements: One has to ask who controls the message production, i.e., who communicates. Then one will have to look at the message itself. The preferred

Fig. 5: LASSWELL *formula*

level of analysis	who?	says what?	through what?	to whom?	with what conse-quence?
element in communi-cative pro-cess	communica-tor, sender, transmitter	message	channel	receiver	effect
approach	control research	textual research	medium research	audience research	uses and effects research
methods	biographies, institutional analysis, "gatekeep-ing", "agenda setting", news bias and selection	content analysis, herme-neutics, semiotics	media theories, media analysis	empirical research (question-naires), cul-tural studies	causes and effects, uses and gratifica-tions, empiri-cal research (question-naires), cul-tural studies

sociological method to achieve this is content analysis or content research. The next element that has to be accounted for, the channel, is the medium which carries the message, e.g., the air and radio waves that carry the radio speech in terrestrial analogue transmission. Questions of channel adequacy, channel capacity, and channel redundancy are important for advertising agencies, TV producers, publishing houses, but also telephone partners, teachers etc. In the next step, the focus lies on the receiver or receivers of the message, such as an audience, spectators, readers, or listeners. This leads to the important field of audience research. Finally, Lasswell allows for the study of media effects to investigate of what consequence, if any, the communicative process has been.

Typically, content research into messages is interested in representation. It is, in fact, the classic method in communication studies (influential studies have been carried out by George Gerbner at the Annenberg School of Communication or by the Glasgow University Media Group). Often this amounts to counting media occurrences of social, ethnic, age or gender groups (it is asked, e.g., "How many coloured persons appeared in American sitcoms in 1977?"), which will then be measured against other sociological data, i.e., statistics. Obviously, quantitative and objective accounts of media texts do not go very far in eliciting the texts' meaning.

Content analysis

The Lasswell formula provides only a narrow notion of what might also be called feedback. Therefore, the linearity and the mechanistic or trivial simplicity of Lasswell's model have frequently been criticized. It is obviously grounded in behaviouristic trigger-response logic. Schmidt / Zurstiege (2000) miss the category of frequency ("how often?") and Faulstich (2002) requires causality ("why?", "what for?"). Klaus Merten (1999) remarks that the communication process is not linear, but that all the factors in a given communicative transaction are interdependent and can be freely combined. Gerbner (1956) increased the number of aspects to ten: "*Someone perceives an event and reacts in a situation through some media to make available materials in some form and context conveying contents of some consequence*" (see Faulstich 2002: 35). Finally, as, among others, Thompson (1988: 7–9) has noted, practical communication presupposed in transmission models cannot account for aesthetic communication (e.g., playfulness, entertainment, beauty, defamiliarization).

Trigger-response logic

Communication studies virtually started with the work of Claude E. Shannon (1916–2001), who worked at the Massachusetts Institute of Technology (MIT) and at the Bell Telephone Laboratories. In the 1930s and 1940s he developed the ideas he synthesized with Warren Weaver in *The Mathematical Theory of Communication* (1949, see fig. 6).

Shannon-Weaver model

Fig. 6: Mathematical communication model (by SHANNON / WEAVER), see UNDERWOOD, http://www.ccms-infobase.com

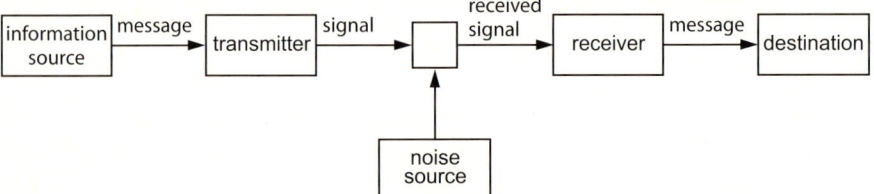

Meaning and effectivity

Whereas SHANNON insisted that problems of meaning are irrelevant to his model and that he was merely concerned with reproducing information as a problem of engineering, WEAVER opened up the information model for sociological interpretation. He added the dimension of semantics and effectivity to the technical problem of sign transmission, i.e., he asked how the transmitted signs relate to their meaning and how the message can be used to determine the receiver's actions. A medium can never be neutral with respect to the meaning of a message because the message does not remain unmodified in the process of transmission.

Linearity

SHANNON and WEAVER hold that communication is a linear process. As SHANNON worked in the Bell Laboratories, it is not surprising that his model works best for the purely technical aspects of telephone communication. There is a speaker, whose sound waves are turned into electrical impulses by the telephone apparatus. Subsequently, these electrical impulses are turned back into sound waves by the receiving telephone device on the other end of the line. The concept can be translated into general terms. An information source (no matter whether this is a machine or a human being) selects a message (words, music). These signs are then transformed or encoded into signals which can be passed on via an appropriate channel. While the signal is in this channel (or medium) it is subject to possible sources of noise which impede the transmission process. This noise may be statistically measured as entropy, a term borrowed from thermodynamics. In any process of sign transmission, there is disorder or noise, but an appropriate code provides so much redundancy that the signal can be decoded by the receiver in spite of the noise factor.

Abstract transmission

The SHANNON-WEAVER model has proved extraordinarily productive, but it has been subjected to such thorough critique that the linear transmission model now seems inappropriate to describe the communication process:
• The model is simply too abstract and not complex enough to account for the communication process.

- It does not allow for a specific and variable social and cultural context.
- Its behaviouristic approach does not account for the fact that human beings are no rigid and unchanging technical units.
- It does not account for the variety of information involved in communication.
- The linear one-way process proposed does not provide for inter-activity, at the simplest level some kind of responding utterance on the phone – unless, that is, one introduces at least NORBERT WIENER's (1948) concept of feedback into the model. The feedback principle is a feature of intelligent systems that allows senders to test and adjust their input in response to information about how their messages have been received.

One of the most interesting aspects in the mathematical communication model is the concept of noise. Initially, SHANNON and WEAVER's concept of "message" did not address the problems of semantics in communication as they focused on channel capacity and physical rather than semantic noise. In a telephone conversation, communication may be impaired (technically) by bad signals, by distractions such as the gurgling of a coffee machine or by an afternoon drowsiness. It may also be stalled (semantically) by a language barrier or an unknown, specialist register, or by the fact that the partners cannot agree on the interpretation of a term such as, for instance, "ideology". Finally, RAYMOND CARVER's short story "A Small Good Thing" provides a harrowing example of psychological noise. Having just learnt that they have lost their son in an accident, the parents are ill-disposed to answer a phone call from the bakery about their failure to collect the boy's birthday cake. The useful concept of noise may therefore be said to encompass technical, semantic, and psychological dimensions. Because of noise, redundancy (from repetitions, re-phrasings, digressions etc.) is essential to every communication process.

The concept of "noise"

❷ US communication studies and Maletzke's field of communication

Good communication is as stimulating as black coffee, and just as hard to sleep after. ANNE MORROW LINDBERGH

The field of communication studies in the US was initially dominated by schools of journalism which were closely connected to the dominant media corporations (LUDES 1998: 37). From these, a number of 'schools' of thought have emerged:

US communication-studies schools

- **Columbia School** (1940s to 1950s: Paul Lazarsfeld, Robert K. Merton)
- **Chicago School** (1900s to 1950s: John Dewey (1859–1952), George Herbert Mead, Gladys & Kurt Lang, Donald Horton / Richard Wohl)
- **Toronto School** (1950s to 1970s: Harold A. Innis (1894–1952), Marshall McLuhan).

Columbia School

The Columbia School was positivist and psychologistic, i.e., it favoured empirical methods such as sample surveys and quantitative analyses, often sponsored by businesses keen on investigating their audiences. In the classic 1949 essay "Mass Communication, Popular Taste, and Organized Social Action", Lazarsfeld and Merton established the "limited effects" research, which argued that only under conditions of (1) monopolization, (2) canalization of pre-existing attitudes and (3) supplementation by face-to-face interaction the mass media crucially determine public opinion.

Effects: The hypodermic needle

This position challenged the critical orthodoxy based on the mass manipulation model, argued by Todd Gitlin, Jim McGuigan, and the Frankfurt School theorists. C. R. Wright (1975) held that media messages inject each audience member (as part of a mass audience) with a hypodermic needle, as it were. Watson (1998: 234) memorably states: "Once upon a time there was a gigantic hypodermic needle full of highly toxic messages which Big Bad Media injected into the unresisting veins of poor princess Audienza".

Agenda-setting

Lazarsfeld's point that the media, however, had the power to structure issues, i.e., reductively prioritize specific kinds of information, led McCombs / Shaw (1972) to formulate the agenda-setting hypothesis. Investigating political campaigns, this research concluded that rather than overtly shaping opinions, the media direct the audience awareness on certain issues. Thus, the mass media attach salience only to certain issues, prioritizing some elements in public discourse at the cost of others.

Chicago School

American communication studies were founded in Chicago. They were focused on journalism and norms derived from ideas of participatory and interactive democracy. George Herbert Mead argued that human beings orientate themselves not just in a natural environment, but also in 'symbolic' interactions or signification processes. John Dewey's instrumentalist approach assessed the potential of symbolic interactions (e.g., in newspapers) for overcoming distance and creating and reformulating communities. It follows that the Chicago School specialized in investigating audiences. In 1956, Horton and Wohl coined the influential term "parasocial interaction" which investigated how TV media personae (such as newscasters) establish semblances of interaction and intimacy with their viewers.

Media communication: models, schools, and theories

In this context, the 'effects' approach to the audience was elaborated by the transactional 'uses and gratifications' model, which presupposes an active individual recipient with rational intentions calculated to maximize media usage. Rather than asking what the media do to the people ('effects'), DENIS MCQUAIL, JAY BLUMLER or ELIHU KATZ asked what the people (as individuals) do with the media. So, why are certain population segments fond of 'blogging' while others tune in to the docu-soap *I'm a Celebrity ... Get Me out of Here* (2002)? In 1972, MCQUAIL et al. suggested a fourfold typology of media-person interactions:

- diversion: escape from routine or problems; emotional release
- personal relationships: companionship; social utility
- personal identity: self reference; reality exploration; value reinforcement
- surveillance: forms of information seeking (in MCQUAIL 2000: 388).

In response to the criticism levelled against the communication models by LASSWELL and SHANNON/WEAVER, these models became far more elaborate. GERHARD MALETZKE's field model of communication (see fig. 7) is based on the work of KATZ and LAZARSFELD. MALETZKE (*1922) tries to avoid a simplistic reductiveness of SHANNON/WEAVER and accounts for socio-cultural variables. He also incorporates bidirectional exchange and the idea of 'feedback'.

Fig. 7: Field model of communication (MALETZKE), see UNDERWOOD, http://www.ccms-infobase.com

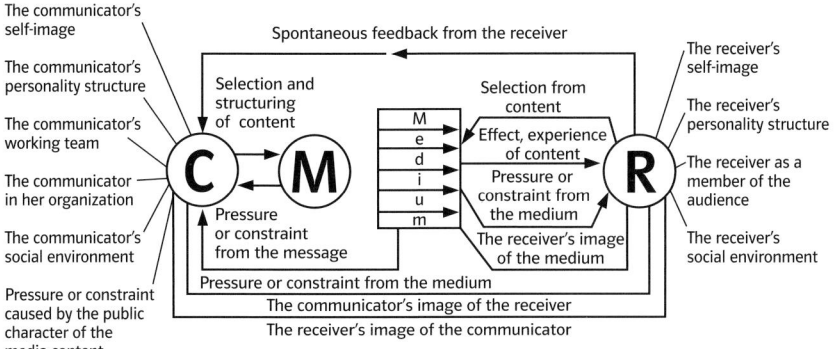

The commu-nicator as "gate-keeper"	Analyses of this factor in communication typically focus on the filtering, editing, and censoring of media messages through institutional constraints on the production side, a process known as "gatekeeping". The information source or encoder is called communicator by MALETZKE, and he distinguishes a number of factors that determine how the communicator shapes the content of the message. Looking at MALETZKE's model with MICHAEL MOORE as a test case will help to specify "agenda-setting" and "gatekeeping".
Self-image, personality structure and social environment	MICHAEL MOORE appears as "writer, filmmaker, and voter" in his bestselling book *Stupid White Men* (2001). He sees himself not only as a professional documentary filmmaker, however, but also as an enemy of the Bush administration. Winning an Academy Award for *Bowling for Columbine* (2002) has also changed not just his image, but probably his self-image as well. MOORE often refers to his childhood in the working-class community of Flint, Michigan, which shaped his personality and drove him to fight against *laissez-faire* capitalism. From these obscure origins, however, he has been turned into a media celebrity and media personality. Ultimately, the values shared within the communicator's social environment are likely to determine his assumptions and views. In a legendary 1998 TV interview, JEREMY PAXMAN, the BBC presenter famous for his irreverent and abrasive style ('the English inquisition'), repeated the same question 14 times to Home Secretary MICHAEL HOWARD. PAXMAN's justification is that the viewer is entitled to a straight answer to a straight question, but his personality, his self image and his journalistic ethos (*"I am always asking myself why is this lying bastard lying to me?"*) also play a part.
The working 'team'	Often the communicator will merely be a label for a collaborative team with specialized roles, working together on a project. To name a film after its director is a gross distortion of the collaborative process of producing a film. MICHAEL MOORE is not just a writer, but also head of a working team devoted to writing 'his' books and making 'his' films, and of course he requires loyalty from his team. He has co-operated with KATHLEEN GLYNN on his TV shows *TV Nation* (1994–95) and *The Awful Truth* (1999–2000). In keeping with standard practice he thanks his team in the "Acknowledgments" sections of his books. His staff is, of course, mentioned in the closing credits of his films. Different media, therefore generate routine operations. Among the chief activities are the production of media content to deadlines and the production of media content for space-slots (defined portions of pages in newspapers and magazines) or time-slots (in television programming). The working team operates under constraints of resources and under the need to generate revenue in order to guarantee profit and produc-

tion value. Public-sector TV (such as the BBC) is largely funded from licence fees. Private-sector TV generates revenue from advertising, subscription or online transactions such as interactive messaging services (in the case of iTV: interactive television).

Resources presuppose organizations. Any book needs not just an author, but also a publisher, a wholesaler and a retailer (i.e., a bookshop), and as the provider of resources the publisher exerts allocative control. Readers of the Penguin edition of *Stupid White Men* can take note of MOORE's account of how Regan Books, a division of Harper/Collins (owned by RUPERT MURDOCH's News Corporation) demanded rewrites before publishing his book, for some time refused to publish it for political reasons and refused to support it when it actually came out, exerting operational control. Similarly, in the case of MOORE's polemic anti-George-Bush documentary *Fahrenheit 9/11* (2004), the funding and distribution was stopped by the Walt Disney Corporation (owners of Miramax films), and subsequently Miramax owners BOB and HARVEY WEINSTEIN bought the rights for $ 6 million. It is, therefore, essential to view a communicator within the organizational context, and investigating the decision-making process within the organization is one object of media studies.

The organization: Allocative control and operational control

The achievements of individual authors have for a long time dominated research into the television play (BRANDT 1980, 1993) and radio play (DRAKAKIS 1981, PRIESSNITZ 1977, 1978, FRANK 1981). In some cases, the director of a film may wish to be removed from the cast list because a 'team' or an 'organization' has taken the project out of the director's hands (in this case, he will appear as ALAN SMITHEE, the only pseudonym accepted by the Directors Guild of America). For a long time, film studies were premised on the *auteur theory*, which proposed a subject-orientated approach to these media for the sake of cultural nobilitation even within the context of the Hollywood industry (see CAUGHIE 1981, GERSTNER/STAIGER 2002). This approach still dominates the discourses in the mass media themselves. It has also been extended to television, where notions of authorship have become particularly problematic (see COWARD 1987).

Media 'authors'

There are successful and long-running book series on important and influential films (Film Classics by the British Film Institute, BFI) as well as on significant and influential directors (BFI World Directors, Wallflower's Directors' Cuts, Conversations With Filmmakers by University of Mississippi Press, Directors on Directors by Faber; in Germany: Schüren/ARTE edition or Bertz + Fischer). MOLLY NESBIT (1995) has drawn attention to the fact that, legally speaking, a mass-media product is authored by capital, that is, the commissioning, producing, and transmitting companies.

Films, directors, companies

Interestingly LEZ COOKE's recent history of television drama opens with a call for new work on individual authors, identifying an under-researched field, but probably also responding to new pressures in the face of 'dumbed down' TV (COOKE 2003: 5). Authors, after all, facilitate interaction with a specific experience and continue to be a factor in meaning-making processes. It may be easier for 'authored' products to transcend generic limitations at the bargaining tables of the mass media.

Media con-glomerates

As a consequence of risk-minimizing diversification and monopolization of financial power, a number of global media conglomerates have emerged, such as AOL Time Warner, Walt Disney, Vivendi, Viacom and Bertelsmann (see fig. 8). Media conglomerates aim at vertical integration (i.e., control over material components, production, distribution and marketing of a given product). Viacom, for instance, owns a film producer (Paramount Pictures), a video distributor (Paramount Home Entertainment), television companies (CBS, MTV, Comedy Central, Showtime), a radio company (Infinity), media retailers (Blockbuster), and print and online publishers (Simon & Schuster, CBS.com, see LACEY 2002: 20). These media conglomerates tend to favour the system which sustains them.

Example: Rupert Murdoch and Fox News

The documentary *Outfoxed: Rupert Murdoch's War on Journalism* (D: ROBERT GREENWALD, 2004), for instance, shows how selective and biased reporting in the channel Fox News (claims: "fair and balanced", "we report, you decide") had a marked impact on the news reporting of other mainstream television channels and news programmes. Founded in 1996, the cable channel has replaced CNN as the most influential news channel in the USA, having topped the CNN ratings since 2002. Blatantly partisan shows such as *The O'Reilly Factor* earned the channel its nickname "Republican TV" by the *New York Times*. Fox News is part of the global conglomerate owned by Australian media tycoon RUPERT MURDOCH. Other media owned by MURDOCH include the tabloid papers *New York Post* (USA) and *The Sun* (UK) as well as the satellite- and cable-TV channels DirecTV (USA), BSkyB (UK), and Star (Asia). Small wonder, then, that MURDOCH's BSkyB in the spirit of vertical integration tried to buy a controlling interest in Manchester United shares – the deal, however, was barred by the British government. *Outfoxed*, on the other hand, may also serve as an example for alternative distribution channels, as it was sold via Internet and shown on private screenings ("house parties") rather than in cinemas.

The public character of the media

The dispute between MOORE and Regan Books as well as the public influence of Fox illustrate the constraints that operate on communicators because they work in the public sphere. Any content

CHAPTER **2** Media communication: models, schools, and theories

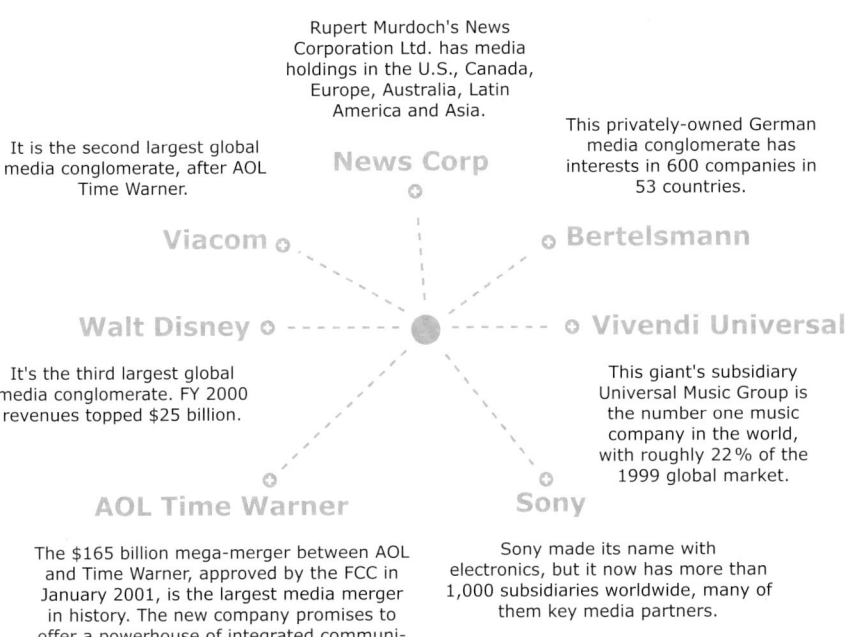

Fig. 8: Media conglomerates in 2001 (see "PBS Frontline: The Merchants of Cool", http://www.pbs.org)

Rupert Murdoch's News Corporation Ltd. has media holdings in the U.S., Canada, Europe, Australia, Latin America and Asia.

News Corp

It is the second largest global media conglomerate, after AOL Time Warner.

This privately-owned German media conglomerate has interests in 600 companies in 53 countries.

Viacom   **Bertelsmann**

Walt Disney ------- **Vivendi Universal**

It's the third largest global media conglomerate. FY 2000 revenues topped $25 billion.

This giant's subsidiary Universal Music Group is the number one music company in the world, with roughly 22% of the 1999 global market.

AOL Time Warner   **Sony**

The $165 billion mega-merger between AOL and Time Warner, approved by the FCC in January 2001, is the largest media merger in history. The new company promises to offer a powerhouse of integrated communication, media and entertainment across all platforms – computer, phone, television and handheld wireless devices.

Sony made its name with electronics, but it now has more than 1,000 subsidiaries worldwide, many of them key media partners.

written or filmed and broadcast, and then published in a book or on TV or a webpage can infringe the law or at least irritate pressure groups, political parties, religious or ethnic communities. Public-relations professionals (so-called 'spin-doctors') shape information according to the preferences of their employers, a practice of disinformation which is euphemistically called 'news management'. Even a link to another website (or, in particular, a 'deep link' which bypasses front page advertising) can constitute a violation of a legal norm. Hardly any published content, therefore, is mediated without 'prior restraint' (which is, however, in legal terms banned by US free speech legislation), unless it is published anonymously in an attempt to mask the communicator.

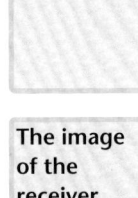

MICHAEL MOORE opens his book *Dude, Where's my Country* (2003) with an ironic address to his readers: "*Greetings, fellow members of the Coalition of the Willing!*" In official usage, Coalition of the Willing refers to those international governments that supported the second war on Iraq. MOORE, of course, does not assume that his readership approves of the war, and his reader address can be seen

The image of the receiver

as an attempt to establish a community of opposition. It is a truism that the audience one has in mind crucially determines what one publishes and how one publishes it, but the text itself may not conform to the communicator's intentions. Literary studies have for a long time recognized the role constructed for a reader in the text and have included the "implied reader" (WOLFGANG ISER, *1926) in their interpretations. Conversely, WAYNE C. BOOTH (*1921) introduced the concept of the "implied author" for the originator constructed in the text. Audience images determine media conventions: Fox is unlikely to air *Bowling for Columbine*.

Constraints from message

MOORE, his team and organization are gatekeepers and agenda-setters. They reject, select and structure content for their books and films, but they do so under constraints from message and medium. For instance, unlike his documentaries, *Stupid White Men* is full of lists and statistics. *Bowling for Columbine*, however, crucially depends on the footage the camera recorded during MOORE's interview with CHARLTON HESTON. Tables of statistics seem to work in books, but not on film. An account of a meeting with HESTON in print would hardly succeed as well as the documentary scene (spontaneously captured by a camera and a microphone) did.

News values

Among others, PIERRE BOURDIEU (1998) and NIKLAS LUHMANN (1996: 57–66) have described how the mass media select what they consider "news value" under specific systemic constraints. In view of the dominance of visual content on television, one might argue for TV news: the 'better' the footage (according to systemic requirements), the higher the projected rating and the more likely the news item to be transmitted. News value makes the communicative process likely to occur. JACKIE HARRISON (in CREEBER 2001: 115) has summed up the values for TV news. The event should
- contain good pictures
- contain short, dramatic occurrences that can be sensationalized
- have novelty value
- be open to simple reporting
- occur on a grand scale
- be negative or contain violence, crime, confrontation or catastrophe
- be highly unexpected, or contain things that one would not expect to happen
- have meaning and relevance to the audience
- be similar to events that are already in the news.

Constraints from medium

DANIEL CHANDLER (1995) neatly summarizes that "*any medium facilitates, emphasizes, intensifies, amplifies, enhances or extends certain kinds of use or experience whilst inhibiting, restricting or reducing other kinds.*" The basic constraint, however, is media access, gov-

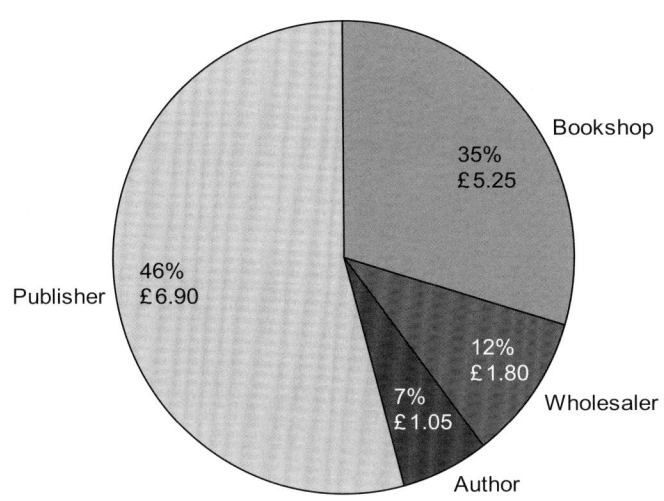

Fig. 9: Breakdown of book costs (from BURTON 2002: 67)

erned, for instance, by cost (cf. fig. 9): From the 1930s to the 1950s, both Warner Bros. and Disney became famous for their cartoon animations on film, marked by big budgets and detailed drawings that devoured enormous amounts of time and money and sought to cash in by global distribution. Since the advent of digital visuality, animated films have been produced merely to boost sales of a toy product line (such as Lego's infantile Bionicle movies, available on DVD, 2003–2004). Today, any programmer familiar with the programmes Flash or Quicktime can achieve stunning visual effects and publish them at little cost on the Internet. This example illustrates the constraints that the medium exerts on both the communicator and the receiver: access to media technology and the skills and competence to operate this technology.

The receiver

Most of the specifications of the communicator also determine the receiver in MALETZKE's model. According to a number of criteria, advertisers regularly segment receivers into personal, social and cultural sub-groups. If I think of myself as a liberal intellectual from Europe then I am likely to read MOORE, and maybe less likely to enjoy the 'Superbowl' final in American Football. On the other hand, I may also enjoy his book if I think of myself as a humorous person or as an unemployed victim of capitalism. The main parameters of self-images are gender, ethnicity, age, education, class, family, nation, and politics. Knowing that I am part of a large community of MOORE *aficionados* will contribute to my enjoyment, and likewise the image that I have formed of MICHAEL

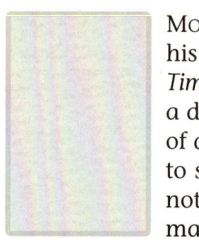

Moore will determine how I read his books. Will I continue to like his work after my best friend (or my wife, my son, *The New York Times*) has declared him a biased polemicist? It will certainly make a difference if I read one of his books on my own or become part of a cinema audience watching one of his films. Although likely to share in the media usage of my peer group, I may, however, not want to see myself as merely one member in Michael Moore's mass audience.

Receivers evolve into users

The digital revolution has redefined the field of media communication. The receiver has been transformed into a user. Users choose from the heterogeneous and potentially unlimited content on digital media and they might be at the same time communicators who publish content on their websites. This content may be visual or aural, narrative or expository, documentary or fictional, and clearly go beyond traditional genres (e.g., newspaper, journal). Information is not 'pushed' at the receiver, but the user 'pulls' it by using links within the space of a communicative network (such as the World Wide Web, WWW). Faulstich (2002: 41) has argued that the concept of mutual interactivity can hardly be incorporated into this model that relies on lines and arrows.

3 Toronto School, media determinism and systems theory

We become what we behold. We shape our tools, and then our tools shape us.
Marshall McLuhan

Toronto School

The Toronto School broke with the central tenets of the empirical and effects- or uses-orientated mass-communication research in the USA. In this view, the media were not merely instruments or contents, but in themselves the shaping element in the history of mankind. The Toronto School has been most influential in its technological determinism, in its enthusiastic focus on the media themselves. In *The Bias of Communication* (1951), economist Harold A. Innis assessed the crucial role of media in civilization and nation building, distinguishing between monumental media (e.g., hieroglyphics carved in stone and the pyramids providing stability for the Pharaohs) and portable media (parchment, paper, print, which are expansive and destabilizing). For Innis, communication and the media were essential in mastering space and time; they were, therefore, the brick and mortar of a culture much more than mere tools. In addition, Innis's analyses of transport and logistics in various contexts (fur trade, ancient Egypt, railways and the press) opened up the path towards a more historical understanding of the media.

The idea of a historical process of "epochs" in the development of the media as well as the emphasis on technological determinism was further elaborated in MARSHALL MCLUHAN's *The Gutenberg Galaxy* (1962) and *Understanding Media* (1964). MCLUHAN's slogan "The medium is the message" inaugurated media studies in that it paved the way towards an analysis of the media beyond their function in channelling contents or messages. MCLUHAN argued that light is the ultimate medium in that it has no content and cannot in itself be carried as a message (the way writing carries language or print carries writing). He was enthusiastic about the relevance and promise of the media as "extensions of man" that are hooked onto the central nervous system. The media – in this broad conception any artefact human beings use – consist of messages that crucially determine human affairs and the history of the world.

The medium is the message: McLuhan

Television, MCLUHAN argued, is a cool medium because it affords synaesthetic, communal experience close to real physical contact – as opposed to hot media which are focused on a particular sense perception, are highly defined and detailed, and further individuality (radio, print). This provocative extension of the term 'media', his denigration of print and contents drew scathing criticism from holders of materialist as well as empiricist or semiotic approaches. GEOFFREY WAGNER bemoaned the "antiprint mania" of "McLuhanacy" (BENJAMIN DEMOTT 1966); ENZENSBERGER (1970) denounced his work as an idiotic and reactionary doctrine of salvation. More recently (and more fundamentally) RAINER LESCHKE (2003: 256–257) chided the attempt to 'interpret' the media as if they were an aesthetic object.

'Hot' and 'cool' media

In his concept of history as media history, MCLUHAN sketched a shift from a unified, tribal, oral culture based on 'hands on' experience to a literate culture (especially after print) that disrupts and splits up experience and has brought about distance, individuality, abstraction and rationality. Beyond this obsolete GUTENBERG galaxy, MCLUHAN found the "global village", a decline of print logic, a retribalization that brings social groups together in communal sensory experience, and a return to an anti-hierarchical wholeness. This was in turn attacked for its unfounded utopianism. With the advent of global networks, however, MCLUHAN was rediscovered and advocated by Internet theorists such as STUART MOULTHROP (who envisaged a GUTENBERG renaissance to replace the post-literate idiot box television, 1993), DERRICK DE KERCKHOVE (who transposed the axiom of participatory media from television to computers, 1995), SHERRY TURKLE (who argued that computer media are a social laboratory that retribalizes users, 1995), or HOWARD RHEINGOLD (who assessed the potential

The "global village"

of virtual communities and transient wireless smart mobs, 1993, 2002).

Media bias, media logic, media event

Both INNIS and McLUHAN insisted on the 'media bias' that locates a direct influence on human beings in the media technologies they use. This has further led to the concepts of 'media logic' (ALT-HEIDE/SNOW 1979), which comprises the notion that 'real world' events are shaped and constructed by their media representations, and of 'media event' (according to BOORSTIN 1980 and DAYAN/KATZ 1992). In the historical, narrow sense, the term 'media event' was used to describe an event which is merely staged for the media and therefore merely a pseudo-event, but now it often refers more generally to an event which attracts particular attention in the media. In fact, most of the shows designated as reality TV or 'docu-soaps' may be termed staged events, in keeping with the media logic of TV. JOSHUA MEYROWITZ (1985) also drew on McLUHAN to argue that electronic media (and especially television) have dissolved boundaries between distinct social, gender or age groups which have all merged in audiences rearranged by the media.

Discourse networks: Kittler

FRIEDRICH A. KITTLER (*1943), a renegade from literary studies, picked up this line of thought and argued against hermeneutics and other meaning-seeking methods in the humanities that media history is a history of material media and that one should give up on the quest for meaning in the media. Instead, he developed a hermeneutics of media technologies and suggested a history of *Aufschreibesysteme* (discourse networks: acoustic and optic storage media such as gramophone, film, and typewriter within a media apparatus). According to KITTLER (1986, 1987), cultural history is the history of media practices. Instead of reading signs, he reads the technologies of storing and processing signs, in other words, he ascribes 'meanings' to hardware and electrical circuits rather than to texts. Around 1800, poetry establishes hallucinatory surrogates of sensual perception, only to be replaced by media technologies around 1900.

Media and war

Another provocative line of argument underlies KITTLER's narrow focus on media and war as determining forces of media development, conveyed by the double meaning of the term "intelligence". The French architect and theoretician PAUL VIRILIO (*1932) provided similar analogies between media practices and warfare. According to VIRILIO, the media (such as television and film) can only be regarded as "weapons of mass distraction" (as the pun circulating during the second Iraq war reads). Arms technologies spur on the development of new media in order to enable total visual control: In *Guerre et cinéma* (1984), VIRILIO bluntly states that cinema is war and war is cinema, and subsequently (for instance in his *L'Écran du désert*, 1991), he read both Iraq wars, the Kosovo

Media communication: models, schools, and theories

war, or the life and death of Princess DIANA, the ultimate media personality, accordingly. This results in an apocalypse of controlled perception, destroyed urbanity and arsenals of increasing pace. Advance intelligence will secure a media advantage in the perpetual state of war, and NORBERT BOLZ (2000: 328) echoes that as knowledge has become universal it is now only advance knowledge (*Vorsprungswissen*) that secures power.

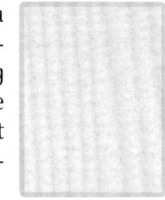

Speed is the second focus in this deterministic narrowing of media theory in VIRILIO's *dromologie* (Greek *dromos*, 'runner, race'). For VIRILIO, the media can also be described as technologies of increased velocity. In contemporary media society, possession of time has replaced control over space. The space of humanity, according to VIRILIO, is in the merciless and destructive grip of unleashed mobility and mediality. Finally, the media "vision machine" is entering the ultimate space of the living body. As KAY KIRCHMANN (1998) argued, VIRILIO's dromology is an anti-utopian version of McLUHAN's vision of the global village.

Media and velocity: Virilio's dromologie

VILÉM FLUSSER (1920–1991) was a polyglot Czech Jew who lived in Brazil and in Europe, teaching in Portugal, France, and Germany, whose nomadic existence equals his nomadic thinking (KLOOCK / SPAHR 1997: 82–84). In *Medienkultur* (1997) he positioned the telematic information society against a deluge of mass-media imagery which victimizes its spectators. Telematics is a neologism combining telecommunication and informatics. Against one-way reality effects, which destroy face-to-face interacting communities, FLUSSER placed the utopian society of telematics. FLUSSER envisioned interactive networks, rather than mass-mediated information packages, which would bring humanity closer together and result in a diversified, multi-relational existence.

Telematics: Vilém Flusser

So far, we have asked in a number of ways how the media relate to human beings. This question is rather irrelevant for the most complex and most abstract transdiciplinary approach to the media, taken by sociological systems theory (NIKLAS LUHMANN, 1927–1998). A disciple of TALCOTT PARSONS, LUHMANN adopts PARSONS's abstract notion of the media. For PARSONS, society as well as social groups and even individuals are social systems. Social systems interact through symbolic exchange, and that is the basis for the systems-theory approach to the media. In the 1950s, PARSONS developed the AGIL pattern that describes the principal aims of social systems (adaptation, goal attainment, integration, and latent pattern maintenance). In order to achieve these goals in a large variety of situations, systems operate with generalized symbolic media of interchange. PARSONS's key examples are power and money. Money, for instance, is a generalized symbolic medium of interchange because (1) it only symbolizes value, (2) it is institu-

Systems theory: Symbolic interchange

tionalized by legal authority, (3) it mediates economic exchange, enables circulation, and (4) it does not constitute a zero-sum situation (i.e., may be increased or decreased in total).

Luhmann: Making communication possible

LUHMANN radicalizes PARSONS's ideas in arguing that society does not consist of classes or people, but of communicative processes. According to LUHMANN, communication is generally unlikely to occur and the 'real' world necessarily remains unknowable, i.e., inaccessible to cognition. Social systems are designed to facilitate communication by reducing the complexity of a chaotic and amorphous world. For LUHMANN, love, truth, and art may also be functional media within social systems. Thus, systems regulate what kinds of information are selected and processed (and therefore, what constitutes meaning). Music may be classified as sound (using the medium air), but within the aesthetic realm of music sound is given a disciplined form – a differentiation which may be lost on your neighbour who thinks 'noise' when you think 'music'. Thus, the arts (such as music) may be described as second-order media which enable communication, a kind of communication which is based on the difference between medium and form. LUHMANN argues that systems are unstable, because these differences are continuously defined and redefined by the boundaries that separate them from their environment.

Autopoietic systems

The basic question that systems theory addresses is how systems communicate. Language facilitates understanding, media of dissemination are intended to reach out to addressees of communication, and, crucially, generalized media of symbolic exchange seek to guarantee success in communication. For LUHMANN, communication is selection and processing rather than transmission. The core element of social systems, LUHMANN argued, is *autopoiesis* (Greek, 'self-creation'), a term transferred from cognitive biology (HUMBERTO MATURANA, *1928; FRANCISCO VARELA, 1946–2001) to sociology by LUHMANN. Autopoietic systems are closed systems which are able to regenerate themselves, continually monitoring and renewing their parts. Within such a system, meaning-making is a process of filtering information from the environment, thus reducing complexity: There is no truthful or essential message which is transported in a transmission process. What we consider the 'reality' comes to us as a product of operations within the autopoietic systems in which we take part.

The system of mass media

LUHMANN proposed a broad definition of media, but he also specifically addressed the mass media. The mass media, LUHMANN argued in *The Reality of the Mass Media* (2000; *Die Realität der Massenmedien*, 1996), operate within a system of their own. (LUHMANN's focus is on media of mass dissemination such as television and radio; he does not address media networks based on telephones

Media communication: models, schools, and theories

or computers.) In the mass media (as in other social systems) it is not the 'objective' environmental set of criteria that determines what counts as information, but the self-referential modes of processing. The role of the mass media in the general self-reproduction of society and in the reduction of complexity is essential. LUHMANN's view of the mass media, however, is very reminiscent of GERBNER's cultivation thesis and may easily be accommodated to established lines of research into, for instance, agenda-setting, media bias or mainstreaming.

LUHMANN's key issue – investigating how systems observe their environment – is also at the heart of the constructivist endeavour (which in its descent from cognitive science (HUMBERTO MATURANA) and cybernetics (HEINZ VON FOERSTER) is closely related to systems theory). Adapting the well-known proverb, one might sum up the approach thus: "cognition lies in the mind of the beholder". Constructivists hold that sense perceptions do not offer mimetic representations or access to a reality, but they construct reality by taking recourse to experience (knowledge, norms, consensus). Perception is a process of testing hypotheses according to plausibility, usefulness, consistency etc. In terms of media studies, therefore, the media do not merely represent a (media-external) reality, but actively shape and construct this reality in an increasingly differentiated set of media practices. Cognitivism has been particularly dominant in recent German media studies (S. J. SCHMIDT 2000, 2003; MERTEN / SCHMIDT / WEISCHENBERG 1994) and it has also been useful in reinvigorating film theory, assigning a more active role to the spectator in neo-formalist approaches (BORDWELL 1989, BORDWELL / CARROLL 1996, BORDWELL / THOMPSON 2001).

Construc-tivism

4 A circular model of media communication

Whoever controls the media – the images – controls the culture.
ALLEN GINSBERG

All of the recent approaches, whether from within cultural studies, constructivism or systems theory, challenge the idea of communication as a linear process. As early as in 1954 WILBUR SCHRAMM replaced the transmission model with a circular model because he saw no beginning and no end to the communication process. He also substituted the apersonal categories of "information source" and "destination" in the mathematical model of communication for the categories "encoder" and "decoder" which can mutually exchange messages provided their fields of experience overlap.

Encoding / decoding

Because media communication is not linear, that is, because it does not originate at one point and end at another, a circular

Fig. 10: Circular model of communication (modified from BURTON 2002: 54)

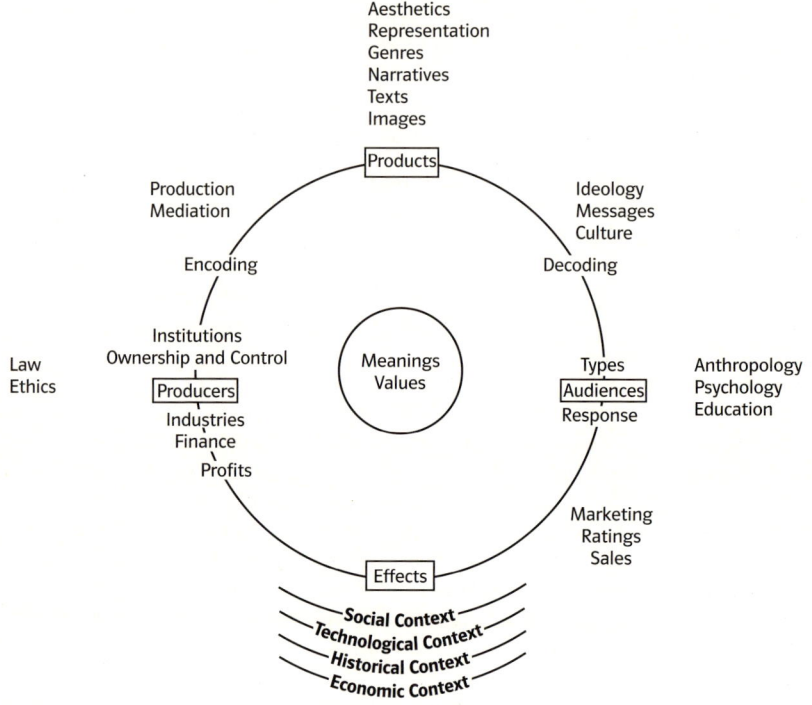

| | Circular model of media communication | model is suited best to represent the process. Our model (fig. 10) is modified from GRAEME BURTON's extension of STUART HALL's half-circular model (BURTON 2002: 54). This circle has four cardinal points: product orientation, audience orientation, context orientation and producer orientation. |

Circular model of media communication

model is suited best to represent the process. Our model (fig. 10) is modified from GRAEME BURTON's extension of STUART HALL's half-circular model (BURTON 2002: 54). This circle has four cardinal points: product orientation, audience orientation, context orientation and producer orientation.

Product orientation

Media **images**, **texts** and **languages**: How do the words, images or sounds structure the signifying process in different media?
Media **narratives**: How do the media tell stories in different ways? Do all media tell stories and do they share certain features?
Media **genres**: How can we categorize or frame media products? What are the rules and functions determining these categorizations? What are the genre repertoires and how do certain features relate to specific media (e.g., how does the medium television and the genre sitcom interrelate)?
Media **representations**: How do the media shape and construe our 'reality'? How do the media stereotype and disseminate collective images?

Media **ideologies**: What is the relationship between values, ideas and power in the media? How are these ideas circulated, and how do they become dominant/hegemonic or subordinate/marginal?
Media **aesthetics**: How can we address media as fields for artistic practice, incorporating questions of technology, or institutions? How do aesthetic forms relate to the media environments in which they appear? How do artistic *avant-gardes* use the media?

Media **audiences**: What are the media audiences? How do media and audiences interact? What do audiences do with different media (and vice versa)?

Audience orientation

Media **marketing**: How do the media inform or draw attention to products or issues? How do marketing and advertising shape the cultural and social environment? What is the relationship between media and consumption? How can we classify audiences (see LACEY 2002: 181–187): e.g., on a social scale of "workers"– professional, white-collar, skilled manual, semi-skilled, unskilled – or according to values (VALS: Values, Attitudes, and Lifestyles Survey) and 'tribes': achievers, believers, makers, strugglers; trendies, traditionalists, rebels; couch potatoes, comedy addicts? How and when do the mass media schedule programmes to attract audiences?
Media **psychology**: How do the media determine individual behaviour? What are the affective and cognitive frameworks of media production and reception?
Media **education**: How can we spread 'media literacy' and 'media competence'? How can we prepare (young and old) people in a climate of increased and diversified media usage? What is the impact of the media on emotional, social and cognitive processes of learning? How do we account for diversity of gender, class, and race in media usage? More specifically, how do we address the problem of violence in the media?
Media **anthropology**: How do the media construct cultures? How are media images and sounds negotiated in lived practice?

Media **sociology**: How do the media construct social reality? How do social groups or individuals interact with and operate the media? How do the media function in social exchange processes?

Context orientation

Media **technology**: How do technology and technological change shape the production or reception of media products, their meanings or integration into media systems? How did the advent of the remote control, the video recorder or the set-top box change television? One may also look at dead technologies: Whatever happened to the videophone and pneumatic delivery? Whatever happened to the telephone used for a radio-like information service (that ran as Telefon Hirmondo, devised by inventor TIVADAR PUSKÁS, from 1893 to 1917 in Budapest)?

Media **history**: This history of media technologies is one aspect of media history. How and why have the media grown in complexity? How did the technologies, systems and institutions evolve? How can we adequately display media history in chronicles, biographies or structural narratives, i.e., narratives focused on particular (mass) media?

Media **philosophy**: How do the media determine what we are (ontology) or how we know or think (epistemology)? How do the media impinge on human existence?

Producer orientation

Media **production**: Why, how, and for whom are media texts produced? What are the professional skills and resources needed? How do the processes work and what are the constraints? How can we best use media tools? For example, how do I prepare a Power-Point presentation, how do I design a homepage, produce a newspaper or video?

Media **industries**: What are the production processes in different media? How are media or media products distributed? What are the costs in various media and who owns the means of production? How are media markets regulated? What are the effects of cross-media ownership (such as RUPERT MURDOCH owning national newspapers and digital TV company BSkyB), transnational ownership (SILVIO BERLUSCONI owning major TV stations in France and Italy) or the influence of global media producers?

Media **institutions**: How do institutions organize and regulate different media? What are the values, interest, the status or the formal characteristics of media institutions that produce, regulate or censor media contents, act as pressure groups or media businesses? Which parts do, for instance, the British Film Institute, the British Audience Research Board (BARB) or the British Board of Film Classification (BBFC) play in British film?

Media **law**: How are the interests of the general public and the individual regulated in the media sphere, for example, how do we preserve copyright, privacy and free speech in the World Wide Web; how do we prevent the global distribution of defamation, pornography and fascism? In this vein, one might investigate "fair use" principles in the Digital Millennium Copyright Act (which passed US Congress in 1998) or notorious cases of plagiarism. These include the copying of LEBBEUS WOODS's chair from a 1987 drawing for the initial sequence of *Twelve Monkeys* (D: TERRY GILLIAM, 1995) and Beatle GEORGE HARRISON's plagiarism of The Chiffon's "He's So Fine" (1963) in "My Sweet Lord" (1970). In 1984, the U.S. Supreme Court famously ruled against a ban of VHS home taping (Sony Corp *vs.* Universal City Studios 1984).

Media **ethics**: How do the media relate to our behavioural norms and how do we react to violations of these norms? How can we (metaethically) describe how we arrive at certain media norms derived from aesthetics, religion or discourse ethics? How do behavioural norms affect the work of media producers (e.g., journalists), institutions (e.g., censorship, see for instance the cases on the BBFC website) or users? Issues include the establishment of 'netiquette', digital manipulation ('thinning') of models in magazine ads, or participatory journalism after the September 11 attacks. The plan by Channel 4 to show a decomposing body filmed in a secluded area of the London Science Museum (*Media Guardian* 4/11/2004) is certainly an issue for media ethics.

3 Media signs and cultural studies

1 Semiotics and cultural studies: From Barthes to Hall

> "[...] there are full professors in this place who read nothing but cereal boxes."
> "It's the only avant-garde we've got."
>
> DON DELILLO, *White Noise* (1985)

Media semiotics

The circular model introduced above reflects text-centred semiotic approaches to the media as well as the cultural studies approach advocated in the seminal essay by STUART HALL, "Encoding / Decoding" (1973/1980). HALL's model of encoding and decoding accounts for the fact that the meaning structures which are encoded by the media producer may not be the meaning structures which are decoded by the audience. HALL's model took a cue from ROLAND BARTHES (1915–1980; *Mythologies* 1957, *S/Z* 1970), and UMBERTO ECO (*1932; *A Theory of Semiotics* 1976). From BARTHES, HALL adapted the term 'reality effect'. It described a crisis of representation which naturalizes images as representations of the real in order to stabilize dominant ideologies. Semiotics provides concepts to analyse texts as systems of signs (Greek *semeion*). Setting apart the contents of signification, semiotic formalism equips the reader with a terminology to overcome the naturalization of media images and to unlock formal meanings of the media, i.e., to read the signs, languages, and codes of the media.

Reading media texts

At the heart of these language analogies is the idea that we can read media texts in a way similar to the way written texts are read: as pieces of fabric (Latin *textum*) woven from images, words, and sounds. A recent British Council conference on literature and media was called "Reading Screens". JAMES MONACO's standard introduction to film studies tells you *How to Read a Film*. Etymologically, photography is 'writing in light' and cinematography 'writing in movement' (Greek *gráphein*, this word covers writing, drawing and engraving). We unlock the codes, i.e., the conventions and rules which are at work to provide meaning in communication. Because meanings are not stable, but are subject to negotiation, one can assume that signs do not have natural or stable meanings but merely potential that may or may not be realized in reading media texts.

Signifier and signified

In 1916, FERDINAND DE SAUSSURE's *Cours de linguistique générale* proposed a two-fold structure of the sign, composed of a *signifiant* (signifier) and a *signifié* (signified). The signifier is a physical

Fig. 11: Ferdinand de Saussure's *model of the sign* (modified)

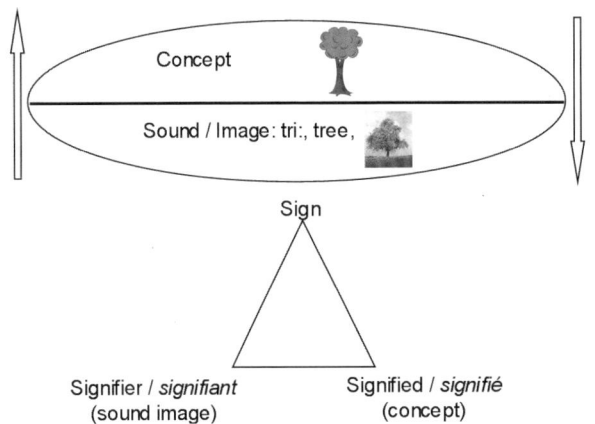

object, sound, a printed word, an image composed of colours and shades etc., for instance, the printed word 'tree' or the photograph of a tree or a photograph of the American president in front of the American flag or the sound of the national anthem. These signifiers carry a whole range of meanings or concepts (signifieds). In the case of symbolic language, the link between signifier and signified is wholly arbitrary, so that 'tree', 'arbre' and 'Baum' relate to the same concept. The mental concepts of a tree may vary considerably and the various meanings of 'tree' may or may not be activated in the process of signification which constitutes the meaning-making.

As an example, let us look at a sign, a still from the movie *Adaptation* (D: Spike Jonze, 2002, fig. 12). Similar to a 16th-century emblem, it is an iconotext that combines an image with an interpretative *subscriptio* or caption. The image is a signifier for an uninhabitable landscape of volcanoes and lava, but the caption reads "Hollywood, CA". This signifies a location, a city and an American state (California). It further signifies the affluent, sunny, image-generating centre of the global entertainment industry. Image and caption generate a humorous paradox: the semantic incongruity produced by the fact that the linguistic information anchors the image of a wasteland of fire with a place-name that suggests the heartland of entertainment. From experience with advertisements, documentaries and news programmes, we may be familiar with the fixing of meaning in an 'anchorage', but the activation of these mutually exclusive concepts (or, in cognitive theory: schemata or scripts) disorientates and generates the atten-

Anchoring meaning

Fig. 12: Still from the movie "Adaptation"

tion which prepares the caption in a subsequent frame ("Forty Billion and Forty Years Earlier"). This next caption anchors the image historically; the lava turns into a primordial soup and the 'forty years' provides a further anchor in the lifetime of the narrator-protagonist, Charlie Kaufman, thus resolving the first humorous incongruity and at the same time supplying the next.

Index, icon, symbol

CHARLES S. PEIRCE (1839–1914) provided an alternative concept of the sign which is less rooted in linguistics. PEIRCE supposed a triadic sign system. The indexical sign has a direct causal connection to its object. The Geiger counter makes radioactivity perceptible and smoke is an index of fire. The iconic sign is marked by a resemblance to its object, often in versions that reduce complexity (as in the case of desktop icons in software programmes). This is true for pictograms, cartoon drawings and maps and often for photographic and filmic signs. One might say that the image of the lava landscape is an index of its object, because it was 'there' when the photograph was taken, but that it is also an icon of the volcanic landscape because it resembles (in flat two dimensions) this specific (three-dimensional) landscape. A symbolic sign is related to its object merely by cultural convention, as in the case of alphabetic writing. Thus, we may read the landscape as desolate and hostile and we know that "Hollywood, CA" stands for an American city in the state of California. The word 'flag' stands for the object 'flag' and the fifty stars in the American flag stand for the states of the USA – but the connection is not physical but based on cultural convention.

Denotation and connotation

The photograph of the American flag therefore covers a general range of meanings. The photograph is an index of the flag, because at one point they shared a physical space. It is also indexical in that it resembles the flag it shows, while the flag symbolizes the United States of America. In other words, it shows on the surface, quite simply, a flag, its apparent, 'literal' or general meaning at face value, its denotative meaning. There is, however, a deep structure of meanings embedded within the flag (or, for that matter, Hollywood), such as patriotism, nationalism, tradition, democracy, militarism etc. This range of ideological, social or cultural implications is the connotative meaning. ROLAND BARTHES argued that 'naturalization' of connotative meanings generates myth – for instance when the connotative meaning of patriotism is automatically read into the myth of the patriotic flag.

Primary codes and secondary codes

There is a conventional shot type, with a certain camera angle and lighting in a particular sequence for filming a president addressing the nation; for instance a medium shot comes before you see him in close-up. These shots may be described as primary codes (or technical codes), the rules of visual narrative. Secondary codes (discourses, conventions, symbolic codes), however, are also at work. For instance, one would not expect the president to wear pyjamas or to use swearwords. What impression would canned laughter instead of the national anthem or rock music and rapid cuts evoke? You would probably think you were viewing a sitcom or a music video instead of a presidential address.

Preferred meaning

The image of the president in front of the flag, singing the national anthem, suggests a meaning anchorage which designates the president as a true patriot. The careful *mise-en-scène* (by KARL ROVE and his team) of GEORGE W. BUSH's "Mission Accomplished" speech on the aircraft carrier USS Abraham Lincoln on May 1, 2003 is a case in point. Bush arrived as co-pilot of a Viking aircraft (labelled "George W. Bush, Commander-in-Chief"). Under a glorious afternoon sun, in front of a stars-and-stripes "Mission Accomplished" banner and dressed in a tight-fitting combat suit he declared to cheering crowds of sailors and aviators that the war in Iraq was over – a scene replete with secondary codes. Encoded within the audiovisual content, therefore, we find a preferred meaning, a bias towards a certain meaning. This is a key element in HALL's model because, on the one hand, the encoder attempts to limit the range of meaning, but on the other hand, the process will never be captured by a mere linear arrow.

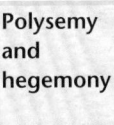

Polysemy and hegemony

What occurs instead is the negotiation of meaning. The sign of the president is polysemic, it is overloaded with meanings, full of multiple codes operating at the same time. Are we free to choose a different reading of this image of a man talking in front of the flag? First of all, the viewer has to own a TV set and he must know how to operate it. Secondly, it is important to know that the man is the president of the USA and that the flag with the stars and stripes is the US flag and that the USA is the most powerful state in the world and a Western democracy, and so forth, that is, you have to activate various frameworks of knowledge. Third, the viewer has to be familiar with the codes of a presidential address on television. Fourth, there will be the logo of a TV company in a corner of the image, signifying an institutional context. If the presidential address is repeated again and again in various media, in fact, you might be led to think that an unseen force controlling the media wants to make sure that everybody watches the president making his address. This, it might be argued, is cultural hegemony, because it is accepted as natural and legitimate by the viewers that the president is ubiquitous. The mass media thus exert subtle cultural force over their recipients (see the section on GRAMSCI below). One question embedded within the signifying process is therefore: Who owns and finances and institutionalizes the signs?

Decoding meaning structures

What you know about the president, however, might induce you to a deviant or oppositional reading. You might be struck by the tanned skin of the president and read this as a sign of laziness, even if it might be a consequence of your maladjusted TV controls. What you make of the middle-aged white, male person will be crucially dependent on your ethnic background, on your age, nationality, gender, religion and job, on your education, on your values and ideologies. That is, from the encoded meaning structure '1', you decode a different meaning structure '2'. Immediately, more questions arise: How can these new and deviant meaning structures be identified and secured, i.e., by measuring ratings and product sales? What feedback do these meaning structures trigger, and how does it, in turn, influence the media meanings and messages? Are we going to see a pale president in the address next year because audience research has suggested that the president's tan does not appeal to an important audience segment? These questions extend the semiotic process into the cultural realm.

Dominant, negotiated, oppositional reading

Because HALL conceives of the audience as actively involved in the meaning-making process, he allows for three potential readings of a message:

(1) dominant-hegemonic or preferred readings encouraged by the producer;
(2) negotiated readings in which audiences struggle with preferred readings, modify and partially reject them according to their own cultural frameworks;
(3) oppositional readings which either disagree with or ignore the suggested meanings.

2 Cultural studies and media cultures

Hardly anyone who enjoys Madonna also enjoys Milton and fans of Abba generally have little enthusiasm for Aeschylus.

ANTONY EASTHOPE (1997)

As our key example, the model of encoding/decoding illustrates, cultural-studies approaches to the media have traditionally seen themselves as interventionist and politically committed. This is particularly true of the Birmingham Centre for Contemporary Cultural Studies (CCCS), where HALL worked from 1964 to 1979, and other centres of cultural studies that conduct research into the media (Centre for Television Research, Leeds; Glasgow Media Group; Open University; Center for Mass Communication Research, Leicester; see G. TURNER 2003: 65–68). In contrast, American mass-communication research starts from the assumption that an open, democratic and liberal society produces choices and that, ultimately, the audience determines what it wants to hear, read, or see (i.e., their media) rather than vice versa. In fact, one can draw a matrix of cultural studies approaches to the media according to the degree to which they accept the pluralist audience activity or insist on the determining factor of media producers and message encoding (see fig. 13).

Inter-ventionism

The key example of STUART HALL shows that study of media culture is at the very core of British cultural studies. GRAEME TURNER concludes that *"within British cultural studies the primary focus of ideological analysis has been on the media, in particular on their definitions of social relations and political problems, and on their implication in the production and transformation of popular ideologies. [...] This was the central concern for the Birmingham centre."* (G. TURNER 2003: 20)

Media in British cultural studies

RAYMOND WILLIAMS (1921–1988) and RICHARD HOGGART, the first director of the CCCS, turned to mass media products in order to liberate the Humanities from the élitist aestheticism of Literary Criticism, which championed minority culture over the anarchy of mass civilization (MATTHEW ARNOLD, *Culture and Anarchy* 1869, F. R. LEAVIS, *Mass Civilization and Minority Culture* 1930). The potential of resistance that this culturalism saw in the home-grown British working-class culture was subsequently challenged by the structuralist turn in cultural studies, but the emphasis on the media remained. Particularly WILLIAMS must be credited with inaugurating an indigenous British media research in his analysis of journalism (*Communications* 1962) and his diagnosis of the incessant flow of TV programming (*Television* 1974).

Culturalism

Whereas culturalism operated within the pragmatic traditions of British academia, in the 1970s, COLIN MACCABE, LAURA MULVEY and

Fig. 13: Critical views of media and society (expanded from BURTON 2002:
48, MARRIS / THORNHAM 2000: 5–17)

Marxism	The media influence society, helps preserve power structure according to class, race and gender; meanings and dominant ideologies as part of the superstructure above an economic power base, i.e. the distribution of wealth, centralized media ownership supports idea of a media oligarchy	Determinist
Neo-Marxism, "Left Leavisite"	Address questions of meaning and dominant ideologies GRAMSCI: "hegemony": dominant ideologies rule because they are accepted as natural, rule by consent and invisible power Frankfurt School: negative effects of powerful mass culture, critical media studies	Determinist
Mass Culture	ARNOLD, F.R. & Q.D. LEAVIS: standardization, cheap emotionality, lit.crit. scrutiny *vs.* passive media diversion	Determinist
Culturalism	HOGGART, WILLIAMS: developing media skills, media education, break with 'minority culture' tradition	Tentatively pluralist
Mass Communication	LAZARSFELD/MERTON: empirical and behaviourist, mass persuasion, propaganda, effects, pluralist societies produce pluralist media, administrative media studies Chicago School: MEAD, COOLEY Toronto School: INNIS, McLUHAN	Pluralist
Semiotics	HALL: study of discourse, reading messages semiotically, circulation model, providing social context to communication model	Tentatively pluralist
Cultural Studies Post-modernism	FISKE, FRITH, MORLEY, HEBDIGE, JENKINS: cultural economy autonomous of financial economy: viewers produce meaning freely, interest in subcultures, audience and 'fandom'	Pluralist
Gender, feminism	TUCHMAN, MULVEY, KUHN, BRUNSDON, ANG, McROBBIE Representations of gender, Institutional role of women Cyberfeminsim: HARAWAY, PLANT	Determinist-pluralist

"*Screen* theory" drew on the work of French theorists CHRISTIAN METZ, JACQUES LACAN and LOUIS ALTHUSSER and psychoanalysis to argue that film and television write the viewer into the text, positioning him or her and almost totally determining the dominant ideological position in a process theorized as "interpellation". In this view, only formally challenging *avant-garde* texts can liberate an audience from the positioning at work even in popular realism – a debate which was fought over TV mini-series that represented the British working-classes such as *Days of Hope* (D: KEN LOACH, Scr: JIM ALLEN, 1975) or *Boys from the Blackstuff* (D: PHILIP SAVILLE, Scr: ALAN BLEASDALE, 1982).

Screen theory

Psychoanalytic *Screen* theories have subsequently been challenged not only from within cultural studies, but also by the so-called 'Wisconsin School' of neo-formalist film analysis (DAVID BORDWELL, NOËL CARROLL, KRISTIN THOMPSON, JANET STAIGER). In the volume with the programmatic title *Post-Theory: Reconstructing Film Studies* (1996), BORDWELL and CARROLL castigated the obscurantism and determinism of most semiotic-psychoanalytic film theory. The development may be followed in the comprehensive anthologies in film theory, provided, e.g., by COHEN/BRAUDY 1999 and STAM/MILLER 2000. In her study *Breaking the Glass Armor* (1988: 4–46), KRISTIN THOMPSON laid out the main tenets of neo-formalism: the focus on aesthetics (but not on high art), the focus on an active spectator (derived from NELSON GOODMAN and cognitivism), the insistence on the artistic value of defamiliarizing the habitual (derived from Russian formalism), the respect for distinct meanings in individual films, and the quest for motivation, agency and function in art.

Neo-formalism

As HEPP (1999) notes, cultural studies have spread from the CCCS not just all over Europe, but also via adapted versions in Australia (GRAEME TURNER), the US (JOHN FISKE, LAWRENCE GROSSBERG), and the Netherlands (IEN ANG). In Germany, there has been a tendency to dissociate the home-grown *Kulturwissenschaft*, from the Anglo-American cultural studies (see SOMMER 2003: 44–89, NÜNNING 2002, NÜNNING/NÜNNING 2003). German *Kulturwissenschaft* is derived from a redefined field of humanities or *Geisteswissenschaft*, and therefore less politically committed, less focused on popular culture and more historically aware than its British counterpart. All in all, however, the influence of cultural studies on media studies in Germany and elsewhere can hardly be overrated (HEPP 1999: 105–108).

International cultural studies

The Italian philosopher ANTONIO GRAMSCI (1891–1937) is another crucial influence in cultural studies. KARL MARX held that social relations are governed by the material base of economic class relations (controlled by those who own the means of production).

Marxism and Gramsci

In this view culture is secondary to economics. Culture is seen in the 'base / superstructure' model as a sphere where ideologies are disseminated by the ruling class according to its interests. GRAMSCI defined hegemony as rule of cultural leaders not by force or coercion, but by the subtle rule of acculturation. This requires the subordinate social group to accept the dominant ideology as legitimate. What seems natural, therefore, is the result of cultural force.

Frankfurt School

Marxism experienced another cultural turn in the critique of mass culture advocated by the Frankfurt School. Its most important theorists include HERBERT MARCUSE (1898–1979), LEO LÖWENTHAL (1900–1993), ADORNO, and HORKHEIMER. Within the Institute for Social Research (founded in 1923, forced to emigrate to New York from 1933 to 1949) the critique of homogeneous mass culture was formulated as a 'critical theory'. In the *Dialectic of Enlightenment* (1944/1947), ADORNO and HORKHEIMER cast a pessimistic view on rationality after Nazi barbarism and coined the derogatory term 'culture industry' for the tailor-made products of capitalist commodification. For them, mass culture is authoritarian and the political consciousness of the working classes are limited and oppressed by standardization and conformity. ADORNO championed aesthetic negativity (BECKETT, BEETHOVEN, KAFKA, SCHÖNBERG) – obstinately resistant forms of expression that preserve their truthful authenticity by rejecting the mass market. In *One-Dimensional Man* (1964), MARCUSE described how mass entertainment indoctrinates and manipulates in order to create affirmative culture, the capitalist version of one-dimensional life. In the Frankfurt School's narrative of a cultural fall from grace, the result is a streamlined culture of conformity, where style and technique have replaced truthfulness.

Mass art

Culturalism as well as hegemony and critical-theory approaches still proposed resistance to the threat of being engulfed in vacuous mass art. In the seminal book *Communications* (1962), however, RAYMOND WILLIAMS challenged the clear-cut distinction between entertainment and art. Subsequently, neo-formalist NOËL CARROLL, in his *Theory of Mass Culture*, argued against the elimination theory (which holds that popular and mass art cannot be differentiated). According to this theory, mass art is a social construction that merely reflects and intensifies class distinction and social status. CARROLL projects a complex binary system of ten criteria, most of which he discredits, however, accepting only one distinction which holds that mass art is consumed by many and *avant-garde* art is consumed by few.

Although he was part of the Frankfurt School, WALTER BENJAMIN deviated from its castigation of mass culture in crucial points. He

Fig. 14: Mass Art vs. Avant-Garde Art (adapted from Carroll 1998)

MASS ART	AVANT-GARDE ART
is common	is distinctive
has passive audience	activates audience
does not require interpretation	requires interpretation
is formulaic, generic	is unique, unconventional
is instrumental and functional	is non-functional, aesthetically autonomous
obstructs emancipation from capitalism	emancipates from capitalism
provides surrogate satisfaction	negates surrogate satisfaction
is mimetic	is anti-mimetic
is consumed by everyone	is consumed in academia
is exoteric and user-friendly	is esoteric and user-unfriendly

amalgamates an aesthetics of the new media with the materialist diagnosis of Marxism, and concludes that new media radically transform not just the contents but the entire field of artistic production. His seminal 1936 essay "The work of art in the age of mechanical reproduction" diagnosed that technical reproduction (as opposed to manual copying) had reached a new standard around 1900. New media of reproduction (photography and film) destroy the aura of the work of art. The aura is the singular cult value of the work of art which originates in its religious use and is re-inscribed by contemplation and the cult of genius in bourgeois culture. Media such as film and photography disconnect art from its tradition and replace the auratic cult value with exhibition value (a different kind of 'what you see is what you get' – WYSIWYG). This destruction of the cult value, Benjamin hoped, would replace (bourgeois) contemplation of the auratic work of art with a politically emancipatory reception by the masses. The shock of rapid movement and an 'abstracted' reception mode would fuse emotional enjoyment and a critical attitude.

Art and mechanical reproduction: Benjamin's aura

Hans Magnus Enzensberger has picked up Benjamin's version of cultural critique and developed his 'constituents' (*Baukasten*) theory of the media against the deterioration of the public sphere through the media (as diagnosed by Jürgen Habermas or Richard Sennett). Habermas's idea of *Öffentlichkeit* translates as 'public sphere' into English, an accessible bourgeois sphere separate from the private family and arcane hierarchical spheres. Habermas provided the picture of a system of bourgeois empowerment against the secrecy of feudal societies. In coffee-houses, bookshops, and newspapers of liberal societies, discourse is (theoretically) transparent and open to everyone. Habermas also noted a process of re-feudalization, however, that started when the media were taken over by the

The public sphere: Habermas

state or by centralized and industrialized interests in the 19th century. In the 1970s, therefore, Marxists such as OSKAR NEGT and ALEXANDER KLUGE (1972) articulated the need for countering the hegemonic mass media power in the public sphere with an alternative public sphere, a plurality of *Gegenöffentlichkeiten*. Subsequently, RICHARD SENNETT (1974) supplied a disillusioned view of the public sphere, which (through media such as radio, television and computers) filters into our bedrooms, which in turn provide the location for the publication of the private spheres of intimacy – PIERRE BOURDIEU (1998: 19), echoing GUY DEBORD, called this a *"relentless search for the sensational and spectacular"*.

'Constituents' theory: Enzensberger

ENZENSBERGER initially argued more optimistically that the egalitarian and perpetually 'present' technological media take culture out of the hands of traditional bourgeois ownership. He pinpointed forms of repressive media use (central control, one transmitter, isolated individual recipients, passive and depoliticized consumers, specialist production, property or bureaucracy as owners). Against these, ENZENSBERGER pitted the appropriation of media production by the audience (decentralization, receivers turning transmitters, mobilized masses, feedback and interaction, political learning, collective production, self-organization). From this vision of independent video co-operatives and alternative web publishers, ENZENSBERGER (1988) retracted to a resigned acknowledgement of TV as a dominant 'zero medium', probably in part responding to a scathing critique of this egalitarian utopianism by JEAN BAUDRILLARD ("Requiem pour les médias" 1972).

Beyond meaning: Baudrillard's hyperreal

For BAUDRILLARD, materialist analysis of the "who owns the media, who uses the media" kind is inappropriate because contemporary media operate in a world of pure signification. This loss of representation is theorized as the 'hyperreal' that does not reflect the world because the world is constituted within the ubiquitous signs of the media. Dissociated from their referents, these 'signs' cannot produce meaning (and cannot be described as mere illusion). Therefore, BAUDRILLARD, for better or for worse, sees television as a meaningless sphere of spectacle. Instead of taking over social responsibility as classes, the masses flock to this void overloaded with meanings. Because of the structural passivity of the media consumer in late capitalism, the media for BAUDRILLARD (1985: 101) are not emancipatory, but apocalyptic, in creating the obscene obesity of overinformation.

In an entirely different vein, the legacy of GRAMSCI and the Frankfurt School is taken up by approaches based on the idea of institutional hegemony and the flexible affirmation of happiness as spending money and pleasure linked to commodities and con-

sumption (GITLIN 1983, 2002, KELLNER 1995, McGUIGAN 1992). The idea of mainstreaming suggests that the mass media accentuate views that seem acceptable to their mass audience, thus excluding deviant or digressive minority views. On the one hand, the mass dissemination of information through the mass media led to an expansion of knowledge, on the other hand, the knowledge-gap hypothesis (TICHENOR et al. 1970) stated that the mass media deepen the educative segmentation within a society. Advanced media technologies and private media ownership are likely to increase this gap; so is the expanding communications strategy of 'narrowcasting' (= a pun on broadcasting: aiming media content at small special-interest audience segments, such as MUTV – Manchester United TV – or HGTV – Home & Garden TV). Privileged media-literate students profit from new media, whereas the uneducated masses remain disadvantaged.

Mainstreaming and knowledge gaps

Similarly, the cultivation theory (GERBNER 1973) holds that the attitudes and ideologies in mass-media messages cultivate audience responses. This botanical metaphor is logically extended by NEIL POSTMAN's project of media ecology to fortify society against superficial and fragmentary image politics on television. In *Amusing Ourselves to Death* (1985) or *Technopoly* (1995), POSTMAN (1931–2003) combined the determinism of McLUHAN and the Toronto School with a humanist scepticism. Against television and digital media, POSTMAN invoked the Bible, PLATO, and humanistic traditions marked by logos – words in speech and print. Thus, POSTMAN bemoaned the decline of typography and the corruption of education. He saw classroom curricula contaminated by ubiquitous computers and audiovisuality, and he castigated the pseudo-events in contemporary media politics (BOORSTIN 1980) as well as the idolatrous worship of technology in contemporary America.

Cultivation and media ecology

Since the pioneering work of STUART HALL, cultural studies have supplied a number of pathbreaking studies of media cultures, focused on audiences and reception, above all in Britain and Australia. These studies have challenged both the *Screen* theory idea of a 'positioned' audience and the communication-studies approach of passive reception.

Significant reception studies

MORLEY's study on *The "Nationwide" Audience* (1980) first tested HALL's model and verified the idea of textual polysemy. MORLEY tested responses of twenty-six separate groups of viewers to an episode of *Nationwide*, steering clear of the categories of 'mass' and 'individual' in examining audience responses. His fine-tuned finding that decodings of apprentices, schoolboys and bank managers were closest to the dominant meaning shattered the assumption of a homogeneous response determined by crass social segmentations. In *Family Television* (1986), MORLEY subsequently criticized

David Morley

the artificiality of his experiment outside the conventional viewing context and everyday viewing style.

Gendered soap operas and girls' magazines: Ang, Modleski, McRobbie

In *Watching Dallas* (written in 1982, published in English in 1985) IEN ANG, a Dutch researcher now teaching in Sydney, Australia, pioneered the study of lived experience with American mass culture in the form of soap opera. Admitting her own pleasure in watching soap operas, she examined forty-two letters responding to the series. At the same time, TANIA MODLESKI (1982) made a case for TV soap opera as providing open, feminine narratives that inscribe a 'mother' as ideal reader. Various studies suggest, of course, that most soaps are tailored to appeal to female audiences. ANGELA McROBBIE drew attention to the fact that popular texts are far from monolithic because in order to be successful they must cater to a wide field of multiple meanings and pleasures. She pointed out that much patriarchal and "modernist" research had failed to address the female contribution to postmodern popular media culture. In reading girls' magazines (*Jackie*) and investigating girls as audiences hitherto marginalized in studies on subculture, such as DICK HEBDIDGE's classic investigation of Punk clothes and dances, *Subcultures: The Meaning of Style* (1979), McROBBIE argued: "*Audiences or viewers, lookers or users are not simple-minded multitudes.*" (McROBBIE 1986: 392)

Bardic television: John Fiske, John Hartley

FISKE and HARTLEY exerted enormous influence with their book *Reading Television* from 1978. They proposed to move beyond the content analyses of American communication studies and to supersede interpretative modes from literary studies with semiotic methods. They characterized television (against literature) as an oral and visual culture whose multiple voices are "*ephemeral, episodic, specific, concrete and dramatic*" (FISKE / HARTLEY 1978: 15). For them, television is bardic, because it moulds experience into a media-specific system of signifying practices, mediating the central concerns and mythologies of a given culture as a consensus of preferred readings.

Activating texts: *Television Culture*

FISKE subsequently radicalized this position in his controversial *Television Culture* (1987). He sees television as a polysemic realm of excess meanings which cannot be controlled. For FISKE, the "*television audience [...] is not a homogeneous mass*", but a wide variety of groups that "*actively read television in order to produce from it meanings that connect with their social experience*" (FISKE 1987: 84). Thus, television may empower an audience in providing 'activated' texts, texts which facilitate a multiplicity of readings against the interests of structuring and controlling agencies within the television apparatus.

The pressure of the polysemy axiom can be seen in the case of ANGELA MCROBBIE as well as in that of ANDREW HIGSON, both of whom were forced to widen the spectrum of their earlier reading of popular media culture. HIGSON's seminal analysis of heritage cinema started from the assumption that these films created an imagined (nationalist) community at the service of hegemonic conservatism. He denounced heritage films (such as *Brideshead Revisited* by Granada TV or *Chariots of Fire*, both from 1981) because of their reactionary anti-narrative pictorialism and the bourgeois reinvention of a golden age (cf. HIGSON 1995, 1996). In a revisionist monograph from 2003, however, HIGSON acknowledged that in view of gendered readings (that highlight the performativity of costumes, for instance) and generic diversification the 'heritage' film need not be seen exclusively as catering to an individual, nostalgic desire to be part of a non-organic, indirect community (in the vein of BENEDICT ANDERSON).

Hegemony to polysemy: Heritage film

The approaches by MCROBBIE and FISKE as well as JIM COLLINS's study of detective fiction and popular television, ANDREAS HUYSSEN's critique of masculinist modernity, and Jean BAUDRILLARD's quarrel with ENZENSBERGER speak for the conflation of philosophical postmodernism and contemporary media culture. Addressing terms such as polysemy, pluralism, post-historicism, postcolonialism, and populism, JONATHAN BIGNELL (2000: 2) argues that "*contemporary media and theories of the postmodern are mutually implicated.*"

Postmodern media culture

BIGNELL's analysis focuses on the question of media and historicity (first put forward by WALTER BENJAMIN) and draws on FREDRIC JAMESON's attack on the nostalgia film and ANNE FRIEDBERG's analysis of cinema and the window-shopping *flâneur*. In the seminal article "Postmodernism, or the Cultural Logic of Late Capitalism" (1984), JAMESON (*1934) assailed the 'nostalgia film' produced by Hollywood-dominated American cinema. According to JAMESON, rather than furthering the process of historical advancement (by commenting on the present through recourse to the past), nostalgia films turn the past into mythical spectacle, thus erasing the idea of a (progressive) historicity itself.

Consumer culture and nostalgia

In his essay "Le public moderne et la photographie" from 1859, CHARLES BAUDELAIRE had deplored the advent of photography as a "*cheap method of disseminating a loathing for history and for painting*" (BAUDELAIRE 1955) which replaced the bodily experience of the male *flâneur*. According to ANNE FRIEDBERG (1993), the gender extension of urban male pleasures through shopping, tourism as well as television and video was appropriated by postmodernist accounts of media culture as a new dominant in analysing consumer experience. Whether or not this centrality of consumer experience will be superseded by new 'male' paradigms of culture

The *flâneur*

clash, fundamentalism, terrorism and warfare, remains to be seen.

Subcultures: Appropriation, poaching, *bricolage*, transcoding

In reviewing cultural-studies approaches to the media from HALL to the 'postmodernist' plurality of FISKE et al., it is clear that HALL's category 'oppositional reading' has drawn particular attention. Their defining characteristic is the highlighting of audience participation in the mass media. In *The Practice of Everyday Life* (1984), MICHEL DE CERTEAU suggested that audiences may actually 'inhabit' a text and contend with the media producer for the ownership of meaning. If audiences do not control the production, at least they exert influence over the consumption of culture. In *Textual Poachers*, HENRY JENKINS (1992: 277–287) found consumer activism, collaborative creativity, alternative readings and social community in television fandom. The Internet affords ample space for parodies and creative reworkings within fan cultures of Hollywood products such as PETER JACKSON's *The Lord of the Rings* trilogy. The terms trans-coding and *bricolage* (mixing, tinkering from French *bricole*, 'trifle') refer to the appropriation, rewriting or taking over of terms/images or consumer products, which, in turn, can be answered by a hegemonic re-appropriation or counter-*bricolage* of subcultures into the mainstream (see STURKEN/CARTWRIGHT 2001: 56–68). Subcultures "*are groups of people that have something in common with each other (i.e., they share a problem, an interest, a practice) which distinguishes them in a significant way from the members of other social groups*" (THORNTON 1997: 1). By definition, this distinction is resistant, oppositional, subordinate, and apart from, or below, kinship and the masses.

Media ethnography and anthropology

The method in these audience studies by HALL, MORLEY or JENKINS may be described as ethnographic in the sense that they observe how people live and interact with the media. Although the audience has played a major part in these approaches, cultural studies have been attacked by the ethno-methodological approach. Cultural ethnology claims that any inquiry into the media must start from the world of everyday experience and practice with due respect for 'common sense' – rather than applying theoretical categories of class or gender. In participant observation methods, for instance, the researcher may overcome the problems of artificial experiments and questionnaires by sharing for a given period the lifestyle and cultural practices of the people he investigates. A recent reader has consequently proposed a re-entry of anthropology into media studies (ASKEW/WILK 2002), (1) for the reason that the media are not seen as separate from other walks of social life (law, economics, religion etc.) and (2) with the interest to counter the dominance of eurocentrism and global capital (ASKEW 2002: 7–8). NICHOLAS MIRZOEFF's reader on visual culture provides exemplary global and transcultural approaches (MIRZOEFF 2002). The most contested category is, of course, the interpretation of what audiences actually do with texts. Critics such as McGUIGAN (1992) or KELLNER (1995), for instance, have criticized fetishisms of audience struggle and audience pleasure.

❸ Case studies in broadcasting and televisuality

"I was born in a house with the television always on."
The Talking Heads, "Love for Sale"
"I was born in a TV."
JAMES LUNA (quoted in MIRZOEFF 2002: 599)

Cultural-studies approaches have clearly invigorated serious study of television since the 1980s (JOHN ELLIS, ROBERT C. ALLEN, LYNN SPIGEL). CECILIA TICHI's *The Electronic Hearth. Creating an American Television Culture* (1991) is an exemplary case, as it engages not just TV itself, but also Hallmark cards, bumper stickers, novels, cartoons, art and ads. Close to *dispositif* or apparatus analyses, TICHI adopts the metaphor of television as an environment, and she uses the slogan "as seen on TV" to delineate the ontological split within the contemporary mediated being. This enables her to read TV culture in all its variety, from TV dinners, TV language, TV rooms, TV furniture, to TV iconography and, finally, TV consciousness. Drawing on RAYMOND WILLIAMS's 'flow' concept and DAVID MARC, TICHI (1991: 104–128) rejects the idea of the vacuous viewer as passive, addicted couch potato in front of his boob tube or idiot box. She replaces it with the notion of the TV viewer as a channel-hopping, backtalking, irreverent editor or *auteur*. As MIR-ZOEFF (1999: 1) stated, the *"average American 18 year old sees only eight movies a year but watches four hours television a day"* – and this alone should suffice to merit more serious TV analysis in German *Anglistik* and *Amerikanistik*.

Television culture: Cecilia Tichi

Historically and in terms of institutional development, television is a descendant of radio. The first news, sitcoms, and sketch and variety shows were, of course, radio programmes. The name soap opera is derived from daytime dramas paid by Colgate-Palmolive and Proctor & Gamble. Radio continues as a low-cost test-case medium for TV shows (see STEWART et al. 2001, on which this section on radio is mainly based). Of course, radio may be defined against TV by its lack of visuality. It has specific codes that convey meaning (voice, sound effects, music, silence). Sounds, for instance, may be classified as action sounds (denoting movement), setting sounds (suggesting surroundings) or symbolic sounds. Radio also

From radio to TV

brings with it a particular media apparatus – it qualifies as a stimulating 'hot' medium in MᴄLᴜʜᴀɴ, it is an inexpensive, steady and readily accessible companion in cars and at work, and in comparison to visual media or print it may be described as 'undemanding' and 'ambient' because it may remain a secondary accompaniment to other activities.

Broadcasting: Radio history

As a broadcast medium it also has a particular national audience and techno-institutional history. Radio is based on late Victorian 'wireless' improvements to the telegraph introduced by Gᴜɢʟɪᴇʟᴍᴏ Mᴀʀᴄᴏɴɪ in 1896 in Britain. In the USA, Canadian-born Rᴇɢɪɴᴀʟᴅ Fᴇssᴇɴᴅᴇɴ used a high frequency alternator for the first radio broadcast (1906). The RCA (Radio Corporation of America) bought Mᴀʀᴄᴏɴɪ's patents in 1919 and established a quasi-monopoly. During World War II, radio was the prime medium for disseminating propaganda commissioned by Jᴏsᴇᴘʜ Gᴏᴇʙʙᴇʟs and others, because broadcasting promised wide range of distribution and was easy to control. Oʀsᴏɴ Wᴇʟʟᴇs's 1938 radio adaptation of H. G. Wᴇʟʟs's *The War of the Worlds* created the first media-specific pseudo-event. His fake radio broadcast on the Martian attack simulated acoustic 'liveness', instilled panic in an estimated one-sixth of the presumed six million audience, and exposed the quasi-religious faith in the media-specific forms of representing (or rather constructing) reality (see Fᴀᴜʟsᴛɪᴄʜ 1981, Cʀᴏᴏᴋ 1999).

Radio in Britain

In Britain, the BBC remained the only official radio broadcaster from 1922 to 1972. It still has a 51 % audience share, with a range of Radio 1 (pop), Radio 2 (easy-listening), Radio 3 (classical) and Radio 4 (speech) and Radio 5 Live (sports). Radio Luxembourg and the 'pirate' north sea stations Radio Caroline (founded in 1964) and Veronica are classic competitors that have been joined by hundreds of regional and local stations. The advent of commercial radio brought a fast-growing market for radio ads with specific qualities (character-driven, short and repetitive dialogue, use of music). Radio also developed medium-specific personalities (disc-jockeys) and formats such as the regular hourly news bulletin or the interactive 'talk radio' phone-in show. Music is of special importance on the radio. The contemporary 'hit radio', identifiable as a brand by jingles and so-called 'radio-idents', offers a 40-song playlist and 600 to 700 rotating tracks selected by a computer system according to the day-part schedule (see below on TV programming). Arguably this music formatting has contributed to a creative stalemate, aggravating the crisis in the music business as a result of illegal file downloads.

TV technology

Television is based on technologies which go back to Pᴀᴜʟ Nɪᴘᴋᴏᴡ's mechanical scanner (1884). The 1920s saw the first experiments with mechanical TV (the Scot Jᴏʜɴ Lᴏɢɪᴇ Bᴀɪʀᴅ's "radio vision"

1924/25) and with an electronic camera and receiver (V. K. Zwory-kin, 1923–1931). Baird started an experimental transmission service and televised a play by Luigi Pirandello in 1930. The 1930s brought the first TV services (Germany 1935, England 1936, France 1938, USSR and USA 1939), but it was only after World War II that national television emerged, with Richard Dimbleby's report of the coronation of Queen Elizabeth in 1953 (watched presumably by as many as 20 million viewers) as a landmark event. Crucial technological steps followed, such as the advent of colour TV (in Britain in 1967), of video in production (magnetic videotape: Ampex 1956), which as a storage device also greatly redefined consumption (home video recorder CBS 1967, Sony Beta VCR 1976, home video camera Sony 1980, DVD 1995). The remote control (invented in the 1950s), for instance, immobilized the viewer and introduced channel-switching with grave repercussions for the TV 'flow', scheduling, narrative construction etc.

Currently, we are faced with high-resolution flatscreens and channel proliferation in satellite, cable and digital TV. This entails the possibility of more, narrowcast channels as well as increased TV/online transactions, such as video-on-demand, home shopping, telephonic messaging, merged Internet access, a choice of camera angles or stills, etc. We have already seen above how it is not just technologies that shape a medium, but the entire institutions and practices that form the media *dispositif* or apparatus.

Future of the TV apparatus

In Britain, there are currently five terrestrial networks that broadcast a national programme, two public-sector channels and three privately organized channels:

Institutions: The BBC and private TV

- BBC One – audience share 36% in 2004 (Sampson 2004: 215)
- BBC Two – in Ireland RTÉ
- ITV (22.8%) broadcasting programmes by companies such as London Weekend Television, Granada, or Carlton (now merged)
- Channel Four (10.2%) – in Wales S4C
- Channel Five (6.7%).

In addition there are countless special-interest channels (both private and public) carried by cable, digital satellite and digital terrestrial television. Public-service broadcasting (PSB) in Britain began with the radio programmes of the BBC (British Broadcasting Corporation), which was founded in 1927 (from private origins). Its first director-general, Lord Reith, conceived of television as a tool for civilizing and educating the nation (in the manner of Matthew Arnold whose ideas were adapted by the culturalists). The BBC also publishes its own magazine (with a historically accurate title, *Radio Times* – its rival, *What's On* was the top-selling British magazine in 2000, Burton 2002: 65).

Regulation and commercial television in Britain	After the war, public-sector TV came under pressure from the American private model. Consequently, ITV (Independent Television) was founded in 1955 as a commercial counterpart to the BBC (composed of various regional companies such as Carlton and Granada, which merged in 2004 and became ITV plc). ITV was nevertheless also harnessed to public service and regulated accordingly by the government. Bodies such as the ITC (Independent Television Commission, now OfCom) and the BBC's board of governors regulate broadcasting in Britain. A fourth terrestrial channel, Channel Four (1982) was unique in having been founded with a mission to cater to minority interests.
BSkyB, public-service television and the Hutton report	In conjunction with Channel Five (1997) and digital satellite TV (Sky Digital 1989, provided by the RUPERT-MURDOCH-owned British Sky Broadcasting, BSkyB), the private sector has expanded. BSkyB is now not only by far the biggest commercial TV company in Britain, but also one of the biggest companies operating in Britain (see SAMPSON 2004: 314). Since the deregulation of the 1990s, even within the BBC a large proportion of the programmes have been produced by private companies and mergers in commercial television. The pressure to reduce costs and increase audience shares has had detrimental effects to the Reithian ethos and destroyed the hierarchical approach to culture, which has been replaced by mandatory entertainment value (see ELDRIDGE et al. 1997, LACEY 2002). Public-service broadcasting came under vicious attack in the aftermath of the Hutton report investigating reports on weapons of mass destruction in the second Iraq war and the ensuing suicide of BBC informant and weapons expert, DAVID KELLY. Lord HUTTON's inquiry having pronounced a verdict of misconduct on the part of the BBC and reporter ANDREW GILLIGAN in January 2004, both the BBC Chairman GAVYN DAVIES and the director-general of the BBC, GREG DYKE, resigned, and subsequently the license-fee system came under review. In March 2005, the BBC board of governors was set to be abolished, following recommendations in a government green paper. The license-fee system, however, was confirmed for another ten years, in spite of attacks from private-sector companies and conservative politicians.
Commercial TV in the USA	The advent of commercial TV in Britain in the 1950s, which was compared to "*small-pox, bubonic plague and the Black Death*" by Lord REITH at the time (see SAMPSON 2004: 213), was stimulated by the American situation. In the US, television from its very inception was a private enterprise dominated by advertising (which accounts for 25% of television time in the US, CASEY et al. 2002: 3). It is regulated by the FCC (Federal Communications Commission). Unlike European nations (SECAM, PAL – Phase Alternating Line), the US adopted the NTSC (National Television Systems Com-

mittee) broadcasting standard. The first programmes were transmitted by General Electric in 1928, and the first radio companies (NBC 1926, CBS 1927); ABC followed in 1943. Driven by commercial interests, television permeated American homes very fast: In 1952, one third of the American population possessed a TV set (20 million) and in February 1955, there were 36 million TV sets in the US, 4.5 million in Britain, and 300,000 in the rest of Europe (BRIGGS / BURKE 2002: 234, 240). Commercial television sells target groups to advertising industries.

Commercial TV brought the archetypal TV commercial – thirty seconds in duration, designed for repetition, miniature genres with micro-Aristotelian structure, based on easily-decodable imagery rich in effects and cultural innuendo, its sound loud and attention-grabbing. The advent of Music Television (MTV) in 1981 contributed to blurring the line between commercial use and synaesthetic pleasure on TV. It relies both on traditions of visualizing music or the modernist *avant-garde* and of selling products (see FRITH et al. 1993, BÜHLER 2002). Since the early 1980s, new channels for music commercial have emerged, in part for specialist tastes, such as VH-1 (1985), BET (Black Entertainment Television), or CMT (Country Music Television). Following the crisis in the music business, however, promo clips have in part been replaced with non-music formats on channels such as MTV. The reality TV series *The Real World* (1992) and the cartoon series focused on the anti-social head-bangers *Beavis and Butt-head* (1993) were influential early moves in this direction, which has culminated in *The Simple Life* (Fox 2003). More recently, inane ads for mobile phone ringtones by companies such as Jamba! (Jamster!) have infiltrated music television channels. Aimed at the youth market, ringtones such as "Axel F." by Crazy Frog (appropriately called "That Annoying Thing" in 1997 by its inventors, Swedes DANIEL MALMEDAHL and ERIK WERMQUIST) have recently climbed the top of the music charts, superseding traditional pop music.

TV commercials and MTV

Promotional music videos (since the inaugural "Bohemian Rhapsody" by Queen, 1975) have arguably influenced other branches of the visual media with their characteristic "clip aesthetics", marked by a flood of dream-like visual cues, rapid cuts, *montage*, and incessant movement. Music videos require trans-disciplinary analysis (music: melody, harmonies, rhythm etc.; language: song lyrics; visuals: effects, symbolism, narrative). BÜHLER (2002: 199–207) contrasts five types of promo videos: (1) performance clips (based on musicians performing and lip-synchronization), (2), visual flood clips (high cut frequency *montage* of disparate images), (3) pseudo-narrative clips (which mix performance and

A short history of the promotional music video

montage of narrative sequences), (4) narrative clips (which illustrate a song's story, often narrated by the lead vocalist; MICHAEL JACKSON's 13-minute "Thriller", directed by JOHN LANDIS, is the classic example), (5) *avant-garde* art clips (focused on merging image and music rather than on advertising the performance).

Art, race and gender construction in music videos

Music-video directors of the 1980s, such as STEVEN BARRON ("Take on Me" 1985), ROBERT LONGO ("Bizarre Love Triangle" 1986), JULIAN TEMPLE or DAVID BYRNE have ennobled the genre with experimental visuality. Clear-cut lines between promotion-video directors and movie directors have been blurred in the work of, for instance, DAVID LYNCH, CHRIS CUNNINGHAM, SPIKE JONZE or MICHEL LONDRY. Cultural-studies analyses by KOBENA MERCER ("Thriller") or RAMONA CURRY ("Open Your Heart", MADONNA) have highlighted the polysemic quality of promotional videos. In "Thriller", the pre-trial JACKSON (who turns into a werewolf and a zombie) illustrates an instable gender and race identity (reinforced by his androgynous image), and MADONNA undermines the voyeuristic catering to the male gaze with her empowering star image, which can be read as liberating.

Networks and syndication

From 1943 to the 1980s, broadcast television in the US was dominated by three national networks – NBC (National Broadcasting Company 1926), CBS (Columbia Broadcasting System 1927) and ABC (American Broadcasting Company 1943). In Canada, there is the CBC (Canadian Broadcasting Corporation) and the private Canadian Television Network (CTV). Independent stations and public-service television (with a hybrid status between commercial and public TV: PBS 1937, ITVS) have only played a minor part in American TV. Networks are composed of regional TV stations, i.e., affiliated stations which share syndication, i.e., rights to air television programmes (which may subsequently be further syndicated in re-runs or on international markets). As in the 1950s, the US networks started to tap into the global markets. The "Kraft Television Theatre" offered live transmission of theatre performance. Paradigmatic TV formats appear in the 1940s and 1950s (*Meet the Press* 1947, *The Ed Sullivan Show* 1949, *I Love Lucy* 1951, *The Tonight Show* 1954, *Bonanza* 1959) and for the first time TV personalities (e.g., MILTON BERLE) emerge. Cable TV has been known in the US since the 1950s. The accelerated development of cable and satellite channels with special-interest narrowcasting, as well as home video, however, prompted the network crisis of the 1980s. Declining network audiences dictated inexpensive programming but also stylistic diversification and new networks appeared (Fox 1987, UPN / Paramount and WB / Warner Bros., both 1995).

What was termed a "vast wasteland" by FCC Chairman NEWTON MINOW in 1961 subsequently became a very complex and heterogeneous landscape indeed. RAYMOND WILLIAMS (1974: 86) theorized broadcast TV as amorphous *"planned flow"* without specific items, instead of a balanced mix, a programming. Programming is at the very core of TV because it is a commercial necessity and determines the TV rhythms, routines and standards, but also reflects and generates cultural values and social trends. The commercial British television channel ITV is unlikely to broadcast one of SAMUEL BECKETT's TV plays in a prime time slot because the company has no interest in alienating viewers who have become used to other (conventional) contents by their experience of ITV programming.

"Flow" vs. programming

With the proliferation of channels and contents, however, programming has become extremely complex, and companies have developed various strategies to maximize and keep audiences (blocking sequences of related shows, counter-programming, lead-ins of popular programmes for less popular ones etc.). Since the 1980s, the US standard of day-part scheduling has been roughly as follows:

Programming since the 1980s

- Early morning (7–11 p.m.: pre-work adults, pre-school children – news, talk)
- Daytime (10 a.m.–6 p.m.: "housewives", children – talk, soaps)
- Early Fringe (6–7 p.m.: elders and adults returning from work – news)
- Prime Access (7–8 p.m.: busy adults at home, children – game shows, comedies)
- Prime Time (8–11 p.m.: family, progressively adult – comedy, melodrama, action-adventure etc.)
- Late Fringe (11–11.30 p.m.: adults – news)
- Late Night (11.30 p.m.–12.30 a.m.: adults, maturing adolescents – talkshow, fiction)
- Overnight (12.30–7.00 a.m.: adults, maturing adolescents – talk, comedy, drama)

The channel proliferation of the 1980s brought a sea-change in television. CALDWELL (1995) theorized the impact of cable TV, of MTV, ESPN and CNN, the visual appropriation of film (as showcase TV) and video art, the 'authorization' of TV by personalities such as STEVEN BOCHCO (*NYPD Blues*), DAVID LYNCH (*Twin Peaks*), DAVID E. KELLEY (*Ally McBeal*) or WILLIAM GIBSON and STEPHEN KING, who worked on the *X-Files*, as well as the advent of televisuality, i.e., the formation of distinctive 'looks' across the cultural range from cheap trash TV to quality 'heritage' television. The results from shifts in technology and institutions can be marked. Because of extensive audience research and various ways of probing into

Televisuality

audience responses (such as the ratings by A. C. NIELSEN in the US, the seminal audience research company founded as early as in 1923, and the BARB figures in Britain), television has become very unstable and flexible. For example, in the area of British television drama there is a notable shift from single plays to umbrellas (i.e., a loosely titled scheduling slots that encompass different and disparate plays, sometimes rotating series in what is known as a 'wheel' in media jargon). Umbrellas and series can be globally marketed and are less risky than single plays.

Serialization

Clear-cut distinctions between sagas (which evolve over lengthy periods of time, such as the soap operas *Coronation Street* – since 1960, on ITV – and *East Enders* or *Neighbours*), retakes (which create a new story around established formulas or personnel, such as *Star Wars* or *Star Trek*), series (which consist of self-contained episodes – permanent dilemma without final closure), serials (in which storylines continue over several episodes) and their shorter descendants, the mini-series (often marketed as authored, extended single plays) have collapsed. In this way, the demise of the single play may be mourned as the sacrifice of an artistic practice on the altar of profitability and entertainment. Arguably, however, the concept of the single play, which descended from theatre and film, has given place to genuine televisual formats. Consequently, the soap opera and the situation comedy have taken over aesthetics and functions that were formerly associated with the single play.

Television formats: Repetition with a difference

In view of television's hybridity it seems impossible to establish a generic typology of television formats. TV mixes fiction and non-fiction, animation film and 'photographic' film, 'live' and recorded material, report, narration and presentation, discontinuous news or reports and homogeneous documentaries, series and one-offs, and specialist programmes for various audience segments (e.g., children's TV). On the one hand, a conventional formula is essential because repetition may reinforce and 'naturalize' a formula and may thus stabilize established commercial success (in so-called 'me too' programmes with minor variation). On the other hand, with the proliferation and diversification of channels there is a growing need for distinction which has fostered generic hybridization.

"Window on the world" I: Documentaries

Within the curious mix of fiction and non-fiction on TV, the documentary has always held a prominent position – in particular within the ethos of public service (for instance, the renowned BBC programme *Panorama*) and the catchphrase of the "window on the world". Semiotics, however, have highlighted the functions of mirroring, distorting and screening (in the sense of selecting) that the television screen also has – documentaries are just as governed by style and convention as fiction films. The term 'documentary' derives from JOHN GRIERSON in the 1920s adapting its French adjectival use (*documentaire*). The documentary ground rules are that the film or programme must always communicate to a certain audience, that it communicates through strong visual images organized in a sequence to make a statement and that the editing of its 'footage' is what really counts (see HAMPE 1997). Typical techniques include the filming of paintings and photographs, of site and stock footage, of footage from fiction film and expert interviews. The observational 'fly-on-the-wall' approach and conventions of *cinéma vérité* (with undirected, raw and poor footage and shaky-cam aesthetics) evoke the illusion of unmediated actuality and unscripted liveness.

Re-enactment, dramatization and re-creation have been part and parcel of documentaries since the 1920s. The documentary ethos might have been undermined by fakes, by playful narrative modes and the reflexivity of the 'fly-in-the-ointment' documentary (NICK BROOMFIELD, see BRUZZI 2000). Traditionally, the documentary is also marked by what BILL NICHOLS termed the documentary "*discourse of sobriety*" (NICHOLS 2001: 39), with a stake in serious politics, economics etc. It is the crucial problem of current documentary formats, therefore, that the interventionist claim of the sober documentary has been given up by the 1990s wave of docusoaps and reality TV.

The "discourse of sobriety"

The derogatory term docusoap describes a new kind of observational documentary that professes little intention to investigate social realities for the sake of the viewers' betterment and education (i.e., along the lines famously suggested by Lord REITH). *The Family* (1974) is often named as a precursor. For instance, the subcategory of the history docusoap alone, at the respectable and educative end, produced a large variety of programmes at the turn of the millennium, such as *The 1900 House* (C4, 1999), *The 1940s House* (C4, 2001), *The Edwardian Country House* (C4, 2002), *The Trench* (BBC 2, 2002), *Surviving the Iron Age* (BBC, 2001), *Pioneer Quest* (History Television, Canada, 2000), *The Frontier House* (PBS, 2002). The main attraction of these programmes is that they merge high ratings with low production costs.

"Window on the world" II: Docusoap

Docusoaps may be regarded as one branch in the wider trend towards reality TV (which in the US includes quiz shows and talk shows and audition shows, such as *Pop Idol*, ITV, 2001 etc.). This phenomenon has its roots in American news programmes designed around emergency services since the late 1980s ("trauma TV", which revolves around crime, accidents, health problems, e.g., *Cops*, Fox, 1989). Subsequently, it has also been used to describe constructed surveillance TV with confessional first-person narra-

"Window on the world" III: Reality TV

tions and online voting elements (*Big Brother*, C4, 2001; *Castaway*, BBC 1, 2000; *Fear Factor*, NBC, 2001; *I'm a Celebrity…Get Me Out of Here*, ITV, 2002). The recent survey by BRENTON/COHEN is aptly titled *Shooting People* and they define reality TV as *"various kinds of unscripted entertainment involving members of the public"* (2003: 8). What is termed 'real' (almost ironically in the title of MTV's classic *The Real World*) actually amounts to raw *cinéma vérité* visuality, no actors, no scripts. SALMAN RUSHDIE denounced the people being shot as *"half-familiar avatars of yourself – these half-attractive half-persons – enacting ordinary life under weird conditions […]"* (in BRENTON/COHEN 2003: 7).

Television genres: Sitcom

The sitcom is the most prominent example of a specific and indigenous television genre. Its archetypal features have emerged since it was first transferred from radio to TV (*Family Affairs*, 1949). It is marked by narrative and spatial stasis, and is focused on the half-hour duration, the predominantly verbal humour of witty dialogues and repartee, the episode-specific predicament, the stereotyped characterization, the perennially static setting and narrative with circular plot constellations, the importance of the series' context, the consistent scheduling, and the season division which cuts across the boundaries of series (see fig. 15). One may differentiate between British and American sitcom, the latter favouring high 'production values', whereas in visually lacklustre British sitcoms such as *The Royle Family* (1998) the tradition of writerly predominance seems to linger at least residually. The sitcom is also a prime example of what has been termed "time porn": television shows and other acts that portray characters as having excessive amounts of spare time. The term reflects the growing competition for time spent by media users in a situation of proliferating media offerings.

Television sitcom and generic hybridity

The most significant trend in recent television history is the marked hybridity of formats, i.e., the emergence of new forms by generic cross-breeding. The television sitcom, for example, is on the one hand defined by a given set of traits, but has on the other hand integrated various new trends within its format:
• The 'ethnic' chat-show sitcom, such as *The Kumars at No. 42* (2001). This generic hybrid mixes an (unscripted) chat show with (scripted) sitcom elements in the house of the bourgeois Anglo-Indian Kumar family. Indulging in the fantasy of becoming a chat show host, the son, Sanjeev Kumar (SANJEEV BASHKAR) has created a TV studio in the garden shed, but his efforts at posing as a TV celebrity are subverted by his family, above all his mother (MEERA SYAL). The show also speaks for ethnic diversification of comedy (just as the faked-ignorance irony in the spoof chats of *Da Ali G Show* (2000, starring SACHA BARON COHEN)

Fig. 15: Sitcom formula (adapted and modified from McQueen 1998 and Clark 2002)

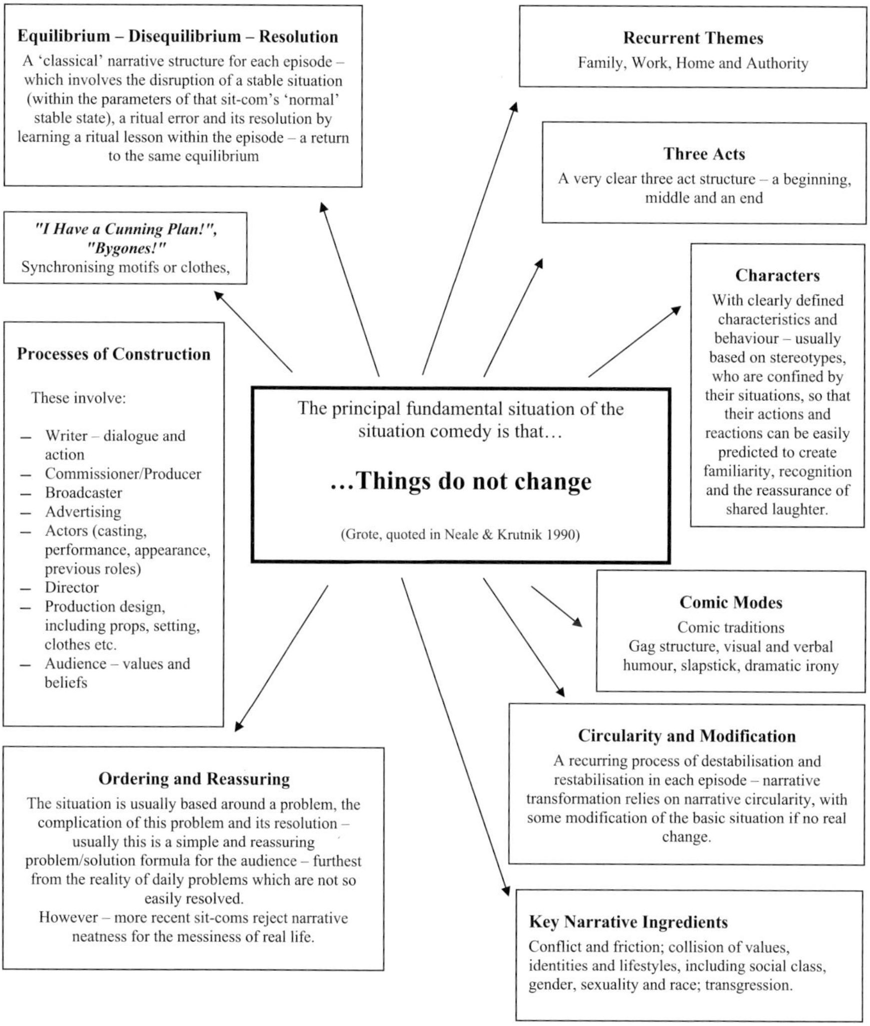

Equilibrium – Disequilibrium – Resolution
A 'classical' narrative structure for each episode – which involves the disruption of a stable situation (within the parameters of that sit-com's 'normal' stable state), a ritual error and its resolution by learning a ritual lesson within the episode – a return to the same equilibrium

Recurrent Themes
Family, Work, Home and Authority

Three Acts
A very clear three act structure – a beginning, middle and an end

"I Have a Cunning Plan!",
"Bygones!"
Synchronising motifs or clothes,

Characters
With clearly defined characteristics and behaviour – usually based on stereotypes, who are confined by their situations, so that their actions and reactions can be easily predicted to create familiarity, recognition and the reassurance of shared laughter.

Processes of Construction

These involve:

- Writer – dialogue and action
- Commissioner/Producer
- Broadcaster
- Advertising
- Actors (casting, performance, appearance, previous roles)
- Director
- Production design, including props, setting, clothes etc.
- Audience – values and beliefs

The principal fundamental situation of the situation comedy is that…

…Things do not change

(Grote, quoted in Neale & Krutnik 1990)

Comic Modes
Comic traditions
Gag structure, visual and verbal humour, slapstick, dramatic irony

Circularity and Modification
A recurring process of destabilisation and restabilisation in each episode – narrative transformation relies on narrative circularity, with some modification of the basic situation if no real change.

Ordering and Reassuring
The situation is usually based around a problem, the complication of this problem and its resolution – usually this is a simple and reassuring problem/solution formula for the audience – furthest from the reality of daily problems which are not so easily resolved.
However – more recent sit-coms reject narrative neatness for the messiness of real life.

Key Narrative Ingredients
Conflict and friction; collision of values, identities and lifestyles, including social class, gender, sexuality and race; transgression.

and the pioneering Anglo-Indian sketch comedy of *Goodness Gracious Me* (1998, also starring Bashkar and Syal).
- The meta-televisual sitcom, such as the real-time *The Royle Family* (1998), which both invigorates the traditions of British working-class humour and reflects on the medium; the Royles assemble in front of the TV set, at times staring back at the

viewer. The series thus undermines the promise of 'real' images made by the window rhetoric by deliberately turning the TV set into the mirror in which viewers watch viewers.

- The reality TV sitcom (*The Office*, 2000, co-written, directed and acted by RICKY GERVAIS and STEPHEN MERCHANT).
- Thematically diversified TV sitcoms addressing history (e.g., *Blackadder*, 1983, which is suffused with anarchism derived from the 1980s' alternative 'punk' comedians, *The Young Ones*, 1982), politics (*The New Statesman*, 1987, *Yes, Minister*, 1980, and *Yes, Prime Minister*, 1986), war (the classic example is *M*A*S*H*, 1972) and religion (*Father Ted*, 1995, *The Vicar of Dibley*, 1994).
- The "unruly woman" sitcom (such as *Roseanne*, 1988, and *Absolutely Fabulous*, 1992, see JANE FEUER in CREEBER 2001: 68–69). A lot of recent sitcoms have revised the traditional family model, which has been substituted for patchwork families with a role reversal (two incompetent 'mothers' and a conscientious but dull daughter in *Absolutely Fabulous*). In general, for younger audiences the traditional utopian family of the sitcom (a landmark of diversification was the successful African-American Dr Huxtable in *The Cosby Show*, 1984) has either become dysfunctional and patchy or has been replaced by sexually active flat sharers and friends (*Seinfeld*, 1990, *Friends*, 1994, *Sex and the City*, 1998).
- The gay and queer sitcom: There are central lesbian and gay characters, particularly after the coming-out of ELLEN DEGENERES in *Ellen* (1994). *Queer as Folk* (1999) examines the pleasures of a young, male, and gay *ménage a trois*.
- The adult animation sitcom (*Beavis and Butt-head*, 1993, *The Simpsons*, 1989, *South Park*, 1997): This is more than doubly addressed to children and adults, cartoons (painted or 'cel' animation, clay animation or CGI), with a penchant for transgressing taboos and ironic, parodic meta-cultural – above all meta-televisual and meta-filmic – comment achieved in part by audio-appearance of TV celebrities.

A number of these hybrid formulas, notably the diversification of narration, gender and ethnicity, thus cut across the reduced complexity of cultural representations in more traditional sitcoms (see fig. 16).

"Dramedy"

As NELSON (2000) has argued, the "dramedy" *Ally McBeal* (1997) may stand as a key example of generic hybridity as it combines

- MTV. There are frequent guest appearances by musicians as well as narrative interiorization by "theme songs", musical visitations, digital effects and lip-synchronization. One should add that *Ally McBeal* also refers to traditions of the Hollywood musical and innovative sound-image dislocations that became the trademark of DENNIS POTTER – and were copied in shows and

CHAPTER 3 Media signs and cultural studies

Fig. 16: Sitcom stereotypes (according to MᶜQᵤₑₑₙ 1998 and Cₗₐᵣₖ 2002)

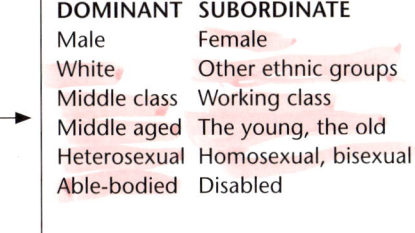

TYPES / STEREO-TYPES	DOMINANT	SUBORDINATE
Laughing with or at them? These are attempts to order the confusion of reality (Dyer): character and narrative shortcuts and simplifications of members of social groups, which can cause offence and reinforce existing prejudices	Male	Female
	White	Other ethnic groups
	Middle class	Working class
	Middle aged	The young, the old
	Heterosexual	Homosexual, bisexual
	Able-bodied	Disabled

MASCULINITY / FEMININITY
Stereotypical Associations

Professional	Domesticated	Rational	Emotional
Strong	Weak	Competitive	Co-operative
Independent	Communal	Aggressive	Passive
Ruthless	Sensitive	Ambitious	Supportive

films as diverse as *Kottan ermittelt* (ORF, 1976–1983) or the ill-fated *Cop Rock* (ABC, 1990), as well as in numerous commercials.

- courtroom drama. This has been exploited for a long time by lawyer series and on reality TV channels such as Court TV. The idiosyncratic eccentricities in the super-rich Boston law firm Fishman & Cage as well as the hypertrophied court cases subvert these televisual clichés.
- home / workplace sitcom (*Cheers*, 1982, *Frasier*, 1993) and soap opera. The court cases are intercut with Ally McBeal's search for 'Mr Right', which frequently turns the powerful female lawyer into a victim of domestic emotionality.
- humorous investigation of 'serious' social issues. The court cases address issues such as feminism, sexual harassment, age discrimination, political correctness, religion, racism, psychoanalysis, commercialism, genetic engineering.

Television narration	Serialization and concomitant semi-'closures' such as the cliff-hanger are typical features of television narration (and in this, TV is a descendant of the Victorian novel as well as the radio). One may, of course, argue that non-fiction TV also narrates in carefully 'scripted' programmes, for instance according to the repertory of narrative functions described by Vladimir Propp (1895–1970). TV news presenters such as Jeremy Paxman (*Newsnight*) or Sir Trevor McDonald (*News At Ten*) appear as vicarious studio editors and selectors, the 'bards' of world news, constructed in the same way as myths, as a conventionalized series of embedded narratives by informed star reporters on location. In a quiz show or game show such as *The Weakest Link* (2000) and *Who Wants to Be a Millionaire* (1998), there is a 'compère' or 'anchor' (in Britain: Anne Robinson, Chris Tarrant) as an embedded narrator (often more or less subtly condescending to the candidates). This (usually male) guide steers through a story of success or failure, with the candidates as protagonists. Other narrative conventions include the studio setting, the theme melody as paratextual framing as well as the audience and the telephone help as 'sidekick' or chorus.

The flexi-narrative

As Nelson (2000: 12) has argued, serial-series hybrids such as *Ally McBeal* respond with a flexi-narrative to a new affective order of a trigger-happy audience with short attention spans for fragmentary images. Features are:

- intercutting of story arcs (beginning-middle-end) within episodes and spanning several episodes
- sound-vision bytes in line with advertisement rhythms
- non-linearity and polysemy, for instance by integration of music.

A recent study (*Narrating TV Series: Towards an Analysis of Narrative Strategies in Contemporary Television*) argues, however, that during the 1990s, the TV series finally came into its televisual own, increasingly beginning to employ playful and experimental narrative techniques, such as multiperspectivity, unreliable narration, voice-over narration, and other kinds of interiorization (cf. Allrath / Gymnich 2005).

The classic TV serial

As Nelson (1997: 144) shows in the case of *Middlemarch*, even the classic TV serial is not exempt from embracing flexi-narrative forms that make it resemble soap opera with its rapidly intercut narratives. It may not be surprising, therefore, that the new adaptation of Dickens's *Bleak House* by Andrew Davies comes in soap opera format, as a 16-episode twice-weekly half-hour series. This is a clear deviation from the traditional classic TV serial, which was reinvigorated in the 1990s by Davies's *Middlemarch* (1994). The trend peaked in 1995's *Pride and Prejudice*, watched regularly by 10 to 12 million viewers. Since then, a great number of mini-series (and movies, see HIGSON 2003) have exploited the new (and largely female) market. Recently, however, expensive heritage television has suffered from sinking revenue in TV advertising and competition for drama from cheap chat and reality formats. Mini-series continue to win awards from the British Academy of Film and Television Arts (BAFTA), for instance the six-part *The Way We Live Now*, but toying around with remakes (*Dr Zhivago*, 2002, *The Forsyte Saga*, 2002) and 'sexier', more popular formats, heritage drama has also become part of the intense debate concerning 'dumbed down' television.

Heritage or costume drama has substituted the earlier tradition of drama on TV in spite of massive production costs, above all because it could be co-produced with American money (invested, for instance, by the Boston-based company WBGH) and sold as British quality and history TV to American public broadcasting (PBS). ROBIN NELSON argues that (in the context of immediate reaction to viewer predilections) these new 'readerly' televisual forms have replaced the 'authorly' communication of television drama – obviously reacting to the technological and commercial shake-up of the TV apparatus since the 1980s. From the 1950s, both in the USA and in Britain, the 'golden age' of television drama spanned decades of interesting work within programming slots such as Armchair Theatre (ABC/ITV, 1956–1968), The Wednesday Play (BBC, 1964–1970) and the Play for Today (BBC, 1970–1984).

The 'golden age' of television drama

In the USA, PADDY CHAYEFSKY (1923–1981) set the standard with his realist *Marty* (1953) – he later wrote a biting film satire on TV (*Network*, 1976, D: SIDNEY LUMET). In Britain, the traditions of Reithian public service, the slots for the single play and the prestige of TV writing for a long time resisted the increasing media pressures on formatting and convention (and occasionally still do). This guaranteed a tradition of interesting and varied work by dramatists such as MIKE LEIGH (*Abigail's Party*, 1977), KEN LOACH (*Cathy Come Home*, 1966), TED KOTCHEFF (*Edna the Inebriate Woman*, 1971), PETER WATKINS (*The War Game*, 1966), JIMMY MCGOVERN (*Cracker*, 1993, *Hillsborough*, 1996), ALAN BLEASDALE (*Boys from the Blackstuff*, 1983), LYNDA LAPLANTE (*Prime Suspect*, 1991–2003), or HANIF KUREISHI (*The Buddha of Suburbia*, 1993), by directors such as ALAN CLARKE (*Elephant*, 1989) or STEPHEN FREARS (*My Beautiful Laundrette*, with KUREISHI, 1985), and producers such as TONY GARNETT and KENITH TRODD. With the exception of DENNIS POTTER, however, the tradition of British TV authors remains underrated in research (on POTTER, see the wave of publications: VOIGTS-VIRCHOW 1995, J. R. COOK 1998, CREEBER 1998, CARPENTER 1998, GRAS/COOK 2000).

Television authors

The prob-lems of studying TV drama	As Caughie (2000) argues, the study of television drama is in a precarious state because (1) television was seen as ephemeral (until 1978, British TV even had a policy of wiping their programmes); (2) unlike Hollywood cinema it remained largely national; (3) there used to be little 'television of (visual) attractions' to be had in TV drama; (4) in the mundane everyday flow of TV, even the textual integrity of Dennis Potter's *The Singing Detective* (1986) – "*one of the significant works of postwar British modernism*" (Caughie 2000: 20) – becomes submerged; (5) prioritizing genre over value and anti-'Lit.Crit.' impulses rejected the canonization of value which still works implicitly in film and literary studies.

4 Intermediality

CHAPTER

1 From primary intermediality to secondary intermediality

The cinema will gradually break from the tyranny of what is visual, from the image for its own sake, from the immediate and concrete demands of the narrative, to become a means of writing just as flexible and subtle as written language.

ALEXANDRE ASTRUC,
"The Birth of a New Avant-garde: La caméra-stylo"

One may also conceptualize theoretical approaches to the media according to their stance on intermediality. In his recent survey on the field of media studies, RAINER LESCHKE (2003) distinguishes various phases and environments in a media-historical perspective:

Intermediality and media theory

(1) primary intermediality
(2) media-specific approaches
(3) general media theories
(4) media ontologies
(5) secondary intermediality

Firstly, approaches determined by a situation of media contact and media rivalry focus on primary intermediality. PLATO (427–348/47 B.C), for example, attempted to define the essence of oral communication against the new media of painting and writing in his *Phaedrus*.

Primary intermediality

Secondly, medium-specificity theories (BLUESTONE 1957) attempt to define the essence of specific media with a view to establish new media practices theoretically. They hold that each separate medium is unique. This results, for instance, in a separate radio theory. Medium-specific theories also hold that the nature of a medium can be explained through analysing media forms or artistic practice as either adequate or inadequate to the media-specific ways of representation. One may, for instance, argue that JAMES JOYCE's modernist novel *Ulysses* (1922) cannot be adequately adapted for the medium of film because film is ill-equipped to bring the narrative complexity of *Ulysses* into media-specific (= filmic) forms. In spite of this, there have been movie versions by SEAN WALSH (*Bloom*, 2003) and JOSEPH STRICK (*Ulysses*, 1967).

Medium specificity

A case in point would be early film studies, both formalist (SERGEJ EISENSTEIN, 1898–1948, RUDOLF ARNHEIM, *1904) and realist (ANDRÉ

Example: Formalist *vs.* realist film theory	Bazin, 1919–1958, Siegfried Kracauer, 1889–1966). In the face of growing importance and complexity of the medium, theorists sought to establish film as a new and specific medium independent of, and different from, earlier aesthetic practice. Dziga Vertov described the essence of film as movement in space, Eisenstein as analytical *montage* of conflicts, Béla Balász (1884–1949) as a new dimension of bodily distance, and Arnheim as aesthetic defamiliarization. Consequently, theorists sought to determine the basics of good cinematic practice, turning towards the analysis not of film but of films and filmmakers, in other words, toward media philology. Bazin's theory of realism favoured the long take (in contrast to Hollywood shot / reverse-shot patterns) and the polyvalent deep focus (which – in contrast to shallow or variable focus – keeps the clarity of the image in the rear of the frame). For Kracauer, film achieved the redemption of physical reality, capturing compensatory visions which had been repressed in bourgeois mass industrialism.
General media theories	Next, general media theories start from an established field of study, which is then applied to a new media situation. For instance, some media (film, photography, computer) have prompted new developments in aesthetic theory, whereas others (telephone) seem, from an aesthetic point of view, irrelevant. Marxist approaches have focused on (repressive) functions of the media in late capitalism; and cultural studies have looked at media polysemy and audience usage. Examples may include not just aesthetic theories, materialist theories, and anthropology or cultural studies, but also Luhmann's systems theory or Schmidt's constructivism.
Media ontologies	Fourthly, general media ontologies (Greek *ōn*, 'being') reverse the point of view of general media theories. They explain the world through recourse to the media, starting from the assumption that established universal models of research have failed in the face of new media practices. Media, these 'ontologists' hold, must be determined not as a function of other social or cultural phenomena, but can only be understood as an autonomous sphere which in itself exerts a dominant influence on everything else. The famous catchphrase for this position is Marshall McLuhan's: "The medium is the message."
Secondary intermediality	Finally, Leschke describes the secondary-intermediality approach, dominated by what used to be called media philology. This approach replaces or augments established fields of study (i.e., literature, theatre, arts, film) with an extended canon of media products. This response to media innovation does not fall back on the old media-rivalry scenario, but instead sees the space in-

between the media, the manifestations and interferences of media change as media hybridity, as its real object of study. The following section will focus on this approach, which has opened a number of promising roads in literary / cultural studies.

2 The intermedial turn: New terminologies

Only that is fruitful what leaves room to the power of imagination. The more we see the more we must be able to add in our minds. The more we add in our minds the more we must imagine to see.

GOTTHOLD EPHRAIM LESSING, *Laocoon*

A song is poetry ('lyrics') with music. A music video is a song with images. LEWIS CARROLL's *Alice's Adventures in Wonderland* is unthinkable without JOHN TENNIEL's drawings, and so is OSCAR WILDE's *Salome* without AUBREY BEARDSLEY's illustrations. In the 16ᵗʰ century emblem books (Greek *émblēma*, 'that which is put in or on') appeared, which consist of a motto, an image (picture, icon or imago) and an explanatory subscription. From our earlier example, the iconotext still from *Adaptation*, we can deduct that film and television may work in similar ways. As BRIGGS / BURKE (2002: 3) argue, speech balloons in 18ᵗʰ century prints herald the cartoon and TINTORETTO's painting *St Mark Rescuing a Slave* (1548) shows St Mark as a precursor of Superman. RICHARD WAGNER's concept of opera integrates various media, and so does the Hollywood film musical. Films may use music and put photography in motion. – All of these aesthetic phenomena are the subject of studies in intermediality. Ideas of intermediality precede its term. JÜRGEN E. MÜLLER (1998: 33) quotes Renaissance thinker GIORDANO BRUNO, who wrote as early as in 1591: *"For true philosophy, music or poetry is also painting, and true painting is also music and philosophy, and true poetry or music is a kind of divine wisdom and painting."*

Crossover and art

BRUNO took his cues from Ancient Greece: According to PLUTARCH, SIMONIDES OF CEOS equated painting and poetry (*"Painting is silent poetry, and poetry painting that speaks"*), and HORACE coined the principle of *ut pictura poesis* or *"as is painting, so is poetry"* (HARVEY 2002). GOTTHOLD EPHRAIM LESSING answered this maxim with a strict separation of painting and poetry in 1776. In his *Laokoon: oder die Grenzen der Mahlerey und Poesie* ("The Limits of Painting and Poetry"), he argued that poetry is an art of time and painting an art of space. This is of course not quite true. For instance, SCOTT MCCLOUD's comics show how rich the potential of (spatial) comic panels (and their captions, speech and thought balloons, motion lines etc.) is for encoding time as simultaneous, momentary, durative, iterative etc. (MCCLOUD 1993). HOLLÄNDER (1995) can refer to

Ut pictura poiesis and Lessing's Laokoon

numerous examples of spill-overs from literature to painting, from OSCAR WILDE's *The Picture of Dorian Gray* (1891) to the mainly literary reception of GIOVANNI BATISTA PIRANESI's engravings *Carceri d'invenzione* (1750/1761) in the Gothic novel and beyond.

Intermedial turn

Even if intermedial discussions, therefore, are not new, it was not until the 1990s that the study of intermediality became a thriving field in literary and media studies (particularly in Europe; see MERTENS 2000). This new field of inquiry has provided enough materials to proclaim an intermedial turn (WOLF 1999). The interest in concepts of intermediality was spawned by the appearance of technical reproduction media in the 1920s and 1930s (WALTER BENJAMIN, BERTOLT BRECHT). BRECHT, for instance, remarked in 1931 that the advent of film also changed the writing of novels, because film audiences include novelists. He concluded that literature needs film (and ALBERSMEIER added in 1995 that film also needs literature). The conceptualization of intermediality, however, is a result of the media convergence and hybridity of media apparatuses which was accelerated by digital media.

Authors in film, TV, and radio

Even at the level of individual authors, intermediality is a fruitful endeavour, as a brief look at the key three modernists of post-1956 British theatre will show. We may still think of SAMUEL BECKETT, HAROLD PINTER and TOM STOPPARD as dramatists, but in fact all of them frequently abandoned the theatre boards to write for film (BECKETT: *Film,* 1965/1979; PINTER: *The Go-Between,* 1971, *The French Lieutenant's Woman,* 1981, *The Trial,* 1993, *The Handmaid's Tale,* 1990, *The Comfort of Strangers,* 1990; STOPPARD: *Shakespeare in Love,* 1998, *Rosencrantz & Guildenstern Are Dead,* 1990, *Brazil,* 1985) or television (BECKETT: *Eh Joe,* 1966, *Quad,* 1982; PINTER: *A Night Out,* 1960, *The Lover,* 1963; STOPPARD: *Professional Foul,* 1977, *Squaring the Circle,* 1984) and radio (BECKETT: *Rough for Radio 1 & 2,* 1976, *All That Fall,* 1957; PINTER: *A Slight Ache,* 1959, *The Dwarfs,* 1960; STOPPARD: *Artist Descending a Staircase,* 1972, *If You're Glad I'll Be Frank,* 1966). All of the texts have been published and the plays have received increasing critical attention (BECKETT: KALB 1991, WULF 1995; PINTER: KLEIN 1985, GALE 2003; STOPPARD: GURALINCK 2001, HODGSON 2002). Interestingly, the key publications on British television drama (CAUGHIE 2000, BIGNELL et al. 2000, COOKE 2003) make a point of bypassing these authors – probably because their aesthetics have remained a footnote in the tradition of British television drama. In the case of SHAKESPEARE and BECKETT, however, the central significance of these authors has been honoured by a television filming of their entire oeuvres – or rather the companies producing these umbrella packages sought to participate in the cultural prestige of these authors (both packages are available on DVD, 19 Beckett plays as *Beckett on Film* (2000–2001), co-produced by RTÉ, Irish Film Board and Channel 4, and 37 Shakespeare plays as *The BBC Television Shakespeare* (1978–1985), co-produced with Time-Life).

Inter-mediality and inter-textuality

Intermediality is an umbrella term for in-between phenomena (Latin *inter*, 'between'), i.e., media forms which appear in various media and operate under constraint of the respective media. The term is an offshoot of the term intertextuality, which aimed at a clearer description of what has been known in literary studies as 'influence studies'. According to the strong position advocated by, among others, JULIA KRISTEVA, intertextuality has been defined as a universal concept against theories that focus on subject agency. JÜRGEN E. MÜLLER (1998: 32) reports that KRISTEVA, in inaugurating the study of intertextuality, included intermediality, or the *"passage d'un système de signes à un autre"* (but then continues to study inter*text*uality).

Terminology

The term intermediality has also descended from interart or comparative art studies. In a pathbreaking 1966 manifesto, Dick HIGGINS, who (adopting the term from SAMUEL TAYLOR COLERIDGE) differentiated between intermedia (which fuses aesthetic practices) and multimedia or mixed media (which combine discreet media). RAJEWSKY (2002: 10) convincingly argues that inquiry should not impose the conceptual restriction on aesthetic products. It is, of course, glaringly imprecise to call computer or video art 'media art' (or, with LINDA BEN-ZVI, BECKETT's plays for TV, film and radio 'media plays') – as if there were a form of art that is not constituted by the media involved.

Inter-mediality *vs.* trans-mediality

Intermediality may be distinguished from *trans*mediality (the quality of phenomena which appear independently of their media set-up, i.e., parody or myth). Thus, basic 'themes' or contents as well as plot elements and character outlines in *Romeo and Juliet* or *Hamlet* are bound to reappear independently of their media genre (e.g., a text, a drama performance, a ballet, a musical, movie or a graphic novel). Certain scenarios have acquired such a dominance that they appear (quasi-mythically) again and again across media boundaries.

Trans-mediality in colonial and postcolonial narratives

JOSEPH CONRAD's *Heart of Darkness* might be compared with MARY KINGSLEY's *Travels in West Africa* (1897) or ADAM HOCHSCHILD's *King Leopold's Ghost* (1999). *Heart of Darkness* was adapted for radio by ORSON WELLES (1945) and gave rise to CHINUA ACHEBE's famous critique in "An Image of Africa: Racism in Conrad's Heart of Darkness" (1977). ACHEBE's equally famous novel *Things Fall Apart* (1958) can be read as a response to CONRAD and W. B. YEATS. More recently, there have been FRANCIS FORD COPPOLA's Vietnam version *Apocalypse Now* (1979), a TV adaptation of *Heart of Darkness* by

Nicolas Roeg (1994) and Danny Boyle's *The Beach* (2000), an adaptation of Alex Garland's novel (1998) which, in turn, derives from Conrad's novel and William Golding's novel *The Lord of the Flies* (1954), which, in turn, reverses Robert M. Ballantyne's *Coral Island* (1858) – and so forth. We have now arrived at the rich intertextual and intermedial field of the Robinsonade and island literature which will yield even more transmedial myths (*The Tempest, Robinson Crusoe, Treasure Island*).

Transmedial horror myths: *Dracula*

Some horror narratives and dystopian narratives (such as *The Lord of the Flies* or Orwell's *Nineteen Eighty-Four*) have easily crossed media boundaries and are therefore best described as transmedial myths. In order to explain their attraction, analyses of horror films have often resorted to psychological models (Kawin 1981). Bram Stoker's novel *Dracula* (1897, itself varying the Romantic vampire in John Polidori's short story "The Vampyre", 1819, vampire melodrama and Sheridan Le Fanu's "Carmilla", 1872) spawned a series of stage adaptations and print narratives (Brian Aldiss's *Dracula Unbound* or Anne Rice's influential *Vampire Chronicles*). Vampires have become so domesticated that they regularly appear in comics, children's books and on *Sesame Street*. Countless films, some of which mix the vampire myth with other Gothic tales and different film traditions have been made. F. W. Murnau's *Nosferatu, eine Symphonie des Grauens*, 1922, set in Bremen, sparked off a copyright row with Stoker's widow Florence. Bela Lugosi starred as an elegant nobleman quipping Swinburne ("there are worse things waiting for man than death") in Tod Browning's *Dracula* (1931), which in turn was based on the streamlined stage versions by Hamilton Deane and John Balderston. Carl Dreyer's *Vampyr* (1931) mixed Le Fanu's "Carmilla" with other stories from his collection *The Glass Darkly*. Vampires figure prominently in the B-movie (i.e., originally the lesser half of a double feature in the cinema) productions from the British Hammer studios, such as *Horror of Dracula* (1958), and in 1979 Werner Herzog remade *Nosferatu: Phantom der Nacht*, casting the notorious Klaus Kinski as the vampire.

Increasing hybridization: AIDS vampires of the 1990s

We have seen that earlier films sucked blood freely from a variety of vampiric traditions, and it is arguably the metaphoric suggestiveness of the immunodeficiency syndrome transmitted via exchange of bodily fluids, AIDS, that accounts for the renewal of the genre in the 1990s. The pleasurable pattern of recognizing repetition with a difference continues in the wake of the successful *Bram Stoker's Dracula* (D: Francis Ford Coppola) in 1992, which for the first time attempted to follow Stoker's convoluted multi-perspective narrative. Neil Jordan's *Interview with the Vampire* (1994) was based on Anne Rice's novel, and in the same year Michael Almereyda's *Nadja* also continued the gay / lesbian theme in vampire film. Further vampires appeared in films by WES CRAVEN (*Vampires in Brooklyn*, 1995), JOHN CARPENTER (*Vampires*, 1998), and STEPHEN NORRINGTON (*Blade*, 1998). In *Shadow of the Vampire* (2000), a meta-movie about the filming of MURNAU's *Nosferatu*, actor Max Schreck (played by WILLEM DAFOE) takes his role as Dracula too seriously. *Van Helsing* (2004) mixes at least three horror myths: Dracula, Frankenstein, and Werewolf. Finally, the TV series *Buffy the Vampire Slayer* (1992), set in Sunnydale, CA, adapts the vampire myth to teenage comedy in order to expand the audience appeal.

MARY SHELLEY's *Frankenstein* palpably inspired MARY LOUDON WEBB's *The Mummy!* (1827) – and in film history both archetypes reappear. BORIS KARLOFF (and his make-up artist JACK PIERCE) created the archetypal creature in the JAMES WHALE movies *Frankenstein* (1931) and *Bride of Frankenstein* (1935), and, more recently, in *Mary Shelley's Frankenstein* (D: KENNETH BRANAGH), ROBERT DE NIRO's portrayal deliberately opposed the KARLOFF legacy. Much earlier, in the 19th-century *Punch* cartoons, the creature already figured as social or national stereotypes, for instance, "The Irish Frankenstein" or "The Brummagem [Birmingham] Frankenstein". KARLOFF also appeared in the 1932 version of *The Mummy* (D: KARL FREUND), updated in a three-part sequel (1999–2001). MEL BROOKS tackled both the Frankenstein and Dracula myths in parody (*Young Frankenstein*, 1974, *Dracula: Dead and Loving It*, 1995) and PAUL MORRISSEY / ANDY WARHOL provided camp versions (*Blood for Dracula*, 1974, *Flesh for Frankenstein*, 1973). Of course, *Dracula* has appeared in video games, and *Frankenstein* may also be adapted to hypertext, as SHELLEY JACKSON's *Patchwork Girl* (1995) illustrates.

More transmedial horror myths: *Frankenstein* and *The Mummy*

One may look at these movies as versions of *trans*medial myths, but also as *intra*medial metafilms or investigate their *inter*medial references. These dimensions should not be conflated. Intramediality involves only one discreet medium, for instance when *Young Frankenstein* parodies Boris KARLOFF in the JAMES WHALE films. When LARS VON TRIER calls the main street in his film *Dogville* (2003) "Elm Street" this is a clear intramedial reference to the movie *Nightmare on Elm Street* (1984). This statement, however, needs specification about the precise nature, quality and rationale of this 'reference', unless one is content with calling the 'reference' an 'analogy', 'source', or 'motif'. In the next step the question must be addressed whether the *Nightmare* reference is to the individual movie or, as a systematic reference, to the horror movie genre. Further, one may check whether it is merely mentioned and discussed or whether *Dogville* itself reproduces the structures of a horror movie. The study of intermediality, therefore, investigates a number of distinct phenomena – media combination, media transfer and

Intermediality *vs.* intramediality

media contact – which nevertheless may appear together in an individual media product (see Rajewsky 2002: 19). A narrow notion of intermediality focuses on the final category of media contact.

Media combination

One may distinguish this narrow notion of intermediality proper from the study of an aesthetic multi-, pluri-, polymediality or media fusion, i.e., the addition of various distinct media. In spite of Richard Wagner's criticism (he aimed at a fusion of individual arts) both operas and movies (as well as, of course, Hollywood musicals) are the result of intense media combination, and, in this sense, *Gesamtkunstwerke* or hybrids. A sound-art installation merges sound with an architectural or 'objective' installation art or sculptural art. Jeffrey Shaw's installation *The Legible City* (1988–1991), for instance, famously combines the physical experience of riding a bicycle and the navigation in a simulated, virtual world, in which the buildings of Amsterdam and Karlsruhe are represented by three-dimensional letters (the letters, in turn, consisting of documents describing urban history). Cycling through a virtual landscape composed of words is clearly different from the monomedial experience of reading a book – an experience in which only one medium is materially present (but which may, of course, be characterized by intermedial contact or by a media transfer, in which some other medium has been replaced).

Film, media combination and remediation: Graphic novels

It is clear that some media result from the (technological) combination of other media (i.e., film), even if they have come to be regarded as distinct. A film divided into titled chapters is not a media combination, because the book is not materially present. In a media combination no medium dominates the other (see Rajewsky 2002: 15, 56–57). A film that mixes cartoon animation and film noir (e.g., *Who Framed Roger Rabbit*, 1988) may be seen as combining media, although, of course, cartoons are, strictly speaking, not materially present in film animation. The increasing number of movies that adapt graphic novels outside of the realm of film animation as live action (following the increasing scope and cultural significance of the graphic novel) should not be regarded as media combinations, but as media transfers (*Road to Perdition*, 2002, *From Hell*, 2001, *Ghost World*, 2001). The trend may have been prompted by successful transfers of computer games to film (*Tomb Raider*: video game 1996, movie 2001). On the other hand, we might argue that in the transfer from cartoon to film, there is an intermedial contact that subtly impinges on both source and target media. Examining *Toy Story* (1995), Bolter/Grusin (1999) argue for a mutual impact between film and computer animation, and they call this phenomenon of refashioning "remediation". When the German TV channel ARD uses a drop-down menu for their trailers they clearly imitate the menu selection familiar from computer software. The term 'remediation' opens up the field of intermedial contact, in which, for instance, 'filmic' writing (a reversal of Jean Astruc's 'caméra stylo') may be explored.

3 Intermedial contact: Some examples

My task which I am trying to achieve is, by the power of the written word, to make you hear, to make you feel – it is, before all, to make you see.
Joseph Conrad, Preface to *The Nigger of the Narcissus*

In order to clarify what happens in media contact, Werner Wolf (2002: 17) distinguished between "extracompositional intermediality" (between given works) and "intracompositional intermediality" (within a given work). In this narrow sense of intermediality within a semiotic entity, one may distinguish a 'contacting' or object medium and a 'contacted' or reference medium. The contacting medium is present in its entire materiality and the contacted medium contributes toward the semantics of the contacting medium. This may be regarded as an extra or excess element within the contacting media product, which is materially present.

Media contact

Film, for instance, is the contacted medium in John Dos Passos's USA trilogy, because it contributes to the effect of 'filmic' writing in the novel (which, nevertheless, remains a novel, a book). In George Eliot's *Adam Bede* (1859), it is Dutch genre painting of the 17th century; and Virginia Woolf addresses post-impressionism in *To the Lighthouse* (1927; see Mosthaf 2000). As Wolf (1999) has shown, modernist works (Woolf's "String Quartet", Thomas Mann's *Zauberberg* and *Tonio Kröger*, the 'Sirens' chapter in Joyce's *Ulysses*) are particularly rich in attempts to fulfil Walter Pater's ideal, aspiring "towards the condition of music". In reverse, film may contact books, for instance when Jean-Luc Godard parodies chapter headings in novels by providing mixed, inconsistent and useless intertitles in his *Pierrot le Fou* (1965). Von Trier's movie *Dogville* equally contacts the 18th century novel with intertitles that designate a prologue and nine chapters. It also contacts (Brechtian) theatre in a transparent, 'alienating' anti-mimetic set in which road names, building outlines and props (such as the dog Moses) are written on the floor in chalk.

'Contacting' and 'contacted' medium

Rajewsky (2002: 26) argues that intermedial contacting is of particular interest for contemporary literary studies, because they systematically cover fields that have been for a long time marginalized and isolated. A good example is the study of ekphrasis.

Ekphrasis: definition

Ekphrasis is defined as "the verbal representation of visual representation" (HEFFERNAN 1993: 3), or, more broadly, "the verbal representation of a real or fictitious text composed in a non-verbal sign system" (CLÜVER 1997: 26). JOHN KEATS's "Ode on a Grecian Urn" is a well-known example. As described by W. J. T. MITCHELL (1994), attitudes to ekphrasis vary from indifference (i.e., the presumption of its impossibility) to hope (i.e., the confidence that imaginative use of language can overcome the problems inherent in the verbal representation of images) and fear (i.e., the awareness of the dangerous distortion that results from the incompatibility of visual and verbal representation). HOLLÄNDER (1995) argues that ekphrasis is inevitably part of spatial description in literature and PETER WAGNER (1995, 1996) expands the term to cover any literary reference to art.

Ekphrasis: A Renaissance example

MARIO KLARER (2001) investigates ekphrasis at a distinct historical moment. He sketches the conflict between neo-Platonic iconophilia in much Renaissance literature and the official iconophobia in Reformation religiosity. One of the more drastic examples of the use of emblems in Renaissance literature is the silenced Lavinia in SHAKESPEARE's *Titus Andronicus* (1594), her arms cut off and her tongue cut out after the rape. In the absence of her own voice and hands (which would have enabled Lavinia to visualize the deed), her uncle Marcus describes the bloody scene with reference to the rape of Philomel by Tereus from OVID's *Metamorphoses*. In this way the graphic visuality of the performance is semiotically balanced and poetically interpreted in SHAKESPEARE's language. The male ekphrasis of the mute Lavinia in SHAKESPEARE's *Titus Andronicus* serves as an example of gendered 'mastering' of women as objects of male wordings. This tradition of reifying the female body by male definition will recur below in the discussion of the male gaze.

Media contacting: TV in postmodern American novels

In an examination of, for instance, intermedial contact between TV (as contacted medium) and written narratives (as a contacting medium), the examples are, significantly, taken from postmodernist American literature (see TICHI 1991, MCHALE 1992 and GRIEM 1996 for more instances of TV narration provided by NORMAN MAILER, BOBBIE ANN MASON, DAVID FOSTER WALLACE, and others). Novels such as THOMAS PYNCHON's *Vineland* (1990) or Don DELILLO's *White Noise* explicitly link TV to ontological multiplication (i.e., parallel worlds) and ontological destabilization (i.e., death). In *Vineland*, characters undergo TV detoxification and there is a sect of 'TV-totallers' called Thanatoids.

In *White Noise* (1985: 50–51), ex-sports-writer Murray Siskind, who teaches popular culture at a liberal-arts college in Middle America

(i.e., in the bland, backward and conservative small-town America also nicknamed 'flyover country'), argues in conversation with his colleague Jack Gladney:

Waves and radiation. [...] I've come to understand that the medium is a primal force in the American home. Sealed-off, timeless, self-contained, self-referring. It's like a myth being born right there in our living room, like something we know in a dream-like and pre-conscious way. [...] You have to learn to look. You have to open yourself to the data. TV offers incredible amounts of psychic data. It opens ancient memories of world birth, it welcomes us into the grid, the network of little buzzing dots that make up the picture pattern. There is light, there is sound. I ask my students, 'What more do you want?' Look at the wealth of data concealed in the grid, in the bright packaging, in the jingles, the slice-of-life commercials, the products hurtling out of the darkness, the coded messages and endless repetitions, like chants, like mantras. 'Coke is it, Coke is it, Coke is it.' The medium practically overflows with sacred information if we can remember how to respond innocently and get past the irritation, weariness and disgust.

> **Don DeLillo:** *White Noise*

In this passage from *White Noise* TV is mentioned and discussed in a novel. It is, therefore, a case of an explicitly demarcated 'thematization' of a contacted medium (TV) in a contacting medium (novel, book). Siskind's micro-lecture contains a comprehensive account of TV (which smacks of McLUHAN, BAUDRILLARD, apparatus and systems theories) that speculates about the quasi-religious repetitive force of its messages (it might have served as an inspiration for HANS MAGNUS ENZENSBERGER's revision of his ideas on TV). It is a case of discursively relevant contact because it addresses the role of television, popular culture, death, and technology in contemporary American society (as is also evidenced in the novel's title *White Noise*, and the chapter subtitle "Waves and Radiation").

> **Explicit system reference**

This is also evident in JERZY KOSINSKI's novelette *Being There* (1971), in which the protagonist Chance is Kaspar-Hauser-like brought up solely on television (and gardening). Chance inherits a Bishop-Berkeley-like attitude of *esse est percipi* ("to be is to be perceived"): "*As long as one didn't look at people, they didn't exist. They began to exist, as on TV, when one turned one's eyes on them*" (12). Chance's simple-minded, bland, repetitive, multiple, past-less and fearless identity prove to be excellent qualifications to become president of the United States. In Chance, KOSINSKI thematically addresses medium-specific traits of TV and the novel. In doing so, he makes a NEIL POSTMAN-like statement about the USA as a media democracy. As GRIEM (1996: 480) has shown, however, in PYNCHON's *Vineland* "*the excessive re-enactment of televisual patterns no longer*

> **Kosinski's** *Being There* **and** **Pynchon's** *Vineland*

seems a symptom of psychotic behaviour but a sign of social competence". According to Brian McHale's analysis (1992: 119), the language (of both narrator and characters) in this novel does not just evoke, but simulates the language of television.

System contamination

Even in the title, which replicates the announcement of the paradigmatic American TV show, Donald Barthelme's short-story "And Now Let's Hear It for the Ed Sullivan Show!" (1963) provides an excellent example of an even more intense case of intermediality, system contamination. The TV format 'television show' is displaced into the genre 'short literary narrative' and the systemic traits of the TV show transform the discourse level, i.e., the core structure, of the literary text. This dislocation results in a narrative voice that elliptically registers the flow of audiovisual content while watching the show – a 'stream of consciousness' that remains, however, at a very selective surface of image- and sound-bites:

The Ed Sullivan Show. Sunday night. Church of the unchurched. Ed stands there. He looks great. […] Ed clasps his hands together. He's introducing somebody in the audience. Who is it? […] Who is it? It's… Don Rickles! Rickles stands up. Eyes glint. Applause.
[…]
Camera straight on Ed. "Before I tell you about next week's … show … please listen to this." Commercial for Silva Thins. Then a shot of old man with ship model, commercial for Total, the vitamin cereal. Then Ed. […] Music comes up. The crawl containing the credits is rolled over shot of Russian dancers dancing […]. Produced by Rob Precht. Directed by Tim Kiley. Music by Ray Bloch. Associate Producer Jack McGeehan […]. (Barthelme 1963: 101, 108)

System contamination: Narrating "watching TV"

As in *White Noise*, TV appears as quasi-religious. It is clear that media specific representation (TV reception: "a couch potato watching") dominates Barthelme's narrative voice in a kind of 'TV eye' (rather than 'camera eye') technique of narrative 'showing'. His narrator registers the viewers' gradual construction of sense from audiovisual content. The voice's parataxis and ellipses parallel in a different medium the rushing sequence that does not leave time for syntactic complexity. Repetitive and meaningless responses equal the showmaster's register ("great", "terrific", "nice") and exhibit the levelling of emotion in an inadequate ekphrasis. The faithful representation of the final credit roll satirizes the emptied excess of meaningless, free-floating signifiers in the TV flow. Apropos of a "submemorable" song that stands for the entirety of the submemorable TV programme, Barthelme's narrator refers to the status of TV as a surrogate experience, when a pornographic tape is accidentally aired by a Californian station: "([…] *unfortunately, the exhibition wasn't on a network. What we really want in this world, we can't have.)"* (Barthelme 1963: 107). The narrative voice is enclosed in brackets when it deviates from registering the TV flow and comments on a rare occasion of memorable TV input. The example is marked as referring to televisual forms of the 1960s: the cable TV or pay-per-view TV pornography and channel hopping requires different forms of system contamination (for an example, see Rajewsky 2002: 129).

4 Media transfers: The case of Shakespeare

By William Shakespeare with additional dialogue by Samuel Taylor.
Credits for 1929 movie of *The Taming of the Shrew*

Artistic processes are marked by routine switching between various media. The work of Shakespeare has been subjected to countless transformations into films, animated films, radio plays, puppet theatre plays, musicals, sketches, cartoons, novels, hypertext etc. This migration of a text/product from one semiotic system into another has been variously called media transfer, secondary intermediality, media change, media switch, and media transformation. The burgeoning industry of Shakespearean film analyses often concentrates on film adaptations (Jorgens 1977, Davies 1988, Donaldson 1990, Wells/Davies 1994, Boose/Burt 1997, Burt 1998, Rothwell 1999, Cartmell 2000, Brode 2000, Burnett/Wray 2000, Jackson 2000, Hodgdon 2002), only occasionally on TV productions (Coursen/Bulman 1988). Almost equally often, one notes a melancholic overtone in accounts of verbal casualties, crippling cameras, and starved imagination (see Cardwell 2002: 36–38); and generic diversification in the context of Hollywood entertainment, adolescent audiences and pornography (*Tromeo & Juliet*, 1997) sounded the danger of "Shakesploitation".

Media transfer and the Shakespeare industry

The movie *Titus* (1999), directed by Julie Taymor, is clearly an adaptation of Shakespeare's most successful play in his lifetime, *Titus Andronicus* (1594). On the other hand, starting with the title, one may characterize the changes and switches. The movie is not called *William Shakespeare's Titus Andronicus* in the vein of *Bram Stoker's Dracula* (1992) or *Mary Shelley's Frankenstein* (1994) by Coppola or Branagh. Neither is it just a Shakespeare adaptation. It has also been characterized as a horror movie or slasher movie and compared to the violent films of Quentin Tarantino. The casting is important in that star actor Antony Hopkins carries his credentials as a Shakespearean actor, but his part as anthropophagic intellectual Hannibal Lecter in *The Silence of the Lambs* (1991) is also connoted. *Titus* makes this overt when Hopkins/Titus snaps his mouth at Chiron and Demetrius before he slits their throats.

Shakespeare adaptation: Titus

Adapting Shakespeare: Stars and casting	Casting and stardom, therefore, introduce categories that are particular to the contemporary media world and essential in the media transfer. To be sure, there is a tradition of Shakespearean star acting (from RICHARD BURBAGE to DAVID GARRICK, EDMUND KEAN, or CHARLES MACREADY), but with the advent of film (with close-ups that furthered individuation) and the commercially driven mass-market, cross-media building of stars in Hollywood, the category 'star' has gained further prominence (particularly since the 1930s). SHAKESPEARE films have turned a number of British actors into male stars (BRANAGH, Sir LAURENCE OLIVIER, JOHN GIELGUD). A cross-over choice may serve both to endear SHAKESPEARE movies to unlikely audience segments and to tap into the cultural prestige of SHAKESPEARE to redefine the star's image (MEL GIBSON or ETHAN HAWKE as Hamlet).
Screen stardom	The screen stardom of Shakespearean actor LAURENCE OLIVIER, who was instrumental in nationalizing (*Henry V*, 1944) or universalizing SHAKESPEARE, shows how acting becomes embedded in the cinematic meaning-making process. Gender, ethnicity and age are essential categories in stardom, according to projected audience segments. A study by LEVY (1990) discovered that American movie stars tended to be blond women and dark-haired men, the male stars lasting longer and being less defined by their physical attractiveness. Stars and celebrities do not merely bring acting skills to a role, but they carry their off-screen persona and their previous roles to 'personify' genres, meanings, and myths. Just as the Hollywood melodrama or the Western, therefore, the heritage film has generated a set of clearly identifiable (mostly British) 'heritage' actors that 'embody' the genre: EMMA THOMPSON, HELENA BONHAM CARTER, HUGH GRANT, COLIN FIRTH (on stars, see DYER 1979, 1986, NAREMORE 1988, GLEDHILL 1991).
Self-conscious inter-mediality in *Titus*	Returning to the example of *Titus*, one may note that its style is elaborately constructed, highlighting its own self-conscious stylishness in the manner of the tableaux vivants that became fashionable in the late 18th century. TAYMOR's movie is full of references to the grotesque decadence of FEDERICO FELLINI or the neo-Jacobeanism of PETER GREENAWAY. Its eclectic visual mix of imperial Rome, and fascism in décor, architectural setting and costumes is palpably inspired by *Richard III* (D: RICHARD LONCRAINE). *Titus* introduces elaborate dream sequences and quotes JEAN-JACQUES DAVID's painting of MARAT in a *tableau vivant*. *Titus* is dominated by the visual climate of Nazi Germany or fascist Italy. Director TAYMOR also provides a pastiche of her Broadway production of *The Lion King* (in her ending) and discusses children and violent entertainment industries in the frame narrative. The revengeful mutilations in *Titus* have been read as a validation of prosthetics in the vein of

Donna Haraway's "Cyborg Manifesto" (Lehmann 2002) or as "*a right wing feminism in which women and sex do not mix*" (Burt 2002: 315). *Titus*, therefore, activates trains of discourse beyond Shakespeare; and it need not be read as an adaptation.

Up to this point, we have implicitly thought about media as media of aesthetic practice (as the study of literary intertextuality implies), but this approach may be restrictive. Marshall McLuhan made the point that one medium may become the content of another medium (as in the case of photography, which may be described as the content of film which, in turn, becomes the content of television or digital media). Jürgen E. Müller (1998: 36) has suggested that we need a revision of older media theories which insisted on the specificity of distinct media. Müller described film as a fusion of other media which generates its own hybrid brand of intermediality: What happens when the photographic shutter freezes time and film sets this frozen time in motion? What happens when the cinematic motion is taken out of the dark cinema and into the data file or the television flow?

Media hybridity

5 Media transfers: Screenplays and adaptation

Complete adaptation to the environment means death. The essential point in all response is the desire to control environment. John Dewey

The classic example for illustrating what happens in a media transfer is literary adaptation. As Murray (1972: 109) states bluntly (and imprecisely): "*The novelist uses words, the film-maker uses pictures; therein lies the simple but major difference between the two art forms.*" Media migration starts as a text transfer from a literary source text, such as a short story or play, or, most often, a novel. Other forms of media transfer, however, should also be considered, for instance the novelization of a movie (such as the novelization of Jane Campion's *The Piano*, 1993, by Campion and Kate Pullinger, 1994), the adaptation of a radio play for the theatre stage or books read as audio art on CD.

Literary adaptation and novelization

Screenwriting – the first step in the transition from word to audiovision, has become a profitable market in which screenwriting coaches (McKee 1999, Field 1984) offer their services in textbooks, DVDs and online courses to literary writers aiming at the most profitable market open to them (on writing for TV and film screens, see, e.g. Brunow 1996, Sternberg 1997, Owen 2003).

Screenwriting as market

Let us consider, for instance, the sequence of transfer texts involved in getting *The Lord of the Rings* from book to film, starting with Tolkien's own sources. The first step is, of course, buying the rights

Script stages: Property	of a given text (which contributes to the popularity of writers such as SHAKESPEARE, who cannot claim royalties for their texts). In the case of *The Lord of the Rings*, for example, J. R. R. TOLKIEN sold the rights to the Hollywood company MGM for £15,000, which, in turn, passed them on to SAUL ZAENTZ, who produced an animated version in 1978 (D: RALPH BAKSHI). Having acquired the rights for *The Lord of the Rings*, ZAENTZ, who controls the merchandising for the TOLKIEN movies, takes earnings from the PETER JACKSON trilogy without being involved in the films in any way (and, as the magazine *Variety* reports, is currently suing the producers of the trilogy, Line Cinema, for an adequate share of the gross profits).
Blueprint, reading material, storyboard, pre-viz	Depending on the nature of the source and of the conceived film, the text travels from property stage to blueprint stage (STERNBERG 1997: 48–79). In this case, PETER JACKSON and his partner FRAN WALSH, produced a 90-page treatment for the company Miramax in 1998. This short treatment was the basis for a two-part script, but Miramax shied away from the risks involved in filming a sequel and demanded a one-part script. With help from PHILIPPA BOYENS, JACKSON and WALSH then wrote a three-part script for the company NewLine, the text thus passing to the reading-material stage. This script was accepted, but it was further transformed in a number of rewrites in a sequence of readings. The script was then complemented by storyboards, a kind of comic-strip visualization of what will be seen in the frame, composed of 'panels', and pre-viz (i.e., pre-visualizations, short and rough preliminary computer animations, digital "animatics").
Visual articulation	The script also provided the cues for the extended process of articulating the symbolically encoded text visually. This is, of course, the great challenge of filmmaking, to create an adequate visual language from the script, to manipulate space (unlike texts) in a concrete and specific manner. In the case of *The Lord of the Rings* this process of visual articulation involved typical stages – casting, rehearsing, location hunting – but also live action scanned into computers, CGI (computer graphic imagery), special tricks in forced perspective, the production of more than 45,000 items (including illustrations, models, armour, latex masks etc.), the building of miniature sets and (larger) so-called "maxiatures".
Special effects and the cinema of attractions	*The Lord of the Rings* is a good example of the increasing importance of special effects in visual articulation. At least from the time of film pioneer GEORGES MÉLIÈS onwards (*Le Voyage dans la lune*, 1905) special effects have played an important part in guaranteeing an attractive visual film articulation, particularly in historical, fantasy or science-fiction films. In a seminal essay, TOM GUNNING (1986) regards special effects as a "*tamed version*" of an innate

quality of film, its *"ability to show something"*. GUNNING analysed early film and finds this exhibitionist quality both in film as vaudeville attraction and in modernist experimentalism (EISENSTEIN's *"montage* of attractions").

19th- or 20th-century novels tend to require a specific set outline, but adaptations of Renaissance dramas provide different challenges. The 1998 movie *Middleton's Changeling* may serve as a simple example. It is an adaptation of the 1622 Jacobean revenge tragedy *The Changeling,* co-written by THOMAS MIDDLETON and WILLIAM ROWLEY. The script was produced by the filmmaker, MARCUS THOMPSON, for High Time Pictures in Oxford. Released through the 'independent' movie company United Independent Pictures, this campy, awkward B-movie is clearly at odds with the typical heritage adaptation of Renaissance drama. During its seven-year production period two cast members (FERNANDO REY, VIVIAN STANSHALL) died, rights to the soundtrack (JIMI HENDRIX) were withdrawn and THOMPSON sank most of his own money in an extremely low budget (for the production history see www.marcusthompson.com).

Adapting Renaissance drama: *The Changeling*

The very title suggests questions of authority. Why MIDDLETON, why not ROWLEY? Why is the author of the play indicated and the article left out? Why base a film on a bloody and sexist Jacobean revenge tragedy which was moderately successful in a number of recent stage productions and was last produced for British TV on BBC 2 in 1993? In addition, there are typical questions concerning the adaptation of SHAKESPEARE or other Renaissance stage plays: What kind of visual language and spatial design fills the void of lacking stage directions (DAVIES 1988)? How does the film as a "performance re-textualized" (DONALDSON 1990) relate to the repeatable text and its flexible performances? What are the effects of the 'alienating' and 'difficult' language, i.e., Early Modern blank verses?

Problems with adapting Renaissance drama

Let us look at an extract from the pre-production typescript:

Typed screenplay

Fig. 17: From the screenplay of Middleton's Changeling
(MARCUS THOMPSON)

```
                                    CUT TO:  │ transition
51   EXT. CASTLE OF SANTA BARBARA BATTLEMENTS.  51 │ slugline
- DAY.
We HEAR a roll of THUNDER and distant gypsy MUSIC │ action text
drifting up from the streets below. VERMANDERO
points out over the city skyline then turns to
ALONSO by his side speaking words we cannot hear.
They then leave frame together.
                                    CUT TO:  │ transition
52  INT. COACH HOUSE. - DAY.              52 │ slugline
DE FLORES takes another draw as BEATRICE sees │ action text
him.
                    BEATRICE                 │ speech prefix
                   (disgusted)               │ parenthetical
                   (26.13.05)                │ time code
                 Oh … De Flores!             │ dialogue
                    DE FLORES                │ etc.
                   (26.14.24)
                      Lady.
BEATRICE slowly walks across to where DE FLORES
is seated in the CARRIAGE. He takes another pull
on the reefer and blows the smoke into her face.
                    BEATRICE
                   (26.22.18)
      What have you done to your face lately?
                   (26.26.01)
    Have you met a good physician? I think you've
  preened yourself. I am sure you used not look so
                     handsome.
                       […]
DE FLORES hands BEATRICE a parcel of cloth which
she unwraps.
                    DE FLORES
                   (35.49.18)
          It was sent somewhat unwillingly;
BEATRICE is shocked to find a severed FINGER within
the bloodstained cloth. The phallic image echoing
the horror of the murder, and forcing BEATRICE to
confront the physical reality of the crime she had
not troubled to envisage. The ring simultaneously
suggesting not only Beatrice's engagement vow to
Alonso and De Flores' sexual intentions, but also
recalling Lollio's thrusting gesture whilst dis-
cussing the subject of wedding rings with Alibius
earlier in the film. Thus the past (the murder),
the present (De Flores' sexual intentions) and the
future (the relationship between Beatrice and De
Flores) are adverted.
                 DE FLORES (cont'd)
                   (35.52.07)
     I could not get the ring without the finger.
```

The text mixes dramatic and narrative passages. The technical outline follows the screenplay conventions (see JAHN 2003): The **scene heading** or **slugline** specifies the location (i.e., is it indoors ("INT") or outdoors ("EXT") and is it day or night) – important information for lighting and setting the film. The script may also specify types of shots or shot transitions ("CUT TO"). The **speech prefix** tells the reader who speaks and the **parenthetical** (also called "wryly") specifies how the lines should be delivered. In this case, the script also provides a **time code** – as a rule of thumb one script page translates to one minute projection time (the fictional or narrated time is, of course, variable). In the **action text** the writer provides technical comments and, more often, paratechnical comments. These comments are typically characterized by the abstract conjunction of writer and reader in the "we" construction ("We HEAR a roll of THUNDER"). Distinct cues for sound and vision are capitalized.

Screenplay glossary

It is interesting to note that the first piece of action text – in keeping with general guiding principles in screenwriting – merely tells us what a viewer might see (and hear), but that the final passage quoted here offers comments which do not necessarily materialize in the audiovisual content of the film. The screenwriter provides a literary and metaphorical interpretation rather than technical comments or visual description. How does he make sure that his audience really sees "a phallic image echoing the horror of the murder" if he can neither force the viewers to think of a phallus nor control that they make the connection to the memory of the murder? One may further note that he even evokes an aural metaphor ("echoing"). What is termed "recalling" in THOMPSON's action text merely expresses the hope on part of the writer that the "abstract bond" to the audience holds, that it will decode or construct the appearance of the ring in a manner similar to the screenwriter himself. The action text of a screenplay, therefore, again illustrates the problems (and potential) of the verbal representation of an audiovisual representation, i.e., ekphrasis.

Action text

6 Narrating novels *vs.* narrating films

What we want is a story that begins with an earthquake and works its way up to a climax.   SAMUEL GOLDWYN

A look at some of the more influential adaptation typologies suggests that there are no hard and fast criteria on how to fit individual films into any of the categories established by critics. The criterion of 'fidelity' is particularly problematic and has been unanimously criticized by 'adaptationists' such as ROBERT STAM,

Adaptation and fidelity

Fig. 18: Adapatation typology

Geoffrey Wagner	Dudley Andrew	Helmut Kreuzer
Transposition: minimum interference	Fidelity of transformation	Appropriation of literary 'raw' material
Commentary: purposely or inadvertently altered	Intersection	Illustration: finding images for literary texts
Analogy: considerable departure, time shifts etc.	Borrowing	Interpretative transformation: enunciation process (discourse) transformed
		Documentation: filming theatre

JAMES NAREMORE, BRIAN MCFARLANE, MORRIS BEJA, HELMUT KREUZER, and IRMELA SCHNEIDER. Adaptation theory tends to view literary adaptations exclusively in hierarchical terms, namely, as dependent upon the earlier *Ur*-text or source text, and therefore in terms of the media transfer. Falling back on the exclusive criterion of a film's relationship to its source text, adaptationists have developed their own typologies.

Medium specificity in film

ERICA SHEEN (2000: 3) has argued against the adaptationist *"rhetoric of possession"* and the concomitant restrictive ideas of meaning in adaptation theory. In view of a virtual literary culture recreated by classic films, she suggests a new New Criticism of *"restoration"* rather than *"fidelity"* (2000: 11). SARAH CARDWELL similarly rejected the old medium-specific adaptationist approach, distinguishing it from the more descriptive comparative approach culminating in MCFARLANE's *Novel into Film* (1996), and the pluralist approach of ERICA SHEEN, DEBORAH CARTMELL et al. CARDWELL is also right, however, to opt for a return to medium-specific issues (for example peculiarities of film *vs.* TV) and to a *"renewed interest in close textual analysis"* (CARDWELL 2002: 73). The term "narrative" clearly cuts across the idea of medium specificity because not only novels and epics, but also cartoons, plays and movies can tell stories. SEYMOUR CHATMAN's model of text types reflects this idea:

Fig. 19: Text types (according to CHATMAN 1990: 115)

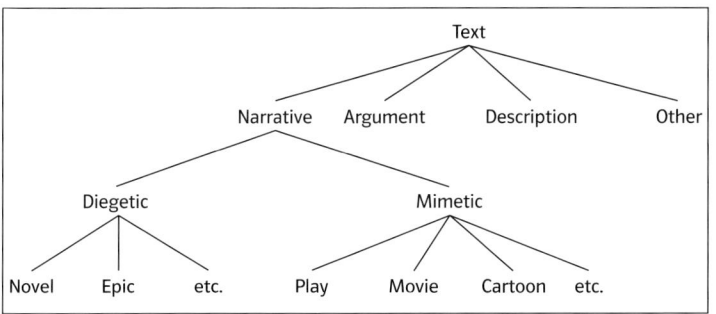

According to CHATMAN (1990: 113), movies are mimetic because they lack *"a 'Narrator' in the narrow sense"*, i.e., the more or less palpable instance of narrative transmission which one finds in diegetic narratives (from Greek *diégēsis*, 'narrative, recital, relation'). Both novels and films, tell stories which unfold in space and time and consist of components connected by causality. BORDWELL / THOMPSON (2001: 61) write: *"We make sense of a narrative, then, by identifying its events and linking them by cause and effect, time and space."* It is clear that film adaptations are most often adaptations of novels, but what happens when (according to CHATMAN) the text type changes from a diegetic to a mimetic narrative?

Films as mimetic narratives

Comparative adaptation studies analyse the semiotic "how" of the media transfer (or translation) from novel to film. Films supply visualizations whereas novels provide printed text which must be mentally visualized by their readers. Both novels and films, however, require the meaning-making processes of comprehension. It is enormously difficult to adapt the discourse level of novels; the iconic and indexical process of meaning-making is necessarily specific and must represent objects. Outside of the symbolic order of language, adaptations have to show "how people live or lived", they have no grammar, and they tend towards neutral narration. Films provide images and sounds, but rather than redeeming an outer reality film treats sounds and images to the process of cinematic construction.

Visual articulation: Comparing films to novels

We can therefore sum up three main characteristics of film narration:
(1) It tends to narrate within a voiceless image-making apparatus and is therefore less anthropomorphist than print narratives. Whereas theorists who insist on the agency of filmic narration have retained the idea of a film narrator (image-maker, *grand imagier*, intrinsic narrator, fundamental narrator, external or cinematic narrator, perceptual enabler / perceptual pilot, see LOTHE

Visual articulation: Film narration

Fig. 20-1: Visual channel: the film shot as 'treated' image (adapted from Bordwell/
Thompson 2001: 155–182)

1. *mise-en-scène* (i.e., control over what appears in the frame)
setting (on location / studio), props, set-design
costumes and make-up
lighting (highlights, shadows) **quality:** hard / soft **direction:** frontal light / sidelight / backlight / underlight / toplight **source:** key light / (less intense) fill light: high key (day) *vs.* low key (night) **colour:** filters, coloured light (cool / warm, harsh, contrasting / smooth, noncontrast-ing)
staging (acting, figure or object movement) **acting:** visual (appearance, gesture, facial expression) *vs.* auditive (voice, voice coaching, effects) **acting style:** individualized *vs.* stylized typing psychodynamic 'method' acting (Konstantin Stanislawski, Lee Strasberg) *vs.* biomechanics (Vsevolod Meyerhold) and gesture acting (Brecht) **position / proxemics:** position (frontality, centrality), address, distance to camera **movement:** (static *vs.* dynamic), stunts
arrangement of screen space (generally as three-dimensional) **balance of distinct components** (symmetry, variation in size) **depth cues:** layering of space into planes (foreground, middleground, background: shallow space *vs.* deep space)
2. cinematography
film stock: monochrome, tinting, toning, exposure, filtering
speed and direction of motion (shooting rate *vs.* projection rate): slow motion, fast motion, freeze frame, time-lapse cinematography, reverse motion
perspective **lens** to manipulate and distort space: wide-angle *vs.* telephoto lens, zoom lens **focus:** deep focus *vs.* selective focus, racking focus (change of focus within shot) **special effects:** superimposition, process (or composite) shots, front or rear projection
framing **aspect ratio:** relation of frame width to frame height **mask / iris:** variations on rectangular frame **split screen** **angle / height:** high-angle (bird's eye), eye level, low-angle **distance:** long shot, medium shot, close-up **mobility:** pan (horizontal), tilt (vertical), roll, tracking or dolly shot, crane shot, Steadicam, computer motion-control, hand-held **duration:** long take *vs.* editing

Fig. 20-2: Auditory channel: film sound

1. varieties of sound
music noise voice (see acting) silence
2. texture / volume
effects, loudness, pitch, timbre, modulation, intonation etc., overlapping, focussed *vs.* unfocussed
3. relationship sound / image
visibility and audibility on-screen *vs.* off-screen sound on-track *vs.* off-track sound (i.e., sound that is narratively implied by the image, but cannot be heard because of presumed distance)
temporality: synchronous *vs.* proleptic (forward) *vs.* analeptic (backward)
relationship to the implied narrative world (diegesis) extradiegetic: on the primary level of discourse intradiegetic: on a secondary level of discourse (e.g., an embedded narrator) heterodiegetic: not part of the story (e.g., non-character narration) homodiegetic: as mental process (interior monologue) or as sense perception

2000, Chatman 1990), others have represented narrative agency in film in more abstract terms (extradiegetic narration, activity of narration, narrative instance, see Bordwell 1985, Branigan 1984, 1992, Deleyto 1991). Adapting a phrase from Mieke Bal, one may conclude that the formula for filmic narration runs thus: Audio-visually encoded narrative information (AV) cues that Y experiences that Z does.

(2) Film narration occurs in a shared presence of narrating instance and perceiving addressee. In the sense that filmic narration is shared perception Béla Balázs argued that film cannot express the variety of tenses. Consequently, Bluestone (1957: 48) holds that *"the novel has three tenses; the film only one"*, because even flashbacks and flashforwards in film must 'happen' on the screen and must be materially perceived by the viewer.

(3) In film, there is a *"general tendency of the medium towards narrative objectivity"* (Deleyto 1991: 222); and it is more difficult to present subjectivity and thought processes in film. The phrase 'camera-eye narration', suggested by Christopher Isherwood's novel *Goodbye to Berlin*, denotes a modernist retreat from intervening in the narrative process (*"I am a camera with its shutter open, quite passive, recording, not thinking"*). The viewer tends to construct the exterior camera perspective as a passive or neutral narrating agent.

This does not mean that film cannot represent 'pastness' or subjectivity through stylistic means, as a few examples (mostly from the detective film, which plays on cognitive processes of presuming and inferring events) will show.

Analysing film: Shots, scenes, sequences, sound

The concepts of narrating and narrated time are useful for films too. In order to research film narration the audiovisual information must be transferred into writing: The film must be segmented, it must be split up in narrative units. These units range from shots clearly demarcated by cuts or dissolves to scenes determined (less clearly and subjectively) by implied temporal and spatial unity and larger sequences (for examples, see KORTE 1999). Any DVD opts for some kind of plot segmentation. Fig. 20 shows the film-making options for creating shots through *mise-en-scène* and cinematography in the first part.

Analysing film sound and music

The second part of fig. 20 supplies a framework for analysing film sound (see for this KOZLOFF 1988, GORBMAN 1987, GRIEM / VOIGTS-VIRCHOW 2002). The field has for a long time been dominated by the rough distinction between counterpoint (sound and image are unconnected, commentary etc.) and parallelism (sound and image are logically connected; following SIEGFRIED KRACAUER). Of particular interest is the role of so-called mood music, for instance ENNIO MORRICONE's classic Western sound in films like SERGIO LEONE's *Once Upon the Time in the West* (1968), MICHAEL NYMAN's structured patterns for movies by PETER GREENAWAY. The elegiac-industrial scores ANGELO BADALAMENTI mixed with popular tunes have become the trademark of DAVID LYNCH (who framed *Blue Velvet* (1986) with a camera pulling in and out of an ear, linking his film both visually and aurally to a dream). LYNCH's oft-quoted claim that he thinks of himself as a "sound man" rather than a director has recently increased interest in the sonic scapes of his films (see CHION 1995, 1999, the essays by DREXLER in GRIEM 1997, ANNETTE DAVIDSON and JOHN RICHARDSON in SHEEN / DAVISON 2004).

Temporality in film

Stories told in movies can deal flexibly with order, duration, and frequency. In BRYAN SINGER's thriller *The Usual Suspects* (1995) the final sequence renders unreliable all the visual information which up to that point seemed to sustain the logic of the suspected criminal 'Verbal' Kint's narrative (in fact, inspired by random cues observed on a notice board in the police office). TOM TYKWER's *Lola rennt* (*Run Lola Run*, 1998) offers three real-time versions of one event. In CHRISTOPHER NOLAN's thriller *Memento* (2000), in which a man who has lost his short-term memory tries to solve a murder mystery, the sequences must be constructed as arranged in reverse order, similar to HAROLD PINTER and DAVID HUGH JONES's *Betrayal* (1983).

Ultimately, the decision who "narrates" a given piece of audio-visual information rests with the audience. Conventional means to delegate narrative control to a frame narrator, or express subjectivity or pastness include point-of-view shots (POV shots), visual effects, *montage* (jump-cuts, dissolves or voice-over narration). Famous examples of extensive POV shooting include DZIGA VERTOV's *Man with a Movie Camera* (1929) and ROBERT MONTGOMERY's *Lady in the Lake* (1946), a sustained attempt to translate RAYMOND CHANDLER's first-person narrative into point-of-view shots representing the visual range of detective Philip Marlowe. The most conventional device to render subjectivity in film is voice-over narration – and it has become so conventional that narrow approaches to film dominated by continuity editing advise against it. This is cleverly satirized in the metafilmic movie *Adaptation* (2002: 67, written by CHARLIE KAUFMAN). Here, a failed screenwriter (also called Charlie Kaufman) sits in an auditorium, listening to a lecture by screenwriting coach Robert McKee:

Subjectivity in film

```
                KAUFMAN (VOICE OVER)
   I should leave here right now. I'll start over.
    I need to face this project head on and - - -
                        MCKEE
   ... and God help you if you use voice over in
                your work, my friends!
```

Adaptation illustrates the narrative potential even within the Hollywood movie industry. It opens with a pastiche of an on-set "Making of" documentary of the earlier JONZE / KAUFMAN film, *Being John Malkovich* (1999). Actor NICOLAS CAGE impersonates the screenwriter of both movies, Charlie Kaufman. *Adaptation* is clearly an intramedial metafilm, which is not just an adaptation, but also about adaptation. At the same time, however, *Adaptation* is intermedial because it takes issue with the very notion of a media transfer. Scriptwriter Kaufman initially declares his intent to write no *"artificially plot driven"* film *"simply about orchids"* without *"sex or guns or car chases"* or *"characters learning profound life lessons"* (KAUFMAN 2002: 5). In other words, he declares his intent to articulate his authorial voice in violation of the established codes of Hollywood cinema – established codes which ironically reappear in the final third of the movie, after Kaufman has been lectured by McKee and his twin brother Donald (also played by CAGE).

Intra-mediality and inter-mediality in *Adaptation*

Plot has been decreed the essential category in Hollywood by the real MCKEE (1999: 16), who deplores the structuralist turn of creative writing towards language and codes – and, in fact warns against *"telling narration"* in film which *"threatens the future of our art"* (MCKEE 1999: 344, his italics). MCKEE (1999: 358) positions the

Classic Hollywood: Archplot, miniplot, antiplot

antiplot (coincidence, nonlinear time, inconsistent realities) and the miniplot (open ending, internal conflicts, multi-protagonists, passive protagonists) against the vast majority of films that follow the archplot principles (causality, closed ending, linear time, external conflict, single protagonist, consistent reality, active protagonist). According to BORDWELL / THOMPSON (2001: 76–78) classic Hollywood cinema has been dominated by

- individual characters as causal agents
- a desire as plot impetus that causes change
- psychological cause and effect in chronological order, clear motivation
- fairly unrestricted narration, measured subjectivity
- a tendency towards narrative closure
- continuity editing.

Continuity editing

Continuity editing (developed with advances in film editing around 1900 to 1910) is important in creating smooth shot transitions and an impression of continuous space and time (cf. BORDWELL / THOMPSON 2001: 262–278). In effect, continuity editing erases traits of the filmic process from the film, as the viewer is not supposed to notice the filmic apparatus. The editing rhythm will move from establishing shots (long shots that introduce the overall setting) to medium shots and close-ups (of shorter duration). In continuity editing, shots tend to keep the eyeline match (implying character relations in directional looking) and over-the-shoulder shots are connected in shot / reverse-shot patterns (to represent conversation). The overall impression of continuous action over a sequence of shots is called "match on action" achieved through central action but also consistent lighting, and symmetrical viewpoints (without crossing the axis of action, according to the so-called 180-degree rule).

Alternatives: *Montage*

Of course, editing patterns can be governed by aims other than narrative continuity, such as graphic or rhythmic effects (in abstract or structural *avant-garde* films as well as in Busby Berkeley musicals). Other possibilities include disruptions of order, duration and frequency, e.g., jump-cuts, disruptive inserts, rapid cutting, ellipses, repetitions and reversals of direction, e.g., the techniques of confrontational or collision *montage* (SERGEJ EISENSTEIN) or parallel *montage* (W. S. GRIFFITH) in order to create conceptual links, such as metaphors, 'poetic' associations, analogies or contrasts.

Invisible style and CGI

Clearly, computer-generated imagery has raised the standards in making extraordinary visual contents "believable", i.e., to keep up the "invisible style" and efface the constructedness even of effects-laden blockbusters, but, as LEHMAN / LUHR (2003: 362) remind us: "*Increasingly, film audiences are aware of the fact that the films they watch are less and less a photographic record of a pro-filmic event and more and more a digital visual construction of something that exists nowhere except in a computer until it is printed onto film.*"

The moment that images are based on digital pixels (regardless of whether they have been recorded by a photographic camera or not) they are open to easy and unlimited alteration and KRACAUER's dubious connection of cinema to 'physical reality' has been fully severed. DZIGA VERTOV's "kino eye" has turned into the "kino-brush". LEV MANOVICH made this point about the redefinition of "*the very identity of cinema*" (2002: 405) in view of morphing, bullet-time (in which a part of the on-screen action is slowed down or paused), and various other image manipulations in movies such as *The Matrix* trilogy (1999–2003, D: ANDY & LARRY WACHOWSKI). He described digital film as "*live action material + painting + image processing + compositing + 2D computer animation + 3D computer animation*" (MANOVICH 2002: 410).

Cinema – digitally redefined

Purely formalist concerns, however, have increasingly been complemented with cultural-studies approaches. The case of DAVID LYNCH shows that, in spite of the specific methodology of film studies, research interests of literary, cultural and film studies overlap to a great extent. In a large number of studies (LAVERY 1995, JERSLEV 1996, RODLEY 1997, BÜHLER 2002, PABST 1999, HUGHES 2001, FÜLLER 2001, HÖLTGEN 2001, SEESSLEN 2003, SHEEN/DAVISON 2004, JOHNSON 2004) his work has been mined predominantly for key concerns of literary and cultural studies, such as:

Overlapping research interest: David Lynch

- narrative complexity and unreliability, metaphors, imagery, symbolism, motifs such as the *Doppelgänger*
- postmodernism, intertextuality and allusive excess
- horror and the fantastic
- popular culture, popular music, American-ness, Reaganism
- the body, violence, sexuality, eroticism and gender
- psychoanalysis, creativity, identity, outsiders and madness.

Another burgeoning field, more specifically in the area of cultural studies, is that of the study of national cinemas in an age of globalization. This manifests itself, for instance, in the "National Cinema Series" published by Routledge and the seminal work on British national cinema by HIGSON (1995, 2003) and STREET (1997). Today, DIANE NEGRA (2005) argues, Irishness has become a racial fantasy of 'à la carte' ethnicity in the US, but arguably also on a global scale. Since the 1990s, therefore, with the economic boom of the Celtic Tiger and a transnationally successful projection of an imaginary cultural identity across genres and media (St. Patrick

National cinema: The case of Ireland

and Celtic mythology, the shamrock and the harp, Guinness and the Emerald Isle, folk music, *Riverdance*, and U2, a literary pedigree from JAMES JOYCE to SEAMUS HEANEY), Irish cinema has turned into a profitable industry. In this, Ireland was aided by traditional links to Hollywood and by its established history as a key site for specific genres, such as political thrillers and rural comedies. Directors such as NEIL JORDAN (*The Crying Game*, 1992; *Michael Collins*, 1996; *The Butcher Boy*, 1997) and JIM SHERIDAN (*My Left Foot*, 1989; *In the Name of the Father*, 1993; *The Boxer*, 1997; *In America*, 2002) have been celebrated as Irish *auteurs*. ALAN PARKER's (*The Commitments*, 1991) and STEPHEN FREARS's (*The Snapper,* 1993; *The Van*, 1996) adaptations of RODDY DOYLE's Barrytown trilogy represent the take-off of a more urban Irish cinema in the 1990s, which has duly sparked a number of recent studies on Irish cinema (BARTON 2004, MCLOONE 2000, MACKILLOP 1999).

Images of Irishness

The national dimension of this cinema is, of course, highly dubious. For decades, Ireland has been firmly established as a site of colonized cinematic images. Ireland is exemplary for displaying both internal and external cultural imagery, e.g., of emigration and music, pubs and landscapes as or *vs.* pastoral heritage (*Man of Aran*, D: ROBERT FLAHERTY, 1934; *The Quiet Man*, D: JOHN FORD, 1957; *Ryan's Daughter*, D: DAVID LEAN, 1970; *The Field*, D: JIM SHERIDAN, 1990; *Waking Ned*, D: KIRK JONES, 1998; *Dancing at Lughnasa*, D: PAT O'CONNOR, 1998) as well as thrillers and melodramas of brutal masculinity, terrorist strife and political corruption (*Hidden Agenda*, D: KEN LOACH, 1990; *Patriot Games*, D: PHILLIP NOYCE, 1992; *Some Mother's Son*, D: TERRY GEORGE, 1996), and traumatic narratives of poverty or corrupt Catholicism (*Angela's Ashes*, D: ALAN PARKER, 1999; *The Magdalene Sisters*, D: PETER MULLAN, 2002).

5 Visuality, orality, literacy

CHAPTER

1 Visual studies and the visual turn

I am eye. I am mechanized eye. I, a machine, am showing you a world, the likes of which only I can see. DZIGA VERTOV, *Kinoglas/Cinema Eye*

We have seen that for a long time questions of intermediality have focused on transfers into the audiovisual media. The reasons are (literally) obvious: As TOM GUNNING's "cinema of attractions" and CGI effects in movies remind us, there has never been more visuality and visual experience is psychologically powerful (see JAY 1993: 11). Recent monographs are quick to point out that video surveillance, camcorders and webcams, computers, DVD, satellite pictures, medical images of body interiors, and television, have prompted a sea-change in human perception. MITCHELL (1986: 9–10) distinguishes five image categories, perceptual, optical, graphic, mental and verbal. Perceptual images are the basic retinal images generated by the 'naked eye' and processed in our brains. Optical images result from mirrors or screen projections as a result of physically aided sight. Graphic images are paintings, drawings, or visual scripts, mental images are generated by the mind as dreams, phantasms and 'visions', and verbal images result from rhetorical operations (figures of speech) that transpose language into imagery.

Image categories

Any account of visuality must start with perceptual images and answer the basic question of what actually happens when a human being sees. We need light in order to see. The study of optics (i.e., of how light is (physically) emitted from incandescent sources and propagated, reflected, and refracted) is therefore essential to visual studies. Optics, however, obviously cannot explain how an eye works. The study of physiology and cognitive psychology seeks to answer the question how an image is formed in the eye and how visual information is processed to and in the brain. Cognitive psychologists propose that vision is achieved by the *"intelligent eye"* (GREGORY 1998: 5), obviously a concept which is at odds with the psychoanalytic account of vision. Some basic assumptions had been formulated in the 1920s by Gestalt psychologists in order to overcome the legacy of behaviourism. For them, visual perception is more than the mere behaviourist reaction to stimuli (in the commonplace phrase, it is more than the sum of its parts). Eyes do not produce pictures, but they produce retinal images that need to be interpreted in the brain.

Optics, perception and cognitive psychology

Perceptions as hypotheses	GREGORY (1998: 10–13) states that "*perceptions are* hypotheses [...] *they can also have or produce, distortions, paradoxes, or fictions.*" Comparing perception to language, he arrives at the speculative mind-design for vision in which the brain 'reads' visual information according to object knowledge (a kind of semantics) and general knowledge (a kind of syntax). To this sensations must be added because emotions affect perception and perception shapes emotions. In any case, for cognitivists such as FREDERIC CHARLES BARTLETT and KENNETH CRAIK visual perception is based on mental representation and marked by problem solving, inference and prediction.
Looking and cognitivism: Schema	If we apply this to film theory, we arrive at conclusions wildly at odds with psychoanalysis: "*Perception in all phases of life is an* activity", writes cognitivist (or neo-formalist) film scholar DAVID BORDWELL (2001: 39). BORDWELL echoes the *Psychology of the Creative Eye* (RUDOLF ARNHEIM 1974) and ERNST GOMBRICH's *Art and Illusion* (1960) which was equally influenced by Gestalt psychology and cognitivism. When we watch a film we process the cues according to schemata (one might also call them default conditions or prototypes); we organize past experience into knowledge structures. We know the cartoon, we know Cubism, we know Hollywood films, the *nouvelle vague* and JEAN-LUC GODARD and we construct meaning according to our prior knowledge of visual content or genre (see BORDWELL 1985, 1989, 2001).
Proliferating visuality	The question of visuality, however, transcends the field of art history or film. MIRZOEFF (1999: 1) concludes from proliferations of visuality that "*modern life takes place onscreen*" and that "*this swirl of imagery* [...] *is not just a part of everyday life, it is everyday life.*" In the climate of casual viewing (that WALTER BENJAMIN theorized as *Zerstreuung*), it is only in specially designed situations (theatres, cinemas, museums) that we consciously regard objects. Through the media we see more, we see across space and time, and we see differently, particularly since the 19th century, which brought the 'iconographical revolution' of photography and film.
History of visual information	Historically, images and statues were important and successful media of communication (particularly in the absence of widespread literacy). Within the Catholic and particularly Orthodox creeds, the kissing of icons (often splendidly painted in gold) adds a tactile aspect to the visuality of devotion. Around 1100, the Bayeux tapestry illustrated the Norman Conquest as a visual narrative; it might be described as a medieval film or cartoon strip. Woodcutting and, above all, printing brought new technologies for the proliferation of images and the lithograph (1796) rendered reproduction of coloured pictures cheaper – ushering in the age of

mechanical reproduction of images. Even before the 19th century, visuality was explored in the *camera obscura* – its principle was known in 10th-century Arabia – and the *laterna magica* (ATHANASIUS KIRCHER, 1646). Let us consider the decisive steps in the proliferation of visuality.

The rise of photography came with attempts to fix *camera obscura* images. CLAUDE and JOSEPH NIÉPCE developed heliography between 1793 and 1826. LOUIS J. M. DAGUERRE, JOSEPH NIÉPCE's former partner, produced his daguerrotypes between 1827 and 1839, triggering a wave of visualization denounced as *daguerréotypomanie* in France. WILLIAM H. FOX TALBOT used silver nitrate for the printing from negatives (calotype, "photogenic drawings") in 1839. Finally, in 1888 GEORGE EASTMAN provided the first portable, inexpensive box camera and printing service for Kodak, selling 90,000 units within five years and supplying the slogan *"You press the button, we do the rest"* (BRIGGS / BURKE 2002: 166).

Photo-graphy

When photography emerged in the 1830s and 40s, it was seen as introducing a superior persuasive veracity into visuality, but this photographic 'realism' was from the very outset undermined by its potential to lie. In the six famous essays *On Photography* (1976), SUSAN SONTAG highlighted the fact that far from revealing everything, the camera was an instrument of deceit, for instance, when HENRY PEACH ROBINSON's pictorial tableau *Fading Away* (1859) made a healthy fourteen-year-old girl look as if she was dying from consumption (see GREEN-LEWIS 1996: 54–55). In the title of his first book illustrated with photographs, TALBOT significantly adopted an artistic metaphor that acknowledged the formative presence of the photographic apparatus (rather than supposing a mere recording of reality), *The Pencil of Nature* (1840). In *On Photography*, SONTAG described the taking of photographs as aggressive appropriations rather than passive recordings. Thus, she held, the camera became central in the 19th-century culture of surveillance, an instrument of power that metaphorically 'assassinates' its objects from a distance.

Photo-graphy as appropria-tion

Photography was a decisive step in the expansion of 'extra-sensual' viewing. It provided the reality effect in fixing or freezing a past event. Other milestones on the way of technologically increasing visual representation are these: telescopes (1590), microscopes (1608), X-ray (1895), space photography (Hubble Space Telescope), endoscopy and in-vivo imagery (both 1990s). Another watershed in increasing visualization was the shift from textual to graphic computer interfaces (GUI, see the section below), as well as the spread of computer graphics (Shockwave, Java, RealPlayer etc.) and digital imaging (PowerPoint, Photoshop, storage on DVD

From 'extra-sensual' viewing to digital imaging

etc.). Digital imagery allows humans to simulate visuality in virtual-reality environments.

Cinema, TV, video

The advent of moving images came with the experiments of EADWEARD MUYBRIDGE (Edward Muggeridge), who produced a serial photography of galloping horses in 1878 (published as *Animal Locomotion*, 1888). In 1895, the LUMIÈRE brothers introduced what they called *cinématographie*, the first public film projection at the Grand Café, Paris. GEORGES MÉLIÈS founded a tradition different from LUMIÈRE's documentaries, he produced the first illusionary fiction film in 1896. Television followed in the 1930s, video from the 1960s to the 1980s, and subsequently the DVD, cable, satellite and digital television. In the 1980s, the advent of VCRs and MTV permeated the western societies with audiovisuality and quickly substantiated the prescient line "Vision came and broke my heart" in the pop-song (and first video to be shown on MTV) with the title that defined the period, the Buggles' "Video Killed the Radio Star" (1979).

Video, VCR and DVD

The appearance of video took visual content out of cinemas or broadcast television programming and into the homes and art galleries, thus restoring the idea of an autonomous work (HANHARDT 1986, CUBITT 1993). As an inexpensive medium of image manipulation it also offered a new potential of inexpensive formal innovation. For instance, video art need not imply a recording camera and therefore played a crucial part in dissociating issues of visuality from an exclusive focus on representation (CUBITT 1993: xvii). The appearance of VCR playback and DVD as market factors prompted the need to produce films that are compatible (technically – aspect ratio – as well as aesthetically) with home viewing on TV screens. Additional material (audio commentary, outtakes, 'making of' documentaries, trailers, interviews etc.) needed to be produced, and the DVD can easily accommodate various versions of a movie (director's cuts, extended versions). Video not only changed the conditions of producing and watching visual content, but also generated media-specific art forms, with NAM JUNE PAIK, BRUCE NAUMAN, and BILL VIOLA as chief exponents.

Panopticism and surveillance

The 1990s expanded the *Global Television* (the title of the MIT collection by SCHNEIDER/WALLIS in 1988) of the 1980s. Video surveillance and videoscreens in public spaces and private use of camcorders, webcams, and cell-phone photography, resulting in a "panopticism" of "*census tools and practices, radars, lasers, sensors, satellites, polygraphs, sonograms, night vision, genetic tests, global positioning systems, space-based telescopes, biometric identification devices, home arrest systems, and numerous other monitoring devices 'jacked-in' to real time communications"*, epitomized by the *"ever-present surveillance camera"* (TURNER 1998: 93–94). Under the condition of perennial and ubiquitous watching we saw coincidental footage of the abduction of JAMIE BULGER from a Liverpool shopping mall in 1993, of the first aeroplane hitting the Twin Towers and of the Tsunami disaster in the Indian Ocean of December 2004. As TURNER (1998: 96–123) demonstrated, surveillance technologies have also informed artistic and cinematic practices from Soviet constructivism and nineteen-sixties films, such as MICHAEL POW-ELL's *Peeping Tom* (1960) and ANTONIONI's *Blowup* (1966), to TONY SCOTT's *Enemy of the State* (1998) or PETER WEIR's *The Truman Show* (1998), to name but a few.

Video-sphere: Iconic, pictorial, visual turn

Media images have prompted what has been variously called an "iconic turn" (BOEHM 1994), "pictorial turn" (MITCHELL 1994), or "visual turn". In *Vie et mort de l'image* (1992), RÉGIS DEBRAY structures media history into the strata of logosphere (writing, images as idols), graphosphere (printing, images as representations) and videosphere (visual media, ambient viewing). For W. J. T. MITCHELL, the pictorial turn *"is [...] a postlinguistic, postsemiotic rediscovery of the picture as a complex interplay between visuality, apparatus, institutions, discourse, bodies, and figurality. It is the realization that spectatorship (the look, the gaze, the glance, the practices of observation, surveillance, and visual pleasure) may be as deep a problem as various forms of reading (decipherment, decoding, interpretation, etc.) and that visual experience or 'visual literacy' might not be fully explicable on the model of textuality"* (W. J. T. MITCHELL 1994: 16).

What is new in visual studies?

Starting from the assumption that all *"media are mixed media"* and that one should not only analyse images, but also *"everyday practices of seeing and showing"* (MITCHELL 2002: 91), the new approach to visuality seeks to merge analysis of art and non-art, visual and verbal signs, both *"the visual construction of the social"* and *"the social construction of vision"* (MITCHELL 2002: 91). Thus, visual studies might be described as art history and aesthetics after a cultural turn, *"so that the next generation of art historians will be skilled with both the concrete materiality of art objects and practices and with the intricacies of the dazzling PowerPoint presentation"* (MITCHELL 2002: 88). LISA CARTWRIGHT (2002: 431), in fact, claims that film studies must not simply analyse films, but *"the conditions of sensual experience in modernity"*.

"Picture theory"

For this approach to visuality, the pictorial rather than textual or semiotic 'views' of the world, MITCHELL has suggested the term "picture theory", which addresses spectators rather than readers. NICHOLAS MIRZOEFF (1999: 13) engages an analysis of what he terms the *"visual event"*, the *"interaction between viewer and viewed"* beyond

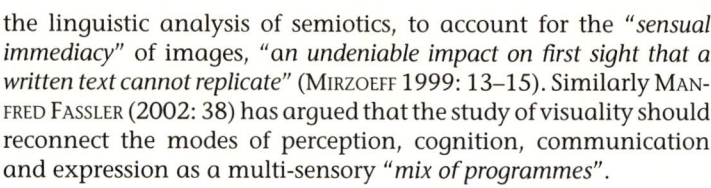

the linguistic analysis of semiotics, to account for the *"sensual immediacy"* of images, *"an undeniable impact on first sight that a written text cannot replicate"* (MIRZOEFF 1999: 13–15). Similarly MAN-FRED FASSLER (2002: 38) has argued that the study of visuality should reconnect the modes of perception, cognition, communication and expression as a multi-sensory *"mix of programmes"*.

Ocular-centrism

This rise of visuality across a range of aesthetic and non-aesthetic practices has prompted the rise of visual studies as a counter-movement against semiotic analysis of images (or, in the words of HANS C. BLUMENBERG, the rational and modern "readability" of the world). FOUCAULT, MCLUHAN, ELIZABETH L. EISENSTEIN or WALTER J. ONG (1912–2003) connected the rise of bourgeois modernity to the primacy of the visual, to ocularcentrism (or, linguistically more correct, oculocentrism). CHANDLER (1997) states that the persistent bias in Western culture to connect vision and reason can be deducted from a number of phrases, etymologies and visual metaphors (phenomenon, Greek *phainómenon*, 'appearing, exposing to sight'; definition, Latin *definire*, 'to draw a line around'; insight, illuminate, clarity, point of view, "I see" etc.). In his introduction to *Downcast Eyes*, MARTIN JAY (1993: 1–2) investigates *"the ocular permeation of language"* in 21 visual metaphors, derived from Latin and Greek (*vigilare, monstrare, specere, scopium, synopsis*), but also incorporating German (*Augenblick, Anschauung*) and French (*savoir, pouvoir*).

Central perspective and scopic regime

In a critique of conventional Western visual arts, MARTIN JAY denounced the *"scopic regimes of modernity"* as *"resolutely ocularcentric"* (1988: 3), arranging and ordering space as transparent for a God-like single eye. Enlisting support from NORMAN BRYSON and JOHN BERGER, he criticizes the technique of perspective painting since the Renaissance which maps the two-dimensional canvas as seemingly three-dimensional by designating a vanishing point (JAY 1993: 54–50). FILIPPO BRUNELLESCHI, ALBRECHT DÜRER and LEONARDO DAVINCI may be credited with developing Renaissance illusionism, a technique which is often called Alberti's Window, with reference to LEON BATTISTA ALBERTI's treatise "Della Pittura" (1435–36). This illusion of realism through the assumption of a mathematical, monocular "absolute eye" led to a widening gap between the spectator and the perceived object, banishing the painter from the pictorial world.

Examples of anti-pictorialism and iconophobia

The relationship between cognition and sensory experience remains a contested field, and often visuality played the part of menial to rational thought (*"eine mickrige Assistentenrolle, wenn überhaupt,"* FASSLER 2002: 44). Whereas Greek culture is generally held to have privileged sight over other senses, there is also the

Hebrew tradition which privileged words (see JAY 1993: 22–33). In Western thought, there also runs a thread of anti-pictorial bias, of ocularphobia (MARTIN JAY) or iconophobia (KENNETH CLARK). Its core manifestations are

- PLATO's allegory of the cave: Chapter 7 of *The Republic* describes the world of appearances as shadow images cast on a screen by marionettes to human captives in a cave and dissociates these flickering shadows from the light in the world of ideas. To PLATO, who valued the interiorized vision of the idea (*eidos*), the eyes are *"those leaden weights of pleasure and desire which bind [man's] soul to earth"*.

- Pentateuch, Exodus 20, 4–5: The Old Testament expounds a clear warning against the dangers of a visual culture. The King James Bible reads: *"Thou shalt not make unto thee any graven image, or any likeness of any thing that is in heaven above, or that is in the earth beneath, or that is in the water under the earth: thou shalt not bow down thyself to them, nor serve them: [...]"*; warnings against idolatry and "humanizing" representations of divinity were frequent in the Christian, Jewish and Muslim churches, reaching a climax in MARTIN LUTHER's maxim *sola scriptura*, and ULRICH ZWINGLI's advice against inner pictures which conceded the value of outer pictures for "the dumb and the weak" ("blöden schwachen", sic!). This culminated in

- Protestant iconoclasm: In the 16th century, Puritan opposition against "counterfeiting" and "representation" of religion renewed the movement of image-breaking (which climaxed in the East in the 8th century).

- the prioritization of literature in aesthetics: In HEGEL's aesthetics, word art is on a higher plane than visual or musical arts because it is closer to philosophy or *Geist*; and ERNST ROBERT CURTIUS argued that images are transparent and do not need interpretation (ZIMA 1995: 2–3, HOLLÄNDER 1995: 132).

The crisis of representation: 'Fear of images' and postmodernity

The expansion of visuality through television and digital media has intensified the critique of its rampant ubiquity, a critique which emerged as *"hostility to visual primacy"* in the mid-19th century (JAY 1993: 14). Thus, GÜNTHER ANDERS (1902–1992) argued from a humanist perspective that the reality effects of a "devouring" wall-to-wall imagery are merely illusory. From a rationalist and Marxist point of view FREDRIC JAMESON mounted his critique of postmodernism: *"The visual is essentially pornographic, which is to say it has its end in rapt, mindless fascination"* ([1990], quoted in MIRZOEFF 1999: 10). For the Frankfurt School, mass media images distort the realities of capitalism; FOUCAULT analysed the expansion of surveillance in modern societies. According to GUY DEBORD (1931–1994) and the situationists, capitalism reduced experience to passive gazing on representations in a "society of the spectacle" (*La Société du spectacle*, 1967). DEBORD's idea of the "integrated spectacle" was evidently a key influence on BAUDRILLARD's formulation of hyperreal simulation in which *"the code eliminates exteriority so that the model takes over from the real"* (BIGNELL 2000: 31). For this crisis of visual representation, one may adapt GERTRUDE STEIN's memorable phrase (from *Everybody's Autobiography*, with reference to her childhood home in Oakland) on TV and digital visuality: *"There is no there there"*.

Fakes, hoaxes and simulation

Increased visuality as well as unlimited manipulation, artificiality and virtual realities arguably result in a media culture of the fake and forgery (GEIER 1999, HÜTTER 2000). A "fake" is a media text which, in contrast to forgery, hints at its own faked nature (RÖMER 2001). There is a long tradition of counterfeit or spurious literature and cases of plagiarism, faking and hoaxing that challenges notions of authenticity and authorship, not least of all in literature (for instance, JAMES MCPHERSON's 'Ossian', THOMAS CHATTERTON's 'Rowley', the 'Ern Malley' case in Australia, see RUTHVEN 2001). Under the condition of media proliferation, however, the "fake" has become both a crucial component of contemporary life and an artistic strategy. In fact, the dividing line between "fake" and "fiction" seems unclear and osmotic, and threatens the documentary ethos in disparate, but related cases, from ORSON WELLES's pseudo-Martian attacks to SOKAL's hoax (the publication of a fake article in the journal *Social Text* in 1996 by physicist ALAN SOKAL in order to expose the follies of deconstructivist appropriations of natural sciences). The digital net world further blurs the line in fake e-mails and the "hacktivism" (a compound of hacker and activism) of rogue Internet sites (see, for instance, the collection at www.museumofhoaxes.com).

Looking and psycho-analysis: Scopophilia

Psychoanalysis, which had an enormous influence on theories of photography and film, offers explanations for this 'fear of images'. According to SIGMUND FREUD (1856–1939), who analysed visual pleasure, there is the pleasure of secret watching (voyeurism) and the pleasure of displaying oneself (exhibitionism). For FREUD, these are forms of scopophilia (= the drive to look, the pleasure in looking). Voyeurism and scopophilia became key terms for analysing the power of visual media such as film. Visual media, according to psychoanalysis, often cater to the gaze of the spectator, to a possessive looking marked by desire and fantasy and the wish to control the observed object. For feminist theorist LAURA MULVEY (1975: 9), mainstream cinema created an *"illusion of voyeuristic separation"* and these voyeuristic pleasures had to be undercut and destroyed in a counter-cinema *"as a radical weapon"* (8).

Mulvey was not alone in describing the gaze as gendered. In *Ways of Seeing* (1972), a book based on his influential BBC series, John Berger denounced the history of painting since the Renaissance as a tradition of male definition (through painting, looking at women) of female objects (as appearing in these paintings, being looked at). Since the pioneering work of Mulvey, ideas which focus on the performativity and construction of gender (Thomas Laqueur, Judith Butler, *1956) have spawned a number of fresh approaches to gender and the gaze. Queer theory questioned monolithic notions of gender and sexuality, and Mulvey's work was complemented by studies on the female gaze (Stacey 1994, who argued for female pleasures and identificatory practices with powerful women stars). Furthermore, research addressed gay male spectators (T. Waugh 1993) and lesbian audiences (R. Lewis 1997) or supplied textual readings of transgender movies such as *The Adventures of Priscilla, Queen of the Desert* (1994, D: Stephan Elliott), *Boys Don't Cry* (1999, D: Kimberly Peirce) or *Orlando* (1992, D: Sally Potter). In addition, research has focused on visuality and transformations of the body, both within a liberationist scenario (Haraway 1991, Jones 1998) and a critique of the (white, European) idealizations of plastic surgery and body engineering (Balsamo 1992). Within film studies, Butler's cues have spawned a number of studies focused on the performativity of costumes (Gaines / Herzog 1990, P. Cook 1996, Street 2001, Bruzzi 1997, 2001).

Gendered gazes

In different ways, the Coke bottle or the McDonald's sign have become icons of "McWorld", the global sphere of visuality dominated by American capitalism (with the Che Guevara portrait as a counter-image appropriated by the advertising industry). As early as in 1977, Jeremy Tunstall's book *The Media are American* appeared, and images of American lifestyle, views, arts and entertainment reach into every nook and cranny of this world: "*In a given Third World household, the TV set is likely to be the most expensive family purchase, and in many places it exists in the absence of a refrigerator or even a bicycle. In the Amazon region of Brazil, battery-powered TV sets are found in river homes without refrigeration or electricity, and neighbors gather to watch the latest American series import outdoors.*" (Sturken / Cartwright 2001: 326) In the US, 98 % of the programme output is domestic, but only 54 % is in Latin America (Western Europe: 73 %; Burton 2002: 82).

Visual colonization

Parallel to tendencies in literary studies, post-colonialism and transculturalism have also redefined the trajectory of visual studies. Using an impetus from Michel Foucault's seminal essay "Des espaces autres" (first formulated in a 1967 lecture), this approach counters cultural imperialism by looking at the heterotopias (i.e., other or counter-spaces) of transcultural resistance. A number of

Transculturalism: Heterotopias and ethnoscapes

studies have focused on diasporic micronarratives in ethnoscapes, according to ethnologist Arjun Appadurai (1996) flexible ethnic groups peopled by refugees, migrant workers, exiles and tourists. This work may rediscover 'other' national or ethnic cinemas (see, for instance, on Black British cinema Malik 1996, Korte/Sternberg 2001); it may focus on the IBC (Inuit Broadcasting Corporation; see Sturken/Cartwright 2001: 331–332); it may look at stereotypical ethnic representations such as the 'blaxploitation' films of the 1970s; it may investigate contemporary Japanese art (L. Bloom 2000). Taking a cue from Edward Said's definition of Orientalism as the idea of otherness, one may focus (negatively) on the imperialist whiteness of soap (McClintock 1994), and the role of visuality in colonization (Terry Smith 2002, Malek Alloula 1986); more positively, one may address Coco Fusco/Guillermo Gómez-Peña's fake, parading in a cage as "Two Undiscovered Amerindians" (1995), or African photography (Olu Oguibe 1996).

2 From orality to literacy: Media history and media differentiation

"O Printing! How thou hast disturbed the peace of Mankind!"
Andrew Marvell (1672)

Early media: Ong and orality

The history of the media is a history of increasing differentiation. Media chronologies tend to start from a media-scarce state, in which our predecessors communicated face-to-face using oral languages. Other forms of communication included beacon fires, torches and smoke signals, drum beating and couriers. Research into orality profited immensely from Walter J. Ong, a Jesuit father working at St. Louis. His PhD thesis was supervised by Marshall McLuhan, and in the spirit of McLuhan's media determinism, Ong wrote his influential book *Orality and Literacy: The Technologizing of the Word* (1982). Many of these approaches posit a 'Great Divide' between oral and literate cultures.

Oral cultures

The Toronto School focused to a great extent on investigating oral cultures. Eric A. Havelock (1903–1988) described a kind of inter-orality among the ancient Greeks, who held assembly speeches and recited plays in amphitheatres in a continuous flow of adoption and adaptation. Even medieval Europe remained a largely oral culture, aided by ritualistic performance (processions, tournaments, public executions, festivals, court masques). Handwritten (and often illuminated) manuscripts monopolized church knowledge and were, of course, read out aloud in public 'hearings'. As the etymology of the 'saga' suggests, mythical stories continued to be read out and the value of oral tradition remained throughout the Middle Ages, in spite of the gradual spread of 'clerks' (i.e., literate clerics, see BRIGGS / BURKE 2002: 7–17). Oral culture obviously survived the coming of print, which the culture of conversation (and rumour) in salons and bookshops of the 18th century testifies to.

According to ONG, oral cultures operate under two basic principles: They rely heavily on bi-directional (face-to-face communication) and they develop mnemonic patterns (rhythms, repetitions, antitheses, alliteration and assonance, formulaic phrases, standard themes and proverbs). The features of oral language are preserved in early written versions of oral narratives (such as the Gilgamesh epos – the oldest preserved oral epic –, the Iliad, the Odyssey, or the Bible). They are additive (or paratactic) rather than subordinative, i.e., they use "… and … and … and" patterns; they are aggregative rather than analytic; they tend to conserve existing narratives rather than incorporating new ones; they are closely related to cultural experience rather than abstract; they are agonistic (i.e., confrontational), empathetic and participatory rather than distanced; they are homeostatic, i.e., they seek to embed new elements into existing and stable patterns. Anthropologist JACK GOODY has described oral cultures as marked by structural amnesia, i.e., a flexible remembering of the past as moulded by the concerns of the present (described as shrinking or telescoping by GOODY / WATT 1963). Written documents, on the other hand, fix the past, and have done so for a long time.

Primary orality and structural amnesia

The Sumerians used cuneiform, logographic characters pressed into soft clay with a stylus. Clay tablets remain the material basis for writing, complemented by animal hides (Near East, 2500 B.C.), carved stone, bone and tortoise shells (China, approx. 1400 B.C.), papyrus (from approx. 2200 B.C.), leather scrolls (Near East, approx. 800), bamboo and silk (China, approx. 500), wax tablets (200 B.C.), and parchment and vellum (made from animal skin, 170 B.C.). Paper first appears in Chinese tombs (produced from soaked, macerated hemp). From about 50 A.D., the codex replaces the scroll as material storing device for writing.

Writing material

Oral languages are instable and volatile. From earliest cave paintings (15,000 B.C.) mankind has sought to stabilize information by storing it in optical signs, and writing is a technology that results from these efforts in that it transfers speech from the oral-aural world to the sensory world of vision, thus transforming our patterns of thought. Writing thus starts with pictures, and logographic writing was first developed in Sumer and Elam (today's Iraq) by around the year 3500 B.C. When it was first discovered

From cave paintings to ideographic writing

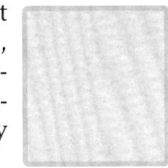

(and, making use of the bi-lingual and tri-scriptural Rosetta Stone, deciphered) in the 'Egyptian craze' after the Napoleonic expedition, this kind of writing was called *idéographique* (Greek *idéa*, 'idea' and *gráphein*, 'to write'). The terms 'ideographic', 'logographic' or 'pictographic' writing are still widely in use. They are, however, not entirely accurate (see DEFRANCIS 1984). In a pictogram, an idea is represented by a picture. In logographic writing, the symbol (often referred to as ideogram) represents or describes a (concrete or abstract) concept, a word or morpheme (rather than evoking a phoneme). Thus "&" or "@" may be regarded as logograms.

Logographic to alphabetic writing

Around 2000 B.C. logographic writing was developed in China. Between 1700 and 1500 B.C., however, the first alphabet was developed by Semitic tribes. All alphabets (Hebrew, Greek, Roman, Arabic etc.) derive from the first Semitic version. Its roots are ideographic (i.e., the written symbols represent images). Logographic writing was further developed by the Egyptians, whose hieroglyphics use about 2,000 characters, arranged according to the principle of rebus. With the rebus idea (which relates a symbol to sound rather than image, for instance, when images of an eye and a can are translated into sound as "I can") a phonetic writing system appears. The great advantage of phonetic writing consists in its flexibility, as reference to sound (other than reference to images of objects) allows for recombination. In syllabic writing the syllables are represented by a relatively high number of individual symbols. In contrast, alphabetic writing further reduces the number of symbols to several dozen by making them represent phonemes, with obvious didactic and mnemonic advantages.

Writing and laws, epics, cults, libraries

Early writing further focuses on law (stone code of Hammurabi, 1700 B.C.; Ten Commandments, 1250 B.C.; Draconian laws in Athens, 620 B.C.), foundational epics and religious myths (Sumerian Gilgamesh, from 3000 B.C.; Jewish Bible, from 950 B.C.; Hindu Mahabharata, from 920 B.C.; Iliad and Odyssey, 850 B.C., with HOMER named as 'author'). The Egyptian *Book of the Dead* (approx. 1500 B.C.) provided information on the afterlife for the deceased, accompanying them on their passage. There are also papyri of literary and administrative nature. Writing stores information for as long as the documents remain intact, and therefore implies the risk of loss. Spectacular information losses occurred during the sacking of Rome (approx. 390 B.C.) or the fire in the library of Alexandria (47 A.D.).

Print is in fact an equally ancient technology, used at least from the 8th century onwards in China for printing of ideograms carved on woodblocks; and even movable types were used in 11th-century China. It was not until the 15th century, however, that inventions

by Johann Gutenberg in Mainz (1450), and, simultaneously, in Korea, inaugurated the spread of printing in Europe and all over the world (with considerable time lag in Russia and the Islamic world, see Briggs / Burke 2002: 16–19). American historian Elizabeth Eisenstein has claimed that print played a major part in the revolutions of the Renaissance, Reformation and Enlightenment, as it standardized knowledge and undermined established authority – with the help of a better communication infrastructure (roads, printed maps since 1472, the Habsburg courier system of the Thurn and Taxis 1490).

'The Great Divide': From handwriting to printing

According to McLuhan's seminal book *The Gutenberg Galaxy* (1962), the shift from the Middle Ages to the Early Modern period is the shift from auditive media (orality) to a visual culture (writing and printing). The ascent of the nation states and of national standard languages as well as the redefinition of the private and public spheres can be related to Gutenberg's invention. The expansion of printing in the subsequent three centuries also sustained and entailed (according to a condensation of Briggs / Burke 2002: 15–105)

The Gutenberg Galaxy

- the rise of European vernaculars (Luther, *Neues Testament* 1522, Tyndale's *New Testament*, Worms 1526, the *Authorized Version* 1611)
- the visualization of literature (diagrams, tables)
- the refinement and uniformity of speech
- the popularization of literature (inexpensive, 'popular' illustrated chap-books)
- the privatization and individualization of reading and the rise of fiction (viewed as potentially dangerous for subordinates and women)
- the redefinition of manuscript literature as private (letters, clandestine publication)
- the rise of a censorship system (such as the Catholic "Index of Prohibited Books" and, later, the media regime of licensing and monopoly in the Restoration period post-1660), with free-speech defenders such as John Milton in his *Areopagitica* (1644); at the same time the rise of encoded (secret) languages and later (in the 18th century) pornographic literature
- the rise of book-trade centres (16th century: Venice, 17th century: Amsterdam, 18th century: London, often sustained by Protestant refugees)
- the rise of a literary field with a book market (Frankfurt Book Fair, 16th century), advertising, 'authorization', copyright and piracy (Copyright Act 1709), and hack writers (called *poligrafi* in Venice and 'Grub Street' writers in London)
- the rise of journalism, as part of everyday life, first in irregular

intervals as pamphlets, then as daily, weekly, bi-weekly and monthly newspapers in the 18th century – in England in 1792 an estimated 15 million newspapers were sold (famous examples include *The Tatler* (1709), *The Spectator* (JOSEPH ADDISON and RICHARD STEELE 1711), and *The Athenian Mercury* (JOHN DUNTON 1691) which in truly interactive fashion promised to answer reader questions)

- the accumulation, destabilization and diffusion of knowledge and the rise of a 'public sphere' in the 18th century (HABERMAS 1962) culminating in the American and French Revolutions, based on writings of the *philosophes* such as VOLTAIRE and ROUSSEAU and the *Encyclopédie* (1751–1756).

Ong: Secondary orality

In his *Orality and Literacy*, ONG coined the influential, but contested concept of secondary orality, which appears at the beginning of the 20th century with the advent of highly technologized media such as radio, television, and the telephone. These media technologies create a post-literate mediatized oral culture that is, however, rooted in forms of literacy. It is interesting to note that media which may be defined precisely by their lack of literacy and visuality have gained ground in recent years – with resurgent use of the radio, the ubiquity of mobile phones and the huge success of audiobooks.

❸ Literacy, memory and electronic media

Everything has been said before, but since nobody listens we have to keep going back and beginning all over again. ANDRÉ GIDE

Memory

In the ancient myth of Mnemosyne (Latin, Memoria), the mother of the muses is the seat of all knowledge (past, present, and future). A common cliché, based on the writings of JAMESON and BAUDRILLARD, holds that with the advent of electronic media, secondary orality and the bombardment with signs, we are losing this knowledge, our cultural memory. This development is characterized as schizophrenic, because the temporal sequence of language is replaced by the experience of incoherent and disconnected simulacra (such as nostalgic movies, music television, Disneyland, fake art), the perpetual present of the 'flow' (RAYMOND WILLIAMS 1974: 86) of televisions.

Example: Ray Bradbury's *Fahrenheit 451*

The classic example of this humanist pessimism is BRADBURY's dystopian novel *Fahrenheit 451*, in which firemen are employed to burn books, while housewives spend their day with interactive soap operas in a wall-to-wall "TV parlor" (BRADBURY 1953: 19–21). Meanwhile, the former humanities élite lives in the wilderness. They have returned to oral history, storing the memory of books in their minds *("bums on the outside, libraries inside")*: *"We'll pass the books on to our children, by word of mouth [...] A lot will be lost that way, of course. But you can't make people listen"* (BRADBURY 1953: 153). In BRADBURY's text, orally transmitted memory is even seen as a final remedy against a different kind of structural amnesia, induced by electronic media. In this climate, there is a growing demand to address the question how societies use media to remember. Drawing on the work of MAURICE HALBWACHS on the social dimension of memory (*La Mémoire collective*, 1950), JAN and ALEIDA ASSMANN have elaborated the concept of communicative and cultural memory. HALBWACHS highlighted the social dimension of memory, and JAN and ALEIDA ASSMANN introduced further differentiations between functional memory (present-day actualizations of memory, a canon of selected memory items appropriated in rituals and traditions) and storage memory (a latent fund of archived material).

Shared narratives and collective memory

Memory generates identity. It is clear that the communal 'we' is created through shared experience, shared norms, values and knowledge. The community of 'worldmates' is either based on direct first-hand, unmediated experience; or it is mediated and may therefore be declared inauthentic or at least 'imagined' (as BENEDICT ANDERSON argued for nations). One may of course also follow ANTONY EASTHOPE and hold that the mediation of signs, language, i.e., 'writing' (of sorts) operates even under the conditions of interpersonal communication in pre-modern communities because identity is necessarily a consequence of construction – or, one may rephrase, mediation (EASTHOPE 1999: 10). To a great extent, a sense of community is constructed from sharing media environments, far beyond the sub-category of history or memory programmes and products with their special connection to national, occasionally and increasingly also transnational, identity, celebrating the *"shared narratives"* of *"continuity, community, and centre"* (DAYAN / KATZ 1995: 170). This is theorized as 'collective' and 'cultural' memory by ASSMANN / ASSMANN (1994).

Communicative memory and media

If the capacity, the technology, tools or skills to store data is the 'hardware' of memorization, then one may speak of the cultural, experiential, and communicative memory 'software'. Patterns essential to memory, repetition and realization are enmeshed within media usage. To use an example one of my students provided: Her idea of the Ferris wheel in Vienna's Prater amusement park (an architectural object of everyday use and experience, but also a symbolic site of memorial heritage, one of PIERRE NORA's *lieux de mémoire*) consists of its present state as well as childhood experience or stories told by parents and grandparents. It is, therefore, part of her short-term communicative memory spanning the

recent past (up to about three generations). To a lesser degree, however, knowledge of the Ferris wheel also depends on history learned in schools (it was built in 1897 to commemorate the 50th anniversary of Emperor FRANZ JOSEPH's ascension to the throne).

Cultural memory and functional memory

Other media images may also contribute to the subject-specific actualizations of the Ferris wheel, such as CAROL REED's *The Third Man* (1949) or the James Bond movie *The Living Daylights* (1986). Aided by photographs, texts and movies, therefore, it enters the expanded long-term cultural memory, which needs, however, not just to be stored in the gigantic media reservoir of cultural memory (or: of documents), but must also be actualized or performed (as monuments, see ASSMANN/ASSMANN 1994: 119–121). In other words, it passes from the (uninhabited) archival storage memory to the (inhabited) functional memory. Sites of cultural memory – the Vietnam Memorial in Washington, the Holocaust Memorial in Berlin or the (projected) 9/11 Memorial in New York – may be described as media of collective memory, media which are created in order to communicate an experience of collective cultural value. These memorial sites that index time (as chronotopes that encode time in a spatial arrangement) are very old media of memory.

Cultural memory and media

The role of the media in cultural memory, which had been somewhat neglected by the pioneers of theorizing cultural memory (PIERRE NORA, MAURICE HALBWACHS, ABY WARBURG), is therefore central. Sign systems (oral language, writing, images) are essential in order to build cultural memory. Media technologies (printing, television, Internet) change the way communities memorize. Specific genres or objects of collective memory are determined by their mediality (ERLL 2004: 14–15). Media events (such as the 9/11 terrorist attack) enter the cultural memory as images transmitted globally via television. Often images and words are tailor-made productions for posterity, 'externalizations' of memory. Sometimes, however, they may enter the cultural memory accidentally, as traces (RUCHATZ 2004: 86). An excellent case of photographic memory externalization is QUEEN VICTORIA, the most-photographed person of the 19th century, whose portraits were widely disseminated through stationers and booksellers on collectible *cartes de visite*.

Memory in oral cultures

Fig. 21 provides an overview over the encoding, the storage, the dissemination and circulation of human knowledge in various media environments (orality, literacy, print, electronics). In oral cultures, rituals and repetitive patterns reduce the complexity of past events because they merely transfer what is needed in order to stabilize a community (homeostatic balancing and structural

Fig. 21: Social memory, communication and media technologies (adapted from ASSMANN/ASSMANN 1994: 131, 139)

	orality	literacy	print	electronics
organization of know-ledge	– closed structure – absolute past – symbolic codes	– open structure – history enters consciousness – alphabet, literal codes	– expansion of knowledge – new sciences – critical tradi-tion: encyclo-pedias	– exploding canon of education – language-free computer-based thought (lan-guages, non-verbal codes) – secondary analphabet-ism
medium = encoding and storage	– volatily of body-based media – multimedia-lity – restricted by human mne-monic capac-ity	– medium sep-arated from code (filtered through writ-ten texts) – autonomous texts – visuality fix-ated on read-ing	– increased abstraction of signs – standardiza-tion	– return of voice (and image) – machines operate through sense percep-tion (no filter-ing in sym-bolic code) – dynamic texts ("process-ing")
communi-cative forms and circulation	– feasts – ritual performance – limited range	– books – recital and reading – transparent space and time	– individual reading and public sphere – mass culture	– audiovisual media – network interaction – globalization

amnesia according to ONG and GOODY). In this closed structure the stored memory is also the performed memory. It depends on a multimedia performance, on the props, sites and performing bo-dies of memory specialists, and particularly on their voice. It is actualized on the occasion of feasts and restricted to the partici-pants of rituals.

Memory in literal cultures

In literal cultures, this structure is opened up; writing expands access to the past, memorization becomes selective and confrontational. Rather than aspiring to retain past models, literal cultures become dynamic and evolutionary. Phonetic writing furthers abstraction beyond the lived-world experience. The sceptical stance towards writing has been criticized as phonocentrism (JACQUES DERRIDA). PLATO's *Phaedrus*, for instance, had Socrates warn against the loss of memory skills through reliance on the exteriorized, disembodied (and therefore, in a way, dead) past of writing or painting. PLATO puts the first passage into the mouth of the Egyptian god Thamus and ascribes the second to Socrates:

[…] for this discovery of yours [letters] will create forgetfulness in the learners' souls, because they will not use their memories; they will trust to the external written characters and not remember of themselves. The specific which you have discovered is an aid not to memory, but to reminiscence, and you give your disciples not truth, but only the semblance of truth; they will be hearers of many things and will have learned nothing; they will appear to be omniscient and will generally know nothing; they will be tiresome company, having the show of wisdom without the reality. [...]
I cannot help feeling, Phaedrus, that writing is unfortunately like painting; for the creations of the painter have the attitude of life, and yet if you ask them a question they preserve a solemn silence. And the same may be said of speeches. You would imagine that they had intelligence, but if you want to know anything and put a question to one of them, the speaker always gives one unvarying answer. And when they have been once written down they are tumbled about anywhere among those who may or may not understand them, and know not to whom they should reply, to whom not: and, if they are maltreated or abused, they have no parent to protect them; and they cannot protect or defend themselves. (PLATO 360–355? B.C.)

Memory in print cultures

From a modernist perspective, WALTER BENJAMIN diagnosed a crisis of experience. In his essay "Der Geschichtenerzähler" ("The Storyteller") from 1936/37 he argued that storytelling is the oral remembering of experience by a wise counselor (*"ein Mann, der dem Hörer Rat weiß"*). This kind of wisdom, however, has become indirect, 'mediated' in the sense of disconnected from the storyteller's sagacious presence (*"mittelbar"*) and has been superseded by information processing in modernity (first in novels, then in the press). In the GUTENBERG galaxy of print, the differentiation and exteriorized storage of memory reached new extremes. The defining myths of a society were fixed and became coherent rather than repetitive, but also lost their absolute status in the relativism of rivalling texts, with detrimental consequences on the value of magic words, oral stories and sacred tradition. ASSMANN / ASSMANN

(1994: 136) argue that GUTENBERG's movable types expelled the remnants of bodily remembering in handwriting (calligraphy, illuminated books) and paved the way towards serialization, abstraction, and bureaucracy, or, in other words, the democratization of culture and the diffusion and mobilization of dynamic cultural memories.

WALTER BENJAMIN's was an early response to media of reproduction, such as the press, film and radio at the beginning of the 20th century. Particularly with TV, after World War II, we fully enter the stage of electronic mediation of memory. On the one hand, knowledge is transported in real-time on a global scale, on the other hand, abstract symbolic codes are no longer the lingua franca of knowledge, which is transported as audio-visual content, via voice or in machine-readable code. It seems that other new media practices sustain the trend diagnosed by ASSMANN/ASSMANN, a trend towards instantaneous, mobile and brief communication. Mobile phones take the real-time long-distance voice communication of telephones to public spaces. SMS, that is, short message service, the transfer of text messages via mobile telephones usually within a 160 character limit, replace public face-to-face interaction with a new public silencing (familiar from walkmen and MP3–players).

Memory and electronic media

ASSMANN (2004: 56) sees the Internet as a kind of stock exchange for data that increases and accelerates data circulation, but at the same time destabilizes long-term accessibility. Real-time and 'now' media, such as radio and TV, ASSMANN/ASSMANN (1994: 140) argue, bring the usurpation of the future by the present and narrow down our experience of time. Without a materially stable written language, the canon of diffused print knowledge is in danger of being dispersed and dissolved, and solitary reading as well as concepts of authorship have lost their quality of defining culture. The idea of instable, instantaneous and dynamic 'word processing' suggests to ASSMANN/ASSMANN (1994: 138) that writing has lost its material base. Invoking a point by historian PETER BURKE, they call for history, literature and the media not just to educate, inform and entertain, but also to act as 'remembrancer', as a medieval collector of 'memory dues'.

Real-time media and long-term accessibility

6 'New media' and cybercultures

CHAPTER

1 Computer-based media and Internet: History and basics

The more elaborate our means of communication, the less we communicate. JOSEPH B. PRIESTLEY

The digital revolution

The term 'new' media tentatively covers a heterogeneous and rapidly changing field. The digital revolution has transformed media practices as well as the entire social and cultural make-up on a global scale. The term new media thus comprises computer-related media, digital storage media such as CD (compact disc) and DVD, multimedia and computer-based networking ("Internet") such as e-mail, chats, and the World Wide Web. Computer networks are mass media, but media practices at the computer screen integrate individual media functions and mass-media functions. Computer-based, digital processes have therefore acted as 'metamedia' in the sense that they have merged traditional media in what has been described above as multi-media convergence or hybridity. MANOVICH (2003: 16) separates the social field of cyberculture (*"the study of various social phenomena associated with the Internet and other new forms of network communication"*: virtual communities, cell-phone usage etc.) from the cultural and technical field of new media (new cultural objects and paradigms).

Computer architecture

The computer is a machine that carries out algorithmic calculating processes in order to store and manipulate data. GOTTFRIED WILHELM LEIBNIZ (1646–1716) is credited with devising the first binary calculating machine in the 1670s. Following LEIBNIZ, CHARLES BABBAGE (1791–1871) unsuccessfully sank enormous amounts of money and time into building the first mechanical, automated calculating machine ("difference engine"). Today's computers combine a storage device (i.e., a hard disk) with a computing device (i.e., a central processing unit, CPU). According to computer 'architect' JOHN VON NEUMANN, a Hungarian WW II émigré working at Princeton, this 'stored-program' computer consists of five components, (1) a calculating unit, (2) a control unit, (3) a memory, (4) an input and (5) an output device, plus a bus that transmits data between the parts.

Computer history

The history of computing since the 1960s has been marked by a replacement of expert-operated giant calculators (Colossus 1942, ENIAC 1945) with relay home-located, personal computers (ATARI, 1970s; APPLE II, 1978) used for office and entertainment purposes (e.g., the inaugural computer game Pong 1974). The history of the computer was for a long time dominated by the American company IBM (International Business Machines). Miniaturization of the computer is closely connected to the development of semiconductor technology that relies on the tiny silicon chips (miniature transistors) developed in the Texas Instruments and Fairchild laboratories in the late 1950s. In 1971, the first microprocessor was produced, an integrated-circuit chip with processing units, subsequently marketed by Intel in the now mythical formative phase of the Californian Silicon Valley.

Storage, software, computer language

A computer must have a data storage device, either mechanical (punched cards or tape), magnetic (disks, magnetic tape) or optical (CD, DVD). A computer also has an operating system ("software", DOS, OS/2, Windows, Mac OS etc.). This is a computer programme directing the calculating processes. Microsoft, founded in 1981 by BILL GATES, provided DOS (Disk Operating System), the software which came to be used in the vast majority of IBM-based personal computers. Programmes, the software used by a computer, are written in computer languages. The idea of a programme-controlled calculating machine was first realized by German KONRAD ZUSE (1910–1995) in 1940s Berlin (Plankalkül). In the 1950s, the first computer languages emerged (JOHN BACKUS (* 1924): FORTRAN, BASIC).

Cybernetics: Wiener and Turing

In 1948, NORBERT WIENER published his seminal work *Cybernetics, or Control and Communication in the Animal and the Machine*. Starting from examining feedback in governors and control mechanisms in antiaircraft guns, cybernetics is related to systems theory in investigating how complex systems are regulated (for instance, how humans and machines interact) in abstract and functional terms. The extent to which new-media language sought to redefine humanity in its discourse can be seen in its use of the triad 'hardware', 'software' and 'wetware' (= human operators). We regularly use the vocabulary supplied by WIENER to describe human-machine interaction (input, output, feedback). ALAN TURING (1912–1954), a mathematician from Cambridge who worked at Bletchley on decrypting the German Enigma encoding in World War II, is famous for providing the theoretical outline for a machine that can solve any mathematical problem on the basis of algorithms (mechanical procedures, such as basic 'if … then' instructions).

Interface: Artificial intelligence (AI) and human-machine interaction

A related concept essential to cybernetics and computer discourse is that of "interface" or the boundary that connects two bodies or spaces – most often used to describe human-computer interaction (as opposed to human-document or human-human interaction). Many of the pioneers of 'new media' concentrated on improving human-machine interface designs. Analysing the difference engine, the prototypical programmable, algorithmic computer devised by CHARLES BABBAGE (1791–1871), ADA LOVELACE (1815–

1852), daughter of Lord Byron, argued that computers lack original impetus. This inaugurated the subsequent debate on AI ("Can computer programmes think like a human mind?" – "How can we describe and develop the non-human thinking of computers?") prompted Turing to tackle the question whether machines can think by devising his Turing test (or: imitation game). Turing predicted that future verbal computers would fool humans in simulation of human conversational interaction (put into practice by Joseph Weizenbaum's 1966 computer programme ELIZA). Douglas Engelbart (*1925), known as the inventor of the mouse, also addressed word processing, speech-recognition, and video-conferencing, and initiated the move towards graphic interfacing.

Interfaces and avatars: From symbolic language to immersion

Engelbart is one of the pioneers of GUI (graphical user interface). In their beginnings, computers were operated using keyboards and symbolic languages. Since then, the move first towards verbal language and then to 'user-friendly' GUI graphics has been seen (according to Charles S. Peirce) as a move from symbolic to iconic ('metaphoric' Windows and Mac desktop design, point-and-click, icons, drop-down menus) and, finally, indexical (immersive, multi-sensory) interface types. The development has brought about 3-D goggles and head-mounted displays, data gloves, body suits, guns, flight sticks and 'joysticks' used in video games and virtual realities etc. Often, a real user is represented by an avatar, i.e., a character representation of a real user within a virtual environment (from Hinduism, in which an avatar is the apparent worldly shape of a God). This character, often a graphic icon, has also become increasingly visual. The changes towards immersive and virtual interfaces have been such that an entire branch of cyberculture theory has come to reject the idea of distinct spheres of 'man' and 'machine'.

The post-human man-machine

A blurring of the human-computer interface is often implicit in critical approaches to cyberspace, cyborgs and virtual reality, for instance, in work by J. C. R. Licklider (man-computer symbiosis as artificial intelligence), Howard Rheingold (virtual community), and Donna Haraway (dissolved boundaries between physical and virtual as well as body and machine as female experience). A poignant formulation of the idea that the history of media is also a history of transcending the boundaries of the human body is N. Katherine Hayles's version of the posthuman: "*In the posthuman, there are no essential differences or absolute demarcations between bodily existence and computer simulation, cybernetic mechanism and biological organism, robot teleology and human goals.*" (Hayles 1999: 3)

The idea of networking computers has been part of the pioneering approaches to the interface. VANNEVAR BUSH (1890–1974) is credited as the 'father' of the Internet. In his essay "As We May Think" (published in *Atlantic Monthly*, 1945) he addressed the problem of information retrieval and expounded his vision of a "*mechanized private library*" based on associative linking, the Memex. Memex is a pre-computer machine that would bring files, microfilms or photographs automatically on a user's desk. The selection, however, would be based on associative linking rather than alphanumeric classification: "*The human mind does not work that way. It operates by association.*" (BUSH 1945: 44)

Associative linking: Bush's Memex

TED NELSON (*1937) built on BUSH's ideas to coin the term 'hypertext' (= extended, generalized text) and famously define it as non-sequential writing. Thus, NELSON inaugurated the development of link-based hypertext nets. In a 1965 paper it becomes obvious that he includes hypermedia in his definition:
Let me introduce the word hypertext to mean a body of written or pictorial material interconnected in such a complex way that it could not conveniently be presented or represented on paper. […] Such a system could grow indefinitely, gradually including more and more of the world's written knowledge. (NELSON 1965: 144)
This hypertext publishing network that NELSON called Xanadu crucially inspired research into computer networks. In the eccentric, self-published book *Computer Lib/Dream Machines* (1974), the visionary NELSON not only attacked the disabling influence of monolithic corporation on computer development ("computer lib") but also envisaged a newly designed, visual and dynamic human-computer interaction ("dream machines").

Hypertext: Ted Nelson

Internet is the name given to a decentralized system of computer networks within which encoded data packages are distributed among connected data servers. Just as cybernetics and human-machine interaction, the Internet is the brainchild of the military-industrial complex of cold-war America (for which BUSH, LICKLIDER, WIENER and others worked). The Internet was devised in the early 1960s, probably as a decentralized communication system for the US military complex which would function even if parts were destroyed by nuclear attacks. Based on technologies by PAUL BARAN (Rand Corporation) and DONALD DAVIES (British National Physical Laboratory), computer scientist LAWRENCE ROBERTS developed the ARPANET for the Advanced Research Projects Agency (ARPA) at the University of California. It started on the 2nd of September, 1969, spreading to Britain and Norway in 1973. With the introduction of TCP/IP (Transmission Control Protocol/Internet Protocol) in 1983, various public and private networks were connected by a common transmission protocol.

Short history of the Internet

WWW (W3): The World Wide Web	In 1991, TIM BERNERS-LEE developed the Hypertext Markup Language (HTML). The combination of this markup language with a network protocol (Hypertext Text Transfer Protocol, HTTP) and an address system (Uniform Resource Locator, URL) inaugurated the World Wide Web which quickly replaced Internet standards such as "Gopher". HTML made web communication so user-friendly and multi-medial that it turned from a specialist application used in academia to a worldwide publication platform. At the beginning of 2003, more than 170 million hosts (i.e., computers with a registered IP address) provided content and, according to "Internet World Stats" an impressive estimated 812 million Internet users. The Web is used for an enormous variety of heterogeneous social interactions. Writing in the Internet magazine *Salon.com*, JAMES PONIEWOZIK noted ironically: "*Any world without handy Internet resources for Brazilian fingernail fetishists is not a world I want to live in.*" WARDRIP-FRUIN and MONTFORT (2003: 791) sum up that the Web is "*a pool that is murky and profound, teeming with the useless and the indispensable; a body of texts we can surf in playfully or sail through with resolve on voyages of many sorts […].*"

2 Cybercultures and cyberarts

99.99 % of what happens is not on the news. LOESJE

Cyberfeminists and webgrrrls: Gender	Thus, the Internet is fraught with a number of problems as well as various enthusiastically propagated promises. It is, for instance, traditionally viewed as a gendered technology. Top searches in the leading search engine google.com in 2004 suggest that the Internet (historically dominated by male, white, and wealthy users) is still largely geared towards the young, male and heterosexual market, in spite of research that suggests increasing use by women. 'Cyberfeminists' such as N. KATHERINE HAYLES, DONNA HARAWAY, MARGARET MORSE and SADIE PLANT have since the late 1980s claimed cyberculture as a feminist sphere. In 1991, HARAWAY's "A Cyborg Manifesto" sought to establish the cybernetic organism of the cyborg (i.e., a hybrid of machine and organism, without origins) as an ironic political and rhetorical myth employed against Western thought. If feminists want to break male-dominated dualisms, HARAWAY argued, they should not seek for an imaginary pre-technological body. SADIE PLANT (1996: 335) acknowledged that network culture "*still appears to be dominated by both men and masculine intentions and designs*", but articulates the Utopia of "*web grrrls*" (the codeword name seeking to avoid the typical search engine results for 'girl', see WAKEFORD 1997) as opposed to the teenage-boy cliché of computer nerds and geeks:

Fig. 22: Google top searches in 2004

	google.com (USA)	google.co.uk (UK)	google.com.au (Australia)	google.de (Germany)
1.	Britney Spears	BBC News	Paris Hilton	Routenplaner
2.	Paris Hilton	Big Brother	Quantas	Wetter
3.	Christina Aguilera	CBBC	Australian Idol	Telefonbuch
4.	Pamela Anderson	Autotrader	Trading Post	Paris Hilton
5.	Chat	Dictionary	Virgin Blue	Chat
6.	Games	Tesco	Delta Goodrem	Christina Aguilera
7.	Carmen Electra	Eastenders	The OC	Bild
8.	Orlando Bloom	Weather	Halo 2	Britney Spears
9.	Harry Potter	British Airways	Ian Thorpe	Aldi
10.	MP 3	National Lottery	Jennifer Hawkins	Arbeitsamt

Cyberfeminism is an insurrection on the part of the goods and materials of the patriarchal world, a dispersed, distributed emergence composed of links between women, women and computers, computers and communication links, connections and connectionist nets. (PLANT 1996: 335)

On the WWW there is a continuous race between control and anarchy, because unlike traditional mass media it is hardly regulated by licensing or regulating bodies. The idea of open source codes presupposes a non-proprietary, collaborative distribution of software (e.g., Linux). This does not mean that there is no pressure from businesses or governments to control contents on the Web and, of course, some of the biggest sites are owned by global media players such as AOL, Microsoft or Lycos. There has also been a trend towards using the Web predominantly for e-commerce functions (amazon, ebay etc.). This has caused a number of problems, such as concern about fraud, and dangers to consumer privacy posed, e.g., by spyware cookies (computer code surrepti-

Control and anarchy

tiously placed on local hard disks), researching consumer habits. In order to control and protect the flow of information, firewalls and data encryption have become profitable branches in the software business.

Zero gate-keeping, identity tourism and culture jamming

Two aspects of the Internet best characterize problems and potential, (1) the fact that it publishes unfiltered content, thus intensifying the erosion of privacy initiated by the expansion of mass media, and (2) its identity tourism (LISA NAKAMURA 2000), i.e., the appropriation of identities in passing (or surfing) and temporary body-mind divorce. NAKAMURA (2000: 234) argues for the potential of performing *"alternative versions of self and race"* in order to *"jam the culture machine"*. Cyberspace is above all a space of confusion and missing "frameworks". Disposable identities and zero gate-keeping causes the ontological destabilisation which has resulted in pranks, hoaxes, gimmicks, jokes, parodies, fakes and what has been termed "culture jamming", i.e., the sabotage of received cultural norms through "hacktivism" (or hacker activism). Often derived from anarchist or situationist opposition to official media and media regulation, groups such as "wu-ming", or "Luther Blissett" have long declared their intentions: *"The media lie. We want to confuse people."* Cases in point are the rogue websites whitehouse.org and etoys.com, the irritating code of jodi.org and the atrocity exhibitions in the "archive on disturbing illustration" (www.rotten.com) or the excrement ratings on www.ratemypooh.com.

Cyberproblems and 'mythinformation'

The most diverse contents may be inaccurate or infringe copyright, without adequate control through legal regulation. Illegal downloads of videos and music (MP3) exchanged on platforms such as Napster have had detrimental effects on the music business. On the Internet one may find forged identities, manipulated images. The Internet is used beside other purposes to sell pornography or to provide a platform for xenophobic, homophobic, misogynous or racist propaganda. Anonymity and masked identities in chatrooms (such as ICQ, 'I seek you', or IRC, 'Internet Relay Chat') may foster cyberstalking. As early as in 1986, LANGDON WINNER pointed out the inherent dangers of 'mythinformed' digital culture: (1) The monitoring of daily activities poses a threat to privacy and public freedom, (2) information is knowledge and knowledge is power, (3) the Web fails to bring about social equality, democratization and a cultural renaissance, and (4) responsibility is deterritorialized by transnational commerce.

Another drawback of computer-based media is that they may widen the gap between those who own or can access information and those who remain offline and thus excluded from information-rich environments. The situation of populations who either do not have access to telephone networks, cables, or to access providers or who put up cultural resistance to computer-based technologies may be aggravated as access to, and familiarity with these technologies is increasingly taken for granted. On the other hand, in various wars and in totalitarian communities the Internet has proved to be a powerful tool for supplying information that was filtered out of more traditional media. As the recent expansion of private 'weblogging' (or 'blogs') or the rapid development of collaborative knowledge bases (wikis, since 1995), illustrate, it remains potentially a medium that increases interactive media participation, not only splintering existing mass media homogeneity and streamlining, but also threatening the integrity of the public sphere.

Participation: Information-rich vs. information-poor

The great promise of Internet media, therefore, is interactivity, even if all too often it merely generates 'interpassivity' (see LEGGEWIE / BIEBER 2004). We have already said that chats, e-mail and WWW are 'pull' media that require user activity. In terms of the obsolete transmission model of communication, recipients have become participants, communicators have turned into organizers, formerly separate technical media now structure communication as versatile 'metamedia' (see GOERTZ 1995: 106). Let us return, therefore, to ANDREW LIPPMANN's definition of interactivity, *"mutual and simultaneous activity on the part of both participants"*. LIPPMANN concludes that true interactivity requires

Interactivity and 'interpassivity'

- **interruptibility**, that is, turn-taking functions which enable the participants in a communication process to alternate with, and interrupt, each other;
- **graceful degradation**, that is, a function which productively regulates the inability of a system to respond, thus preventing communication from collapsing;
- **limited look ahead**, that is, the absence of predetermined communication paths;
- **no default**, that is, the absence of 'boring' default patterns;
- **impression of infinite database**, that is, a potentially unlimited communication environment.

Following GOERTZ (1995: 108), one might argue that interactivity is high when a communication process is (1) high in selectivity, (2) has a large potential for modification, (3) increases the scope of selections and modifications and (4) is non-linear. If compared to the cinema, the DVD raises the selectivity and scope of film, and similarly pay-per-view increases the selectivity of TV, but in both cases there is still no opportunity to modify contents.

As J. YELLOWLEES DOUGLAS (2001: 42–43) and others have remarked, this definition applies admirably to technology-free human-

Interactivity as mental process	human interaction. Going to the movies, however, does not meet LIPPMANN's criteria, such as "interruptibility", "absence of a clear-cut default path or action" or "impression of an infinite database". The definitions of interactivity by JAN ESPEN AARSETH and BRENDA LAUREL both start from a basic subjective level at which any kind of fictional novel or film can be addressed:

In terms of literature a fiction is a representation of an unreal event or object; something invented or imaginary; a lie. In terms of literature, a fiction is a portrayal of invented events or characters, usually in the form of prose [...], constructed in a way that invites rather than dispels belief. A successful fiction must, therefore, be interactive, just as a lie needs a believer in order to work. (AARSETH 1997: 50)

There is another, more rudimentary measure of interactivity: "You either feel yourself to be participating in the ongoing action of the representation or you don't". (LAUREL 1991: 20–21)

At this level, of course, interactivity is not specific to Net media, and one may invoke the standard texts of reader-response theory and affective stylistics (STANLEY FISH, HANS-GEORG GADAMER, WOLFGANG ISER). DAVID S. MIALL (1999: 169) argues, for instance, that hypertext theorists have misread books as static:

Reading is an interactive process: at any given point during a reading a group of readers is likely to bring a varied range of assumptions, experiences, or feelings to the text.

VR as externalized interactivity	Thus, we may see the evolution of virtual reality and computer media as yet another attempt to build the interactivity of mental processes into human-machine interaction (for instance, as the pushing of buttons or clicking of mouses). Other terms such as 'participation', 'play', 'use', creep in. JANET MURRAY (1997: 74) refers to *"participatory"* texts as texts which are *"responsive to our input"*. MURRAY also concentrates on the subjective aspect of the notion of interactivity: *"Agency is the satisfying power to take meaningful action and see the results of our decisions and choices"*. Provided one sees mental and emotional processes – "filling-in", inferences, hypotheses, empathy, sympathy – as interactive operations and as meaningful choices, then movies, novels, sculptures, paintings may also qualify.

Virtual reality and immersion	Recent publications (BOLTER / GRUSIN 1999, GRAU 2001) have pointed out that the concept of virtual reality is anything but new. It is, on the contrary, founded on the search for illusionistic experience which culminates, for instance, in the panoramas. Virtual experience strives for eradicating the medial experience, in other words, immersion is founded on a total experience of aesthetic message at the expense of medium and form. As RYAN (2001: 11) points out, however, immersion in textual worlds need not be the passive experience it is made out to be through association with popular

arts, it *"does not mean that immersive pleasure is in essence a lowbrow, escapist gratification"*. Ryan (2001: 13, 28) goes on to scan the continuum of virtual reality, distinguishing an optical dimension (the virtual is an illusion as opposed to the real), a technological (the virtual is computer-mediated) and a scholastic one (the virtual is something potential). She argues against reducing the virtual to the optical aspect and thus equating it negatively with fake.

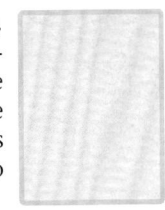

Hypertext has been claimed as a fulfilment of contemporary critical theory (Landow 1992) or postmodern literature (Coover 1992), as a redefinition of writing, authoring, and publishing. Since its heyday, however, an increasing disillusionment with what has been termed "cyberhype" has become evident (a hype is artificially stimulated media activity; originally the word refers to a drug injection, derived from 'hypodermic'). Coincidentally with the bursting of the e-commerce bubble, most of the recent publications in the field have articulated reservations about the artistic or social potential of the Internet (cf. Porombka 2001, Maresch / Rötzer 2001, Simanowski 2002, Coover 2001, even Snyder 1998).

Hypertext and cyber-hype

The new media, particularly those relying on the Internet (or Net for short), have generated their own subcultures, distinguished as "new age cyber-hippies", "Net defenders", "Marxist theoreticians", "Net promoters", "Net(-hype) haters and cyber-punk provo-geek techno-luddites" by Weinstein / Weinstein (1997). Especially in Europe, the digerati (i.e., digital literati) are conflated with the protagonists of rampant American neo-liberalism. In an outspoken attack on Californian subculture and cyberspace ecstasy, for instance, Hans Ulrich Reck (2002: 20–22) denies the potential of current 'media art', which having embraced the ubiquitous techno-industry has lost the critical difference essential to artistic processes. Maresch / Rötzer (2001: 7–26) decry both the commercialization of the Internet (online-shopping, e-trade, e-banking) and increasing dystopian control mechanisms. The adventurous computer nerd has been replaced by the e-consumer whose privacy is blatantly violated by state apparatuses and greedy corporations in a wild and expanded marketplace.

Digerati, Net subculture and expanded markets

It is fascinating to see that the theorists of hyperfiction have described the effect of an extra burden on the new reader-writer. The ideal recipient of hypertext is clearly at odds with the 'scanning' surfer who is invariably treated in the standard research into Net usability (Morkes / Nielsen 1997). The superficial reader, diverted by pop-ups, other links, or browser functions (forward-backward navigation or 'history' buttons), the fickle and transient content surfer of usability research is a far cry from the truly inter-

Surfer vs. 'wreader'

active "wreader" required by hyperfiction. This has led to the kind of disappointment voiced by novelist ROBERT COOVER, one of the first champions of hyperfiction, who has subsequently seen the Net as fallen from textual grace into the hands of non-interactive, linear, commercial visualization, a regression to the 'authoritarian' cinema (COOVER 2001).

Hypertext vs. cinema

According to LEV MANOVICH (2001: 61), therefore, hypertext is yet another stage in the externalization of satisfying mental processes – this time not by viewing edited images (cinema), but by following programmed links: *"If the cinema viewer, male or female, lusted after and tried to emulate the body of a movie star, the computer user is asked to follow the mental trajectory of the new media designer"*. Reader-response theory as well as audience-centred cultural-studies approaches, however, teach us not to paint too bleak a picture. Historian ROGER CHARTIER argues: *"[...] to be sure, the creators [...] always aspire to pin down their meaning and proclaim the correct interpretation that sets out to constrain reading (or viewing). But without fail, reception invents, shifts about, distorts."* (1994: ix-x)

Hyperfiction and media art

The field of hyperfiction or media art has been described in a number of ways. Approaches range from a primarily technological determination of a vast field where science, technology, and literature intersect (WILSON 2002) to a complete rejection of the 'newness' of new media and a reintegration into traditional concepts (GENDOLLA et al. 2001), from an insistence on the crucial role of the Web for a sub-section of this art (excluding Flash media, hypertext etc., WILSON 2002) to a rejection of such a claim conveyed in the coinage "interfictions" (SIMANOWSKI 2002). There is no consensus on what to call the work in this field – "information art", "Web art", "literature in electronic space", "digital literature", "interfiction", "interactive fiction", "hyperfiction", "new media art" (SCHWARZ/SHAW 1996), "interactive art" (DINKLA 1997), "Net literature", or "computer literature" (see fig. 23). AARSETH (1997) speaks about cybertext; and in a collection published by GENDOLLA et al., for instance, contributors variously address *ars digitalis* (NORBERT M. SCHMITZ), media art (PETER M. SPANGENBERG) or a fleeting oeuvre ("flottierendes Werk", SÖKE DINKLA) whose tremors seismographically register the movements in world culture. SIMANOWSKI (2002) brackets off collaborative writing projects from hyperfiction and (linear) multimedia art.

Varieties of digital literature

The Electronic Literature Organization (ELO) has provided a number of rapidly changing, tentative subdivisions of 'digital' literature. The current version (www.eliterature/org/about) reads as follows:
- Hypertext fiction and poetry, on and off the web.
- Kinetic poetry in Flash and using other platforms.

Fig. 23: Definitions of 'electronic' or 'digital' literature and art

WILSON (2002)	HEIBACH (2003)	SIMANOWSKI (2002)	BÖHLER/SUTER (1999)
Information Arts Intersections of Art, Science, and Technology (Kinetics & Robotics, Sound, Virtual Reality, Motion & Gesture, AI, Information Systems, Speech, Computer Media, Telecom/Radio/Telephone, Microbiology, Animals & Plants, Ecology, Body & medicine, Math & Algorithms/AL, Particle Physics & Nanotechnology, Dynamic Systems, Geology & Chemistry, Rapid Prototyping, Space Science, GPS) **Web Art** (2002: 560) "The Web is essential, however, for art that builds on connections between remote persons or makes use of persons located in distant locations."	**Literature in electronic space** Literature as language art (writing, speech, multimedia performance, visual poetry) "an electronic space that enables user action and interaction: computer and computer networks" "computer networks as social connectors" (Heibach 2003: 27) polydirectional, instantaneous; dynamic and process-oriented, unframed	**Interfictions** (from Ziegfield 1989: Interactive Fiction) Fictional *vs.* non-fictional contents, prefers 'fiction' over problematic term 'Net art', 'fiction' as transmedial term (comprises text, image, sound); prefix 'inter-' introduces basic traits of the digital media, i.e. interactivity and intermediality and also refers to the most popular of these media, the Internet	**Hyperfiction** Opens up a new, virtual space for narration, an electronic hypertext that defines text as texture or web which is in a continuous process of weaving and extending Hypertexts are complex literary webs in which multiple narrational processes become directly obvious through their structural linking, these processes are open for the reader to follow (cf. BÖHLER/SUTER 1999: 15–16)

- Computer art installations which ask viewers to read them or otherwise have literary aspects.
- Conversational characters, also known as chatterbots.
- Interactive fiction.
- Novels that take the form of emails, SMS messages, or blogs.
- Poems and stories that are generated by computers, either interactively or based on parameters given at the beginning.

- Collaborative writing projects that allow readers to contribute to the text of a work.
- Literary performances online that develop new ways of writing.

Precursors of digital art

HEIBACH (2003) states a research consensus when she argues that there are precursors of digital art in traditional media: There was initial, reactive and creative interactivity, in which the user began process, controlled process, and created process. Collective creativity was tested in mail art, telephone art, and happenings. Literary interaction was crucial in Dada poetry, cut-up, *collage*, conversation art, and letter art. Word art, concrete and visual poetry, intermedia, video poetry (Brazil), and multi-sensory synaesthetic art are important inspirations for the Web artists. Finally, challenges to traditional meaning-making by emphasis on structure and coincidence were tried in aleatory art and Oulipo, the movement "ouvroir de littérature potentielle" which based its art on mathematics and permutation. HEIBACH proposes a threefold typology which distinguishes (1) collective production, (2) intermedia, and (3) media and code critique.

Computer games

One of the most prominent of the many 'recreational' functions of the computer is the computer game, which has been investigated as a defining new media practice. This is why it was introduced at the ZKM in Karlsruhe among other forms of media art (FURTWÄNGLER 2001). Unlike books or television, the game must be interactive in the sense that its user is a player who invests *"non-trivial effort"*, as AARSETH argued, and receives system feedback. There is a great variety of game genres, from the initial arcade games (*Pong, Pac Man*) and racing and flying simulations (which put the user into a driver's seat or cockpit, as it were), sports games (in which users switch players), combat games and first-person shooters (with graphic interfaces simulating POV camera footage), adventure games (with quest narratives, the prime example is *Myst*) and multi-purpose simulation games (*Sim City*) to networked multi-player games. There is a general drift from text-rich environments ("text adventures") to movie simulations ("full-motion video games").

Game psychology and accommodation

One of the earliest researchers into gaming (a field now covered by the emergent game studies), SHERRY TURKLE, investigated the video game in the 1980s. TURKLE paid particular attention to the psychology of video and computer gaming as requiring undivided attention, as providing the pleasure not of 'identifying with', but of 'becoming', of being infatuated with a challenge, of having complete control and attaining perfection. Beside these attractions, TURKLE argued, the stories seemed irrelevant. In the words of

GRAHAM NELSON, an adventure game is *"a crossword at war with a narrative"* (quoted in FURTWÄNGLER 2001: 200). The ludic pleasures of computer games mainly consist in user-accommodation to role-governed behaviour in win-lose situations – and even level-design and modifications represent only very limited versions of interactivity (see MERTENS 2004).

From this observation, there sprang an unresolved debate within the analysis of computer games, between narratologists (MARIE-LAURE RYAN) and ludologists (JAN ESPEN AARSETH, MARKKU ESKELINEN, GONZALO FRASCA). While it is true that positions are not as clear-cut as this paragraph will make it seem, ludologists hold that rule-governed computer games cannot be adequately described by analytical tools used in analysing text narratives, whereas narratologists insist that such an analysis is useful. Afraid of being engulfed by approaches borrowed from film studies or literary studies, ludologists, who are often in closer relation to gaming communities, seek to establish the medium specificity of computer games. They hold that stories are mere 'gift wrappings' of the game processes which (unlike print or film narratives) are not based in interpreting or making sense of a sequence of events. On the other hand, categories such as character, plot, point of view, setting, are clearly essential both for analysing computer games and for designing them.

Narratology vs. ludology

7 Conclusion

CHAPTER

GLSTNBRY FSTVL
seasnd w msts n fruitless mellwnss
n pungent smlls f grss ovr hay
we flp nto ponchos fr a mnts rest
n try nt t pln t rst f t day
GRAHAM FRANCIS (Orange Prize for creative use of SMS, *Guardian* text-message poetry contest, www.guardian.co.uk/textpoetry)

Future media

Let us return to the beginning of this book by stating the obvious again. Without a doubt rapid technological change is set to transform the media world immensely within ever shorter time spans. Today, mobile telephony and SMS messaging as well as online services are widely regarded as the most significantly expanding future media practices. CD, DVD and (certainly) VHS are in the process of being superseded by services which depend on increased connectivity of mobilized Net media. The latest edition of the Communications Industry Forecast (CIF, published by media merchant bankers Veronis Suhler Stevenson 2004) reports an increased media usage concentrated on Internet music, video games and radio as well as increasing Internet activities by businesses based in traditional media (newspapers, magazines, TV companies).

Media 'mega-trends'

These are the 'megatrends' according to the CIF:
- Media usage is growing. In 2004, average media consumption in the US was up to 10.4 hours per day (from 9.3 in 1999). Consumers spent 3,599 hours using media in 2002, that is more than 10 hours per day and an increase of 1.8 percent over the previous year as consumers continued to indulge in more creative and escapist media.
- Communications spending is set to increase, driven by cable and satellite TV, filmed entertainment and video games and Internet.
- The communication industry's growth outpaced the US Gross Domestic Product (GDP), remaining the fifth-fastest-growing sector of the U.S. economy in the 2002–2007 period.
- Increasingly, we are becoming media multitaskers that operate in various media at the same time. *"Consumers are increasingly using two or more media simultaneously with the plethora of media choices and competition for attention accelerating. The result is a media generation that is consuming more information in less time than ever before."* (JAMES RUTHERFORD, VSS)

- Consumers spent most of their time with television in 2002 as they continued to increase cable & satellite television viewing. Next to television, radio commanded the most attention from consumers climbing 4.3 percent in 2002 as a result of longer commutes and the emergence of satellite radio. Consumers spent less time with broadcast television, recorded music, consumer magazines, daily newspapers and home videos. Use of these media is forecast to decrease slightly or, at best, remain stable.

Future of media studies

We have already stated the dynamics and the increased urgency to expand and update media studies under the permanent threat of obsolescence. In spite of the need to register the trends sketched in the CIF and elsewhere, it seems important to highlight the history of the media and to explore how they have always shaped our notions of reality. We are, after all, not just consumers as the CIF seems to suggest. In general, we need to address with a long attention-span the mediality of cultural practices rather than trying to keep up with the latest of the 'new' media. The structure of this book reflects the most likely candidates for intensified research:

- Net-based media interaction
- Visual studies that transcend art and art history and reflect the cultural variabilty and potency of vision
- The role of the media in cultural memory
- Intermediality both as research into adaptation and media transfer and as new discoveries in media contact, reflecting the hybridity of remediation

New media, old methods?

The ludology *vs.* narratology debate sketched above is a telling example. Methods that are based on experience with older (but still vibrant) media (TV, film studies, literary studies) are unlikely to become obsolete. The study of narratives and reader-response theory, for instance, have much to offer beyond the confines of books, performance studies have profitably begun to inspire research into *Inszenierungskultur* outside of theatres and the study of computer games would be infinitely poorer without the analysis of moving images that has been the business for film studies for decades. In the face of increasing media hybridity, we are going to see increasing methodological hybridity in media studies.

Literary into media studies?

Media studies is a seductive field. A worrying trend in Britain, for instance, shows enrolment in media studies up, enrolment in modern languages (particularly German) down (WARD 2004). Politicians such as the British culture minister TESSA JOWELL support the growth of media studies: "*I believe in the modern world media literacy will become as important a skill as maths or science. [...] Decoding our media will be as important to our lives as citizens as understanding great literature is to our cultural lives."* (BUCKINGHAM 2004) In view of growing enrolment numbers my hope seems not entirely unfounded that this book will encourage colleagues and students alike to integrate media studies into the revised curricula of a modularized study of English-language cultures. In 1991, the title of ANTONY EASTHOPE's *Literary Into Cultural Studies* suggested that the man had a mission – a mission both to transform media and communication studies with the study of textuality and to widen the scope and methodology of literary studies to encompass signifying practices across the media divides. It would be wrong to update EASTHOPE's agenda to "literary into media studies", "communication into media studies" or "cultural into media studies" because this would establish unnecessary boundaries and blinkered points of view.

Redesigning media studies: a dilemma

At the same time, one should not be too sanguine about the prospects of a revamped media studies because in spite of decades of cultural studies it seems to be incomparably harder to integrate ABC's *Desperate Housewives* (2004), a computer game by Electronic Arts or the *Guardian* mobile SMS poetry into a humanities curriculum than a movie by INGMAR BERGMAN. Thus, English studies are beleaguered on all sides: on the one hand asked to perform compensatory functions and preserve in the cultural memory the biotopes of cherished cultures threatened by rapid media upheavals – on the other hand pressurized into acknowledging the emerging cultural practices in order to remain relevant to the next generation of media users. In any case, the time has come to move on from showing film adaptations and passing this off as merging literary into media studies.

Mission statement

With some delay, the OED registers new personalities such as media barons, media junkies or media darlings, new occupations such as media consultants, new spaces such as media rooms or media centres, new languages such as mediaspeak. The curriculum proposed in this book does not prepare for a specific job in the media business. Its job is to help us tell the media event from the media hype, to distinguish the media market from the media circus, and to turn media-shy into media-savvy or media-wise students.

Bibliography

1. Foundations of media and communication studies

There is no shortage on general introductions to the field. For a first orientation, here is a short survey with brief comments:

Einführung in die Medienwissenschaft (HICKETHIER 2003).
An excellent up-to-date, German-language introduction to media studies.

Einführung in die Medienwissenschaft. Konzeptionen, Theorien, Methoden, Anwendungen (RUSCH 2002).
An edited volume, which provides a multi-perspective introduction from diverse positions, with a distinct constructivist bias on scrutinising the interdisciplinary set-up of media studies itself.

Einführung in die Medienwissenschaft. Probleme, Methoden, Domänen (FAULSTICH 2002).
An eight-module introduction with an aggressive stance against media ontology and 'unscientific' approaches.

Einführung in die Medientheorie (LESCHKE 2003).
A comprehensive guide to media theory with harsh critical readings of standard theoreticians as fashionable nonsense.

Kursbuch Medienkultur: Die maßgeblichen Theorien von Brecht bis Baudrillard (PIAS et al. 1999).
Attempts to develop a media-theory canon in confrontation with the instrumental mass communication approach and beyond technical definitions of the media. Here are the texts attacked by FAULSTICH and LESCHKE.

Texte zur Medientheorie (HELMES/KÖSTER 2002).
An inexpensive and historically informed German-language anthology.

Metzler Lexikon Medientheorie – Medienwissenschaft (SCHANZE 2002).
A useful, but not exhaustive dictionary compiled by a group of researchers from the former SFB "Screen Media" in Siegen.

Media Studies: A Reader. 2nd ed. (MARRIS/THORNHAM 1999).
An anthology of sixty-five essays focused on broadcasting and the press. Shorter sections on "media and social power", "production", "text", more comprehensive coverage of "text" and "reception", with case studies on "soap opera", "news", "advertising" and "new media".

Media and Meaning: An Introduction (STEWART/LAVELLE/KOWALSKI 2001).

Media Studies: The Essential Introduction (RAYNER/WALL/KRUGER 2001).

More than Meets the Eye. An Introduction to Media Studies, 3rd ed. (BURTON 2002).
Basic introductions for the British market, aimed at A-level students and undergraduates. Lucid style, functionalist and empiricist: images, statistics, examples, glossaries, activities. Low on theory.

Einführung in die Kommunikationswissenschaft, 3 Vols. (MERTEN 1999–2000).
Representative and comprehensive introduction to communication studies with constructivist sympathies.

McQuail's Mass Communication Theory. 4th ed. (MCQUAIL 2000).
The standard English-language introduction to mass communication, which reproduces the prevalent functionalist and empiricist attitude (LUHMANN, BAUDRILLARD, VIRILIO, KITTLER, ASSMANN are not even mentioned).

ADORNO, Theodor W. & Max HORKHEIMER: *Dialectic of Enlightenment.* (1944/47) New York: Continuum, 1990.

ALTHEIDE, David L. & Robert P. SNOW: *Media Logic.* Beverly Hills, CA/London: Sage, 1979.

ANDERS, Günther: *Die Antiquiertheit des Menschen.* 2 Vols. Munich: C.H. Beck, 1956 & 1980.

APPADURAI, Arjun: *Modernity at Large: Cultural Dimensions of Globalization.* Minneapolis: University of Minnesota Press, 1996.

ASKEW, Kelly & Richard A. WILK (Eds.): *The*

Anthropology of Media: A Reader. London/ Malden, MA: Blackwell, 2002.

ASKEW, Kelly: "Introduction." In: ASKEW/ WILK 2002, pp. 1–17.

BARTHES, Roland: *Mythologies*. London: Vintage, 2000 [1957].

BARTHES, Roland: *S/Z*. New York: Hill & Wang, 1974 [1970].

BASSNETT, Susan: *Studying British Cultures*. London: Routledge, 1997.

BAUDRILLARD, Jean: "Requiem for the Media." In: WARDRIP-FRUIN/MONTFORT 2003, pp. 278–300 ["Requiem pour les medias" 1972].

BAUDRILLARD, Jean: "The Masses: The Implosion of the Social in the Media." In: MARRIS/THORNHAM 2000, pp. 98–108. [1985].

BERNARDI, Daniel: *'Star Trek' and History Race-ing towards a White Future*. New Brunswick NJ: Rutgers UP, 1998.

BIGNELL, Jonathan: *Postmodern Media Culture*. Edinburgh: Edinburgh UP, 2000.

BIGNELL, Jonathan: *Media Semiotics: An Introduction*. Manchester: Manchester UP, 2002.

BOCK, Wolfgang: *Bild – Schrift – Cyberspace. Grundkurs Medienwissen*. Berlin: Aisthesis, 2002.

BOLZ, Norbert: "Wirklichkeit ohne Gewähr." In: HELMES/KÖSTER 2002, pp. 326–331. [2000].

BOORSTIN, Daniel: *The Image: A Guide to Pseudo-Events in America*. New York: Athenaeum, 1980.

BRAND, Stewart: *The Media Lab: Inventing the Future at MIT*. New York: Viking/Penguin, 1988 [1987].

BRANSTON, Gill & Roy STAFFORD: *The Media Student's Book*. 3rd ed. London: Routledge, 2003.

BRIGGS, Asa & Peter BURKE: *A Social History of the Media: From Gutenberg to the Internet*. Cambridge: Polity Press, 2002.

BUCKINGHAM, David: "Survival Skills." *Media Guardian* July 27, 2004. <http://media. guardian.co.uk/> Accessed June 2005.

BURKE, Seán (Ed.): *Authorship: From Plato to the Postmodern. A Reader*. Edinburgh: Edinburgh UP, 1995.

BURTON, Graeme: *More than Meets the Eye. An Introduction to Media Studies*. 3rd. ed. London: Arnold/Hodder, 2002.

CARROLL, Noël: *A Theorie of Mass Art*. Oxford: Clarendon Press, 1998.

CAUGHIE, John (Ed.): *Theories of Authorship*. London: Routledge, 1981.

CHANDLER, Daniel: "Processes of mediation." Media and Communication Studies (MCS) University of Aberystwyth. 1995. <http://www.aber.ac.uk/media// Documents/short/process.html>Accessed January 2004.

CLARK, Vivienne & Richard HARVEY (Eds.): *GCSE Media Studies*. London: Longman, 2002.

CRAIG, Robert. T., & David A. CARLONE: "Growth and transformation of communication studies in US higher education: Towards reinterpretation." *Communication Education* 47.1 (1998), pp. 67–81.

CURTIS, Polly: "Media calling", Education Guardian <http://education.guardian. co.uk> June 19, 2003. Accessed September 1, 2003.

DAYAN, Daniel & Elihu KATZ: *Media Events*. Cambridge, MA: Harvard UP, 1992.

DE CERTEAU, Michel: *The Practice of Everyday Life*. Berkeley: University of California Press, 1984.

DEMOTT, Benjamin: "Against McLuhan." In: *Supergrow: Essays and Reports on Imagination in America*. Piscataway NJ: Transaction, 2003, pp. 33–45. [1966].

DEBRAY, Régis: *Vie et Mort de l'Image. Un Histoire du Regard en Occident*. Paris: Gallimard, 1992.

DEBRAY, Régis: *Einführung in die Mediologie*. Bern: Haupt, 2003.

EASTHOPE, Antony: *Literary into Cultural Studies*. London: Routledge, 1991.

ECO, Umberto: *A Theory of Semiotics*. Bloomington IN: Indiana UP, 1976.

ELM, Theo und Hans H. HIEBEL (Eds.): *Medien und Maschinen. Literatur im technischen Zeitalter*. Freiburg: Rombach, 1991.

ENZENSBERGER, Hans Magnus: "Constituents of a Theory of the Media." In: MARRIS/ THORNHAM 2000, pp. 68–91. [1970].

ENZENSBERGER, Hans Magnus: "Die vollkommene Leere." *Der Spiegel* no. 20 (1988), pp. 234–244.

FAULSTICH, Werner (Hg.): *Grundwissen Medien*. 5th ed. Munich: Fink, 2004.

FAULSTICH, Werner: *Einführung in die Medienwissenschaft*. Munich: Fink/UTB, 2002.

FISCHER-LICHTE, Erika: *Ästhetik des Performativen*. Frankfurt/Main: Suhrkamp, 2004.

FLUSSER, Vilém: *Medienkultur*. Frankfurt/ Main: Fischer 1997.

FRIEDBERG, Anne: "The Mobilized and Virtualized Gaze in Modernity: Flâneur/Flâneuse." In: MIRZOEFF 2002, pp. 395–404. [1993].

GERBNER, George: "Towards a General Model of Communication." In *Audio-Visual Review* 4 (1956), pp. 171–199.

GERBNER, George: "Cultural Indicators – The Third Voice." In: *Communications Technology and Social Policy.* Ed.: George GERBNER/ Larry GROSS/William H. MELODY. New York: Wiley, 1973, pp. 553–573.

GERSTNER, David A. & Janet STAIGER: *Authorship and Film.* AFI Film Readers. New York: Routledge, 2002.

GITLIN, Todd: *Inside Prime Time.* New York: Pantheon, 1983.

GITLIN, Todd: *Media Unlimited. How the Torrent of Images and Sounds Overwhelms Our Lives.* New York: Metropolitan Books, 2002.

GREIS, Andreas, Gerfried W. HUNOLD, & Klaus KOZIOL (Eds.): *Medienethik.* Francke/ UTB: 2003.

HABERMAS, Jürgen: *Strukturwandel der Öffentlichkeit.* Neuwied/Berlin: Luchterhand, 1962. [*The Structural Transformation of the Public Sphere,* transl. 1989].

HALL, Stuart: "Encoding/Decoding." In: MARRIS/THORNHAM 2000, pp. 51–61. [1973/1980].

HARTMANN, Frank: *Mediologie. Ansätze einer Medientheorie der Kulturwissenschaften.* Wien: Facultas, 2003.

HELMES, Günther & Werner KÖSTER (Ed.): *Texte zur Medientheorie.* Stuttgart: Reclam, 2002.

HEPP, Andreas: *Cultural Studies und Medienanalyse. Eine Einführung.* Opladen/ Wiesbaden: Westdeutscher Verlag, 1999.

HICKETHIER, Knut: *Einführung in die Medienwissenschaft.* Stuttgart: Metzler, 2003.

HIEBEL, Hans H. (Ed.): *Kleine Mediengeschichte. Von den ersten Schriftzeichen zum Mikrochip.* Munich: Beck, 1997.

HÖRISCH, Jochen: *Der Sinn und die Sinne. Eine Geschichte der Medien.* Frankfurt/Main: Eichborn, 2001.

HORTON, Donald & Richard R. WOHL: "Mass Communication and Parasocial Interaction." *Psychiatry* 19 (1956), pp. 215–229.

INGLIS, Fred: *Media Theory: An Introduction.* Oxford, Cambridge, MA: Blackwell, 1990.

INNIS, Harold A.: *The Bias of Communication.* Toronto: University of Toronto Press, 1951.

JAMESON, Fredric: "Postmodernism, or The Cultural Logic of Late Capitalism." In: *Postmodernism, or The Cultural Logic of Late Capitalism.* Duke: Duke UP, 1991. [1984].

JENKINS, Henry: *Textual Poachers: Television Fans and Participatory Culture.* New York: Routledge, 1992.

KATZ, Elihu et al. (Eds.): *Canonic Texts in Media Research: Are There Any? Should There Be? How About These?* Cambridge: Polity Press, 2003.

KELLNER, Douglas: *Media Culture. Cultural Studies, Identity and Politics between the Modern and the Postmodern.* London/New York: Routledge, 1995.

KIRCHMANN, Kay: *Blicke aus dem Bunker. Paul Virilios Zeit- und Medientheorie aus der Sicht einer Philosophie des Unbewussten.* Stuttgart: Klett-Cotta, 1998.

KITTLER, Friedrich A.: *Aufschreibesysteme 1800–1900.* Munich: Fink, 1987.

KITTLER, Friedrich A.: *Grammophon, Film, Typewriter.* Berlin: Brinkmann & Brose, 1986.

KLOOCK, Daniela & Angela SPAHR: *Medientheorien. Eine Einführung.* Munich: Fink/ UTB, 1997.

KORTE, Barbara, Klaus-Peter MÜLLER (Eds.): *Anglistische Lehre aktuell. Probleme, Perspektiven, Praxis.* Trier: WVT, 1995.

KRALLMANN, Dieter & Andreas ZIEMANN: *Grundkurs Kommunikationswissenschaft.* Munich: Fink/UTB, 2001.

KRÄMER, Sybille: "Sprache – Stimme – Schrift. Sieben Gedanken über Performativität als Medialität." In: WIRTH 2002, pp. 323–346.

KÜBLER, Hans-Dieter: *Mediale Kommunikation.* Tübingen: Niemeyer, 2000.

LACEY, Nick: *Image and Representation: Key Concepts in Media Studies.* Basingstoke: Macmillan/St. Martin's Press, 1998.

LACEY, Nick: *Media Institutions and Audiences: Key Concepts in Media Studies.* Basingstoke: Palgrave, 2002.

LACEY, Nick: *Narrative and Genre: Key Concepts in Media Studies.* Basingstoke: Palgrave, 2000.

LASSWELL, Harold D.: "The Structure and Function of Communication in Society." In: *Mass Communications.* Ed.: Wilbur

SCHRAMM. Urbana: University of Illinois Press, 1960, pp. 117–130. [1948].

LAZARSFELD, Paul F. & Robert K. MERTON: "Mass Communication, Popular Taste, and Organized Social Action." In: MARRIS/THORNHAM 2000, pp.18–30. [1948].

LESCHKE, Rainer: Einführung in die Medientheorie. Munich: Fink/UTB, 2003.

LUDES, Peter: Einführung in die Medienwissenschaft: Entwicklungen und Theorien. Berlin: Erich Schmidt, 1998.

LUHMANN, Niklas: Die Gesellschaft der Gesellschaft. 2 Vols. Frankfurt/Main: Suhrkamp,1997.

LUHMANN, Niklas: Die Realität der Massenmedien. 2nd ed. Opladen: Westdeutscher Verlag, 1996.

MACDONALD, Myra: Exploring Media Discourse. London: Arnold, 2003.

MALETZKE, Gerhard: Kommunikationswissenschaft im Überblick. Grundlagen, Probleme, Perspektiven. Opladen/Wiesbaden: Westdeutscher Verlag, 1998.

MALETZKE, Gerhard: Kommunikationswissenschaft im Überblick: Grundlagen, Probleme, Perspektiven. Opladen/Wiesbaden: Westdeutscher Verlag, 1998.

MARCUSE, Herbert: One-Dimensional Man: Studies in the Ideology of Advanced Industrial Society. Boston: Beacon Press, 1964.

MARRIS, Paul & Sue THORNHAM (Eds.): Media Studies. A Reader. 2nd ed. New York: NYU Press, 2000.

McCOMBS, Maxwell E & Donald L. SHAW: "The agenda-setting function of the press." Public Opinion Quarterly 36 (1972), pp. 176–187.

McGUIGAN, Jim: Cultural Populism. London: Routledge, 1992.

McLEOD, Donald. "Media Studies: Popular in class, but lacks respect." Education Guardian June 9, 2005. <http://www.education.guardian.co.uk> Accessed June 2005.

McLUHAN, Herbert Marshall: The Gutenberg Galaxy. The Making of Typographic Man. Toronto: University of Toronto Press, 1962.

McLUHAN, Herbert Marshall: Understanding Media. The Extension of Man. London: Routledge & Kegan Paul, 1964.

McQUAIL, Denis: McQuail's Mass Communication Theory. 4th ed. London: Sage, 2000.

MERTEN, Klaus, Siegfried J. SCHMIDT & Siegfried WEISCHENBERG (Eds.): Die Wirklichkeit der Medien. Opladen: Westdeutscher Verlag, 1994.

MERTEN, Klaus: Einführung in die Kommunikationswissenschaft. Vol. 1. Münster/Hamburg: LIT, 1999.

MERTEN, Klaus: Kommunikation. Eine Begriffs- und Prozessanalyse. Opladen: Westdeutscher Verlag, 1970.

MEYROWITZ, Joshua: "Images of Media: Hidden Ferment – and Harmony – in the Field." Journal of Communication 43 (1993), pp. 55–66.

MEYROWITZ, Joshua: No Sense of Place. The Impact of Electronic Media on Social Behavior. Oxford/New York: Oxford UP, 1985.

NEGT, Oskar & Alexander KLUGE: Öffentlichkeit und Erfahrung. Frankfurt/Main: Suhrkamp, 1972.

NESBIT, Molly: "What Was an Author?" In: BURKE 1995, pp. 247–262. [1987].

NÜNNING, Ansgar & Vera (Eds.): Konzepte der Kulturwissenschaften. Stuttgart/Weimar: Metzler, 2003.

PIAS, Claus et al. (Eds.): Kursbuch Medienkultur: Die massgeblichen Theorien von Brecht bis Baudrillard. Stuttgart: DVA, 1999.

POSNER, Roland: "Kultursemiotik." In: A. & V. NÜNNING 2003, pp. 39–72.

POSTMAN, Neil: Amusing Ourselves to Death. New York: Penguin, 1985.

POSTMAN, Neil: Technopoly: The Surrender of Society to Technology. New York: Vintage, 1995.

PROSS, Harry: Medienforschung: Film, Funk, Fernsehen. Darmstadt: Habel, 1972.

RAYNER, Philip et al.: Media Studies: The Essential Introduction. London & New York: Routledge, 2001.

RUSCH, Gebhard: Einführung in die Medienwirtschaft. Wiesbaden: Westdeutscher Verlag, 2002.

RUTHERFORD, James: Communications Industry Forecast 2003 <http://www.vss.com/articles/articles_2003/article_081103.html> Accessed April 2005.

SAXER, Ulrich: "Mediengesellschaft: Verständnisse und Missverständnisse." In: Politikvermittlung und Demokratie in der Mediengesellschaft. Ed.: Ulrich SARCINELLI. Bonn: Bundeszentrale für politische Bildung, 1998, pp. 52–73.

SCHANZE, Helmut (Ed.): Metzler Lexikon

Medientheorie Medienwissenschaft. Stuttgart/Weimar: Metzler, 2002.

SCHMIDT, Siegfried J.: "Medienkulturwissenschaft." In: V. & A. NÜNNING 2003, pp. 351–370.

SCHMIDT, Siegfried J.: Kalte Faszination. Medien, Kultur, Wissenschaft in der Mediengesellschaft. Weilerswist: Velbrück Wissenschaft, 2000.

SCHRAMM, Wilbur: "How communication works." In: The Process and Effects of Mass Communication. Ed.: Wilbur SCHRAMM. Urbana: University of Ilinois Press, 1954, pp. 3–26.

SENNETT, Richard: The Fall of Public Man. New York: Knopf, 1974.

SHANNON, Claude E. & Warren WEAVER: The Mathematical Theory of Communication. Urbana IL: University of Illinois Press, 1949.

SOMMER, Roy: Grundkurs Cultural Studies / Kulturwissenschaft Grossbritannien. Stuttgart: Klett, 2003.

STANITZEK, Georg & Wilhelm VOSSKAMP (Eds.): Schnittstelle. Medien und kulturelle Kommunikation. Köln: Du Mont, 2001.

STANITZEK, Georg: "Kriterien des literaturwissenschaftlichen Diskurses." In STANITZEK/VOSSKAMP 2001, pp. 51–76.

STEWART, Colin, Marc LAVELLE & Adam KOWALTZKE: Media and Meaning: An Introduction. London: British Film Institute, 2001.

TAYLOR, Andrew & Andrew WILLIS: Media Studies: Texts, Institutions and Audiences. Oxford: Blackwell, 1999.

THORNTON, Sarah: "General introduction." In: The Subcultures Reader. Ed.: Ken GELDER & Sarah THORNTON. London/New York: Routledge, 1997, pp. 1–7.

TICHENOR, Phillip J., George A. DONOHUE & Clarice N. OLIEN: "Mass Media Flow and Differential Growth in Knowledge." Public Opinion Quarterly 34 (1970), pp. 159–170.

TUNSTALL, Jeremy: The Media are American. London: Constable, 1977.

TURNER, Graeme: British Cultural Studies. An Introduction. 3rd ed. London: Routledge, 2003.

VIRILIO, Paul: Desert Screen: War at the Speed of Light. London: Continuum, 2002. [L'écran du desert. Chroniques de guerre 1991].

VIRILIO, Paul: Ground Zero. London: Verso, 2002.

VIRILIO, Paul: The Virilio Reader. Oxford: Blackwell, 1998.

VIRILIO, Paul: War and Cinema. The Logistics of Perception. London: Verso, 1989. [Guerre et Cinéma 1984].

WAGNER, Peter: History of British, Irish and American Literature. Trier: WVT, 2003.

WARD, Lucy: "Career warning over rise in 'soft' subjects." Education Guardian <http://education.guardian.co.uk> August 19, 2004. Accessed September 13, 2004.

WATSON, James: Media Communication: An Introduction to Theory and Process. Basingstoke: Macmillan, 1998.

WILLIAMS, Kevin: Understanding Media Theory. London: Arnold, 2003.

WILLIAMS, Raymond: Communications. London: Penguin, 1962.

WILLIAMS, Raymond: Television. Technology and Cultural Form. London: Fontana, 1974.

WIRTH, Uwe (Ed.): Performanz. Zwischen Sprachphilosophie und Kulturwissenschaften. Frankfurt/Main: Suhrkamp, 2002.

WRIGHT, C.R.: Mass Communication. New York: Random House, 1975.

ZAKON, Paul: Hobbes' Internet Timeline. <http://zakon.org/robert/internet/timeline/#Growth> Accessed January 2004.

2. Literary studies, cultural studies, media studies and Anglistik

BACH, Gerhard & Johannes-Peter TIMM: Englischunterricht. 3rd ed. Francke/UTB, 2003.

BACHLEITNER, Norbert: "Hypertext als Herausforderung der Literaturwissenschaft. Probleme der Rezeption einer Form digitaler Literatur." In: FOLTINEK/LEITGEB 2002, pp. 245–266.

BÖKER, Uwe & Christoph HOUSWITSCHKA (Eds.): Einführung in das Studium der Anglistik und Amerikanistik. Munich: Beck, 2000.

BORCHERS, Hans, Gabriele KREUTZNER, Eva-Maria WARTH (Eds.): Never-Ending Stories: American Soap Operas and the Cultural Production of Meaning. Trier: WVT, 1994.

BORRMANN, Andreas & Rainer GERDZEN: Vernetztes Lernen – Hypertexte, Homepages & was man im Sprachunterricht damit machen kann. Stuttgart: Klett, 1998.

DECKE-CORNHILL, Helene & Maike REICHART-WALLRABENSTEIN (Eds.): *Fremdsprachenunterricht in medialen Lernumgebungen.* Frankfurt/Main: Lang, 2002.

DONATH, Reinhard (Ed.): *CD-ROMs im Fremdsprachenunterricht.* Stuttgart: Klett, 2001.

DONATH, Reinhard (Ed.): *Kreative Textarbeit mit dem PC.* Stuttgart: Klett, 2000.

DONATH, Reinhard: *E-mail-Projekte im Fremdsprachenunterricht. Authentische Kommunikation mit englischsprachigen Partnerklassen.* Stuttgart: Klett, 1996.

DONATH, Reinhard: *Internet und Englischunterricht.* Stuttgart: Klett, 1997.

FELDMANN, Doris, Fritz-Wilhelm NEUMANN & Thomas ROMMEL (Eds.): *Anglistik im Internet. Proceedings of the 1996 Erfurt Conference on Computing in the Humanities.* Heidelberg: Winter, 1997.

FOLTINEK, Herbert & Christoph LEITGEB (Eds.): *Literaturwissenschaft: intermedial – interdisziplinär.* Wien: Verlag der österreichischen Akademie der Wissenschaften, 2002.

GOETSCH, Paul and Dietrich SCHEUNEMANN (Eds.): *Text und Ton im Film.* ScriptOralia 102. Tübingen: Narr, 1997.

GRABES, Herbert (Ed.): *Literatur in Film und Fernsehen: von Beckett bis Shakespeare.* Königstein,Ts.: Scriptor, 1980.

GRIEM, Julika (Ed.): *Bildschirmfiktionen.* Tübingen: Narr, 1997.

HANDKE, Jürgen (Ed.): *The Mouton Interactive Introduction to Phonetics and Phonology.* New York/Berlin: Mouton de Gruyter, 2000.

HANDKE, Jürgen (Ed.): *The Interactive Introduction to Linguistics.* CD ROM. Munich: Hueber, 2001.

KALLENBACH, Christiane & Markus RITTER (Eds.): *Computerideen für den Fremdsprachenunterricht.* Berlin: Cornelsen, 2000.

KEITEL, Evelyne et al.: *Neue Medien im Alltag.* 4 Vols. Lengerich: Pabst Science Publishers, 1999–2003.

KLARER, Mario: *Einführung in die anglistisch-amerikanistische Literaturwissenschaft.* Darmstadt: Wiss. Buchgesellschaft, 1998.

KLEIN, Eberhard, Karlfried KNAPP, Fritz-Wilhelm NEUMANN, Hans Wolfgang SCHALLER (Eds.): *Kulturkommunikation: Anglistik in der Remediatisierung der Informationsgesellschaft.* Trier: WVT, 2000.

KORTMANN, Bernd & Edgar W. SCHNEIDER (Eds.): *A Handbook of Varieties to English.* New York/Berlin: Mouton de Gruyter, 2004.

KRANZ, Dieter & Paul TIEDEMANN: *Internet für Anglisten. Eine praxisorientierte Einführung.* Darmstadt: Wiss. Buchgesellschaft, 2000.

KREUTZNER, Gabriele: *Next Time on "Dynasty." Studien zu einem populären Serientext im amerikanischen Fernsehen der achtziger Jahre.* Trier: WVT, 1992.

LEGUTKE, Michael & Dietmar RÖSLER (Eds.): *Fremdsprachenlernen mit digitalen Medien.* Tübingen: Narr, 2003.

LIEBELT, Wolfgang: *Literaturverfilmungen im Unterricht: Vorschläge für die Unterrichtspraxis.* Hildesheim, 1999.

LUDWIG, Hans-Werner, Elmar SCHENKEL & Bernhard ZIMMERMANN: *Made in Britain: Studien zur Literaturproduktion im britischen Fernsehen.* Tübingen: Narr, 1992.

LUDWIG, Hans-Werner & Thomas ROMMEL: *Studium Literaturwissenschaft. Arbeitstechniken und Neue Medien.* Tübingen/Basel: Francke/UTB, 2003.

MEYER, Michael: *English and American Literatures.* Tübingen/Basel: Francke, 2004.

MÜLLER-HARTMANN, Andreas, & Marita SCHOCKER-VON DITFURTH: *Introduction to English Language Teaching.* Stuttgart: Klett, 2004.

NEUMANN, Fritz-Wilhelm: "Anglistik im Internet: Die neuen Ressourcen." In: BÖKER/HOUSWITSCHKA 2000, pp. 329–348.

NÜNNING, Ansgar & Vera: *Grundkurs anglistisch-amerikanistische Literaturwissenschaft.* Stuttgart: Klett, 2001.

NÜNNING, Ansgar: "Zehn Thesen zum Thema 'Literaturwissenschaft und/oder/ als Kulturwissenschaft: Prolegomena, Plädoyer und Projekte für einen kulturwissenschaftlich ausgerichtete Literaturwissenschaft." In: FOLTINEK/LEITGEB 2002, pp. 39–66.

RÜSCHOFF, Bernd & Dieter WOLFF: *Fremdsprachenlernen in der Wissensgesellschaft: zum Einsatz der Neuen Technologien in Schule und Unterricht.* Ismaning: Hueber, 1999.

SCHMITZ, Ulrich (Ed.): *Linguistik lernen im Internet.* Tübingen: Narr, 2004.

SCHNEIDER, Ralf (Ed.): *Literaturwissenschaft in*

Theorie und Praxis. Eine anglistisch-ameri-kanistische Einführung. Tübingen: Narr, 2004.

SCHNELL, Ralf (Ed.): *Konzeptionen der Medien-wissenschaften I: Kulturwissenschaft, Film-und Fernsehwissenschaft. Zeitschrift für Literatur-wissenschaft und Linguistik* 132 (2003).

SCHWERDTFEGER, Inge C.: *Medien und Fremd-sprachenunterricht.* Hamburg: Buske, 1973.

SEITER, Ellen, Hans BORCHERS, Gabriele KREUTZNER, Eva-Maria WARTH et al. (Eds.): *Remote Control. Television, Audiences and Cultural Power.* London/New York: Rout-ledge, 1989.

STRATMANN, Gerd, et al. (Eds.): *Filme. anglistik & englischunterricht* 36. Heidelberg: Win-ter, 1988.

THALER, Engelbert: *Musikvideoclips im Eng-lischunterricht.* Munich: Langenscheidt-Longman, 1999.

VIEHOFF, Reinhold: "Von der Literaturwis-senschaft zur Medienwissenschaft – und kein Weg zurück." In: FOLTINEK/LEITGEB 2002, pp. 67–96.

WEIAND, Hermann-Josef: *Film und Fernsehen im Englischunterricht: Theorie, Praxis und kritische Dokumentationen.* Kronberg: Scriptor, 1978.

WESKAMP, Ralf: *Fachdidaktik: Grundlagen und Konzepte Anglistik-Amerikanistik.* Berlin: Cornelsen, 2001.

3. Intermediality, media hybridity, media transfer and adaptation

ALBERSMEIER, Franz-Josef: "Literatur und Film. Entwurf einer praxisorientierten Textsystematik." In: ZIMA 1995, pp. 235–268.

ANDREW, Dudley: "Adaptation." In: *Con-cepts in Film Theory.* Ed.: Dudley ANDREW. Oxford: Oxford UP, 1984, pp. 96–106.

AUSLANDER, Philip: *Liveness. Performance in a Mediatized Culture.* London/New York, 1999.

BARTHELME, Donald: "And Now Let's Hear It for the Ed Sullivan Show!" In: *Guilty Pleas-ures.* New York: Dell/Delta, 1963, pp. 101–108.

BEJA, Morris: *Film and Literature.* New York: Longman, 1979.

BLUESTONE, George: *Novel into Film.* Berkeley:

University of California Press, 1957.

BOOSE, Lynda E. & Richard BURT (Eds.): *Shakespeare, the Movie.* London & New York: Routledge, 1997.

BRADBURY, Ray: *Fahrenheit 451.* New York: Del Ray/Ballantine, 1991 [1953].

BRODE, Douglas: *Shakespeare in the Movies.* Oxford: Oxford UP, 2000.

BRUNOW, Jochen (Ed.): *Schreiben für den Film. Das Drehbuch als eine andere Art des Erzäh-lens.* 4th ed. Munich: Edition Text + Kritik, 1996.

BRUSBERG-KIERMEIER, Stefani & Jörg HELBIG (Eds.): *Shakespeare in the Media: From the Globe Theatre to the World Wide Web.* Frankfurt/Main: Lang, 2004.

BUCHLOH, Paul G., Jens Peter BECKER & Ralf J. SCHRÖDER (Eds.): *Literatur und Film: Stu-dien zur englischsprachigen Literatur in Buch und Film.* Kiel: Kieler Verlag Wissen-schaft und Bildung, 1985.

BURNETT, Mark Thornton & Ramona WRAY (Eds.): *Shakespeare, Film, Fin de Siècle.* Basingstoke, London: Macmillan, 2000.

BURT, Richard (Ed.): "Shakespeare and the Holocaust: Julie Taymor's *Titus* is Beauti-ful, or Shakesploi Meets (the) Camp." In: *Shakespeare after Mass Media.* Ed.: Richard BURT. New York: Palgrave, 2002, pp. 295–330.

BURT, Richard: *Unspeakable ShaXXXspeares: Queer Theory and American Kiddie Culture.* New York: St. Martin's Press, 1998.

CARDWELL, Sarah: *Adaptation Revisited. Tele-vision and the Classic Novel.* Manchester/ New York: Manchester UP, 2002.

CARTMELL, Deborah: *Interpreting Shakespeare on Screen.* Basingstoke, London: Macmil-lan, 2000.

CHATMAN, Seymour: *Coming to Terms: The Rhetoric of Narrative in Fiction and Film.* Ithaca NY/London: Cornell UP, 1990.

CLÜVER, Claus: "Ekphrasis Reconsidered: On Verbal Representations of Non-Verbal Texts." In: Ulla-Britta LAGERROTH et. al. *Interart Poetics. Essays on the Interrelations of the Arts and Media.* Amsterdam: Rodopi, 1997, pp. 19–34.

COURSEN, H.R. & J.C. BULMAN (Eds.): *Shake-speare on Television. An Anthology of Essays and Reviews.* Hanover NH/London: Uni-versity of New England Press, 1988.

DAVIES, Anthony: *Filming Shakespeare's Plays.* Cambridge: Cambridge UP, 1988.

DeLILLO, Don: *White Noise*. New York: Penguin, 1986 [1985].

DONALDSON, Peter S.: *Shakespearean Film – Shakespearean Directors*. London: Hyman, 1990.

DREXLER, Peter & Lawrence GUNTNER (Eds.): *Negotiations with Hal: Multi-Media Perceptions of (Shakespeare's) Henry V*. TU Braunschweig: Seminar für Anglistik & Amerikanistik, 1995.

FREY-VOR, Gerlinde: *Coronation Street: Infinite Drama and British Reality. An Analysis of Soap Opera as Narrative and Dramatic Continuum*. Trier: WVT, 1991.

GIDDINGS, Robert & Erica SHEEN (Eds.): *The Classic Novel from Page to Screen*. Manchester: Manchester UP, 2000.

GRIEM, Julika: "Screening America: Representations of Television in Contemporary American Literature." *Amerikastudien* 41.3 (1996), pp. 465–481.

HABICHT, Werner & Günther KLOTZ (Eds.): *Shakespeare-Jahrbuch* 129 (1993). Special media issue.

HARVEY, Judith: "Ut pictura poesis." (2002), Chicago School Theory of Media Glossary <http://chicagoschoolmediatheory.net/glossary2004/utpicturapoesis.htm> Accessed December 2004.

HEFFERNAN, James: *Museum of Words: The Poetics of Ekphrasis from Homer to Ashbery*. Chicago: University of Chicago Press, 1993.

HEFFERNAN, James: "Ekphrasis and Representation." *New Literary History* 22.2 (1991), pp. 297–316.

HELBIG, Jörg (Ed.): *Intermedialität: Theorie und Praxis eines interdisziplinären Forschungsgebiets*. Berlin: Erich Schmidt, 1998.

HODGDON, Barbara (Ed.): *Screen Shakespeare*. Special issue *Shakespeare Quarterly* 53.2 (2002).

HOLLÄNDER, Hans: "Literatur, Malerei und Graphik. Wechselwirkungen, Funktionen und Konkurrenzen." In: ZIMA 1995, pp. 129–170.

JACKSON, Russell (Ed.): *The Cambridge Companion to Shakespeare on Film*. Cambridge: Cambridge UP, 2000.

JORGENS, Jack: *Shakespeare on Film*. Bloomington: Indiana UP, 1977.

KALB, Jonathan: *Beckett in Performance*. Cambridge: Cambridge UP, 1989.

KAUFMAN, Charlie: *The Shooting Script: Adaptation*. London: Nick Hern Books, 2002.

KOSINSKI, Jerzy: *Being There*. New York: Bantam, 1972 [1971].

KREUZER, Helmut: *Arten der Literaturadaption*. In: Wolfgang GAST (ed.). *Literaturverfilmung*. Bamberg: C. C. Buchners, 1993, pp. 27–31.

KREWANI, Angela: *Hybride Formen: New British Cinema – Television Drama – Hypermedia*. Trier: WVT, 2001.

LEHMANN, Courtney: "Crouching Tiger, Hidden Agenda: How Shakespeare and the Renaissance Are Taking the Rage Out of Feminism." In HODGDON 2002, pp. 260–279.

McCLOUD, Scott: "Time Frames." In: WARDRIP-FRUIN/MONTFORT 2003, pp. 711–736. [1993].

McHALE, Brian: *Constructing Postmodernism*. London/New York: Routledge, 1992.

McKEE, Robert: *Story. Substance, Structure, Style and the Principles of Screenwriting*. London: Methuen, 1999.

MERTENS, Mathias: *Forschungsüberblick Intermedialität. Kommentierungen und Bibliographie*. Hannover: Revonnah, 2000.

MOSTHAF, Franziska: *Metaphorische Intermedialität: Formen und Funktionen der Verarbeitung von Malerei im Roman – Theorie und Praxis in der englischsparchigen Erzählkunst des 19. und 20. Jahrhunderts*. Trier: WVT, 2000.

MÜLLER, Jürgen E.: "Intermedialität als poetologisches und medientheoretisches Konzept: Einige Reflexionen zu dessen Geschichte." In: HELBIG 1998, pp. 31–40.

MURRAY, Edward: *The Cinematic Imagination: Writers and the Motion Pictures*. New York: Frederick Ungar, 1972.

NAREMORE, James (Ed.): *Film Adaptation*. New Brunswick NJ: Rutgers UP, 2000.

NÜNNING, Vera & Ansgar NÜNNING (Eds.): *Erzähltheorie transgenerisch, intermedial, interdisziplinär*. Trier: WVT, 2002.

OWEN, Alistair (Ed.): *Story and Character. Interviews with British Screenwriters*. London: Bloomsbury, 2003.

PAECH, Joachim: "Intermedialität: Intermediales Differenzial und transformative Figurationen." In: HELBIG 1998, pp. 14–30.

PETZOLD, Dieter (Ed.): *Fantasy in Film und Literatur. anglistik & englischunterricht 59*. Heidelberg: Winter, 1996.

PHELAN, Peggy: *Unmarked. The Politics of Performance*. London/New York: Routledge, 1993.

RAJEWSKY, Irina O.: *Intermedialität*. Tübingen; Francke/UTB, 2002.

ROTHWELL, Kenneth S.: *A History of Shakespeare on Screen: A Century of Film and Television*. Cambridge: Cambridge UP, 1999.

SCHMIDT, Johann N.: "In Love with Shakespeare: Der Barde und das zeitgenössische Hollywood-Kino." *Shakespeare-Jahrbuch* 137 (2000), pp. 86–99.

SCHMITZ-EMANS, Monika: "Die Intertextualität der Bilder als Gegenstand der Literaturwissenschaft." In: FOLTINEK/LEITGEB 2002, pp. 193–230.

SCHNEIDER, Irmela & Christian W. THOMSEN (Eds.): *Hybridkultur: Medien, Netze, Künste.* Köln: Wienand, 1997.

SHEEN, Erica: "INTRODUCTION." IN: GIDDINGS & SELBY 2000, PP. 2–13.

STAM, Robert: *Literature through Film. Realism, Magic and the Art of Adaptation.* Oxford: Blackwell, 2005.

STAM, Robert & Allessandra RAENGO (Eds.): *Literature and Film. A Guide to the Theory and Practice of Film Adaptation.* Oxford: Blackwell, 2005.

STERNBERG, Claudia: *Written for the Screen. The American Motion-Picture Screenplay as Text.* Tübingen: Stauffenburg, 1997.

STERNBERG, Claudia: „Film und Literaturwissenschaft." In: SCHNEIDER 2004, pp. 213–240.

SUNARA, Nives: *Immer wieder Hamlet. Shakespeare's Tragödie im Film – immer wieder anders.* Trier: WVT, 2004.

THOMPSON, Marcus: *Middleton's Changeling.* United Independent Pictures. <http://www.uipl.co.uk/mc/mcscript.htm> Accessed January 2003.

THOMSEN, Christian W. (Ed.): *Hybridkultur.* Arbeitshefte Bildschirmmedien 46. Siegen: Universität Siegen, 1994.

VOIGTS-VIRCHOW, Eckart (Ed.): *Mediated Drama – Dramatized Media.* Trier: WVT, 2000.

VOIGTS-VIRCHOW, Eckart (Ed.): *Janespotting and Beyond. British Heritage Retrovisions since the Mid-1990s.* Tübingen: Narr, 2004.

WAGNER, Geoffrey: *The Novel and the Cinema.* London: Tantivy Press, 1975.

WAGNER, Peter (Ed.): *Icons – Texts – Iconotexts. Essays on Ekphrasis and Intermediality.* Berlin: De Gruyter, 1996.

WAGNER, Peter: *Reading Iconotexts: From Swift to the French Revolution.* London: Reaktion Books, 1995.

WEBER, Alfred & Bettina FRIEDL (Eds.): *Film und Literatur in Amerika.* Darmstadt: Wiss. Buchgesellschaft, 1988.

WEISS, Tanja: *Shakespeare on Screen.* Frankfurt/Main: Peter Lang, 1999.

WELLS, Stanley & Anthony DAVIES (Eds.): *Shakespeare and the Moving Image: The Plays on Film and Television.* Cambridge: Cambridge UP, 1994.

WOLF, Werner. "Das Problem der Narrativität in Literatur, Bildender Kunst und Musik." In: NÜNNING/NÜNNING 2002, pp. 23–104.

WOLF, Werner: *The Musicalization of Fiction: A Study in the Theory and History of Intermediality.* Amsterdam: Rodopi, 1999.

WOLF, Werner: "Intermedialität: Ein weites Feld und eine Herausforderung für die Literaturwissenschaft." In: FOLTINEK/LEITGEB 2002, pp. 163–192.

WOLF, Werner: "Intermediality Revisited: Reflections on Word and Music Relations in the Context of a General Typology of Intermediality." *Word and Music Studies* 4.1 (2002), pp. 13–34.

WULF, Catharina (Ed.): *The Savage Eye/L'Oeil Fauve. A Collection of Critical Essays on Samuel Beckett's Film and Television Plays. Beckett Today/Aujourd'hui* 4. Amsterdam/Atlanta GA: Rodopi, 1995.

ZIMA, Peter V. (Ed.): *Literatur intermedial: Musik – Malerei – Photographie – Film.* Darmstadt: Wiss. Buchgesllschaft, 1995.

4. Film

ALBERSMEIER, Franz-Josef (Ed.): *Texte zur Theorie des Films.* Stuttgart: Reclam, 1995.

ALTMAN, Rick: *Film/Genre.* London: British Film Institute, 1999.

ANDERSON, Benedict: *Imagined Communities. Reflections on Origins and the Spread of Nationalism.* London/New York: Verso, 1991.

BARTON, Ruth: *Irish National Cinema.* London/New York: Routledge, 2004.

BORDWELL, David & Kristin THOMPSON: *Film Art. An Introduction.* 6th ed. New York et al: McGraw Hill, 2001.

BORDWELL, David & Noël CARROLL (Eds.): *Post-Theory: Reconstructing Film Studies.* Madison WI: University of Wisconsin Press, 1996.

BORDWELL, David: *Narration in the Fiction Film.* London: Routledge, 1988. [1985].

BORDWELL, David: "A Case for Cognitivism." *Iris* 9 (1989): pp. 11–40. <http://www.geocities.com/david_bordwell/caseforcog1.htm> Accessed September 2004.

BRANIGAN, Edward: *Narrative Comprehension and Film.* London/New York: Routledge, 1992.

BRANIGAN, Edward: *Point of View in the Cinema: A Theory of Narration and Subjectivity in Classical Film.* Berlin/New York/Amsterdam: Mouton, 1984.

BRUZZI, Stella (Ed.): *Fashion Cultures: Theories, Explorations, and Analysis,* London: Routledge, 2001.

BRUZZI, Stella: *New Documentary: A Critical Introduction.* London/New York: Routledge, 2000.

BRUZZI, Stella: *Undressing Cinema. Clothing and Identity in the Movies.* London: Routledge, 1997.

BÜHLER, Gerhard: *Postmoderne auf dem Bildschirm auf der Leinwand: Musikvideos, Werbespots und David Lynchs Wild at Heart.* St. Augustin: Gardez!, 2002.

CHION, Michel: *The Voice in the Cinema,* ed. and transl. Claudia GORBMAN. New York: Columbia UP, 1999.

CHION, Michel: *David Lynch.* London: British Film Institute, 1995.

COHEN, Marshall & Leo BRAUDY (Eds.): *Film Theory and Criticism.* 5th ed. Oxford: Oxford UP, 1999.

COOK, Pam & Mieke BERNINK (Eds.): *The Cinema Book.* 2nd ed. London: British Film Institute, 1999.

COOK, Pam: *Fashioning the Nation. Costume and Identity in British Cinema.* London: British Film Institute, 1996.

DELEYTO, Celestino: "Focalisation in Film Narrative." In: *Narratology: An Introduction.* Eds.: Susana ONEGA & José Angel Garcia LANDA. London/New York: Longman, 1996, pp. 217–233. [1991].

DREXLER, Peter (Ed.): *British Cinema. Journal for the Study of British Cultures* 5.2 (1998).

DYER, Richard: *Heavenly Bodies: Film Stars and Society.* Basingstoke/London: Macmillan, 1986.

DYER, Richard: *Stars.* London: British Film Institute, 1979.

FIELD, Syd: *Screenplay. The Foundations of Screenwriting.* 3rd ed. New York: Dell, 1984.

FÜLLER, Ralfdieter: *Fiktion und Antifiktion: Die Filme David Lynchs und der Kulturprozess im Amerika der 1980er und 90er Jahre.* Trier: WVT, 2001.

GAINES, Jane & Charlotte HERZOG (Ed.): *Fabrications. Costume and the Female Body,* London & New York: Routledge, 1990.

GALE, Steven H.: *Sharp Cut: Harold Pinter's Screenplays and the Artistic Process.* Lexington, KY: University Press of Kentucky, 2003.

GLEDHILL, Christine (Ed.): *Stardom: Industry of Desire.* London: Routledge, 1991.

GORBMAN, Claudia: *Unheard Melodies. Narrative Film Music.* Bloomington/Indianapolis: Indiana UP/British Film Institute, 1987.

GRIEM, Julika & Eckart VOIGTS-VIRCHOW: "Filmnarratologie: Grundlagen, Tendenzen und Beispielanalysen." In: NÜNNING/NÜNNING 2002, pp. 155–183.

GUNNING, Tom: "The Cinema of Attraction: Early Film, Ist Spectator, and the Avant-Garde." In: STAM/MILLER 2000, pp. 229–235. [1986].

HAMPE, Barry: *Making Documentary Films and Reality Videos.* New York: Henry Holt, 1997.

HELBIG, Jörg: *Geschichte des britischen Films.* Stuttgart/Weimar: Metzler, 1999.

HICKETHIER, Knut: *Einführung in die Film- und Fernsehanalyse.* 3rd ed. Stuttgart/Weimar: Metzler, 2001.

HIGSON, Andrew (Ed.): *Dissolving Views. Key Writings on British Cinema.* London: Cassell, 1996.

HIGSON, Andrew: *Waving the Flag: Constructing a National Cinema in Britain.* Oxford: Oxford UP, 1995.

HIGSON, Andrew: *English Heritage, English Cinema. Costume Drama since 1980.* Oxford: Oxford UP, 2003.

HILL, John & Pamela CHURCH GIBSON (Eds.): *Film Studies.* Oxford: Oxford UP, 2000.

HÖLTGEN, Stefan: *Spiegelbilder: Strategien der ästhetischen Verdopplung in den Filmen von David Lynch.* Hamburg: Kovac, 2001.

HUGHES, David: *The Complete Lynch.* London: Virgin Books, 2001.

JAHN, Manfred: "A Guide to Narratological Film Analysis." *Poems, Plays, and Prose: A Guide to the Theory of Literary Genres.* English Department, University of Cologne, 2003. <http://www.uni-koeln.de/~ame02/pppf.htm> Accessed January 2005.

JERSLEV, Anne: *David Lynch: Mentale Landschaften*. Wien: Passagen Verlag, 1996.

JOHNSON, Jeff: *Pervert in the Pulpit: Morality in the works of David Lynch*. Jefferson NC/London: McFarland, 2004.

KAWIN, Bruce: "The Mummy's Pool." In: COHEN/BRAUDY 1999, pp. 679–690. [1981].

KLEIN, Joanne: *Making Pictures: The Pinter Screenplays*. Columbus OH: Ohio State UP, 1985.

KORTE, Barbara & Claudia STERNBERG: "'If you want to know about London ... it's a laundrette in Peckham'. Black British Directors and Screenwriters Visualise the Metropolis." In: *Proceedings. Anglistentag 2000 Berlin* Eds.: Peter LUCKO & Jürgen SCHLAEGER. Trier: WVT, 2001, pp. 139–154.

KORTE, Helmut (Ed.): *Einführung in die systematische Filmanalyse: Ein Arbeitsbuch*. Berlin: Schmidt, 1999.

KOZLOFF, Sarah: *Invisible Storytellers. Voice-Over Narration in American Fiction Film*. Berkeley CA: U of California Press, 1988.

LEHMAN, Peter & William LUHR: *Thinking About Movies. Watching, Questioning, Enjoying*. 2nd ed. Oxford etc.: Blackwell, 2003.

LEVY, Emanuel: "Social Attributes of American Movie Stars." *Media, Culture & Society* 12.2 (1990), pp. 247–267.

LOTHE, Jakob: *Narrative in Fiction and Film. An Introduction*. London, New York: Oxford UP, 2000.

MACKILLOP, James (Ed.): *Contemporary Irish Cinema. From* The Quiet Man *to* Dancing at Lughnasa. New York: Syracuse UP, 1999.

MALIK, Sarita: "Beyond 'The Cinema of Duty'? The Pleasures of Hybridity. Black British Film of the 1980s and 1990s." In HIGSON 1996, pp. 202–215.

MANOVICH, Lev: "What is Digital Cinema?" In: MIRZOEFF 2002, pp. 405–416.

McLOONE, Martin: *Irish Film. The Emergence of a Contemporary Cinema*. London: British Film Institute, 2000.

MONACO, James: *How to Read a Film*. 2nd ed. Oxford/New York: Oxford UP, 1981.

MURPHY, Robert (Ed.): *British Cinema in the 1990s*. London: British Film Institute, 2000.

NAREMORE, James: *Acting in the Cinema*. Berkeley: University of California Press, 1988.

NICHOLS, Bill: *Introduction to Documentary*. Bloomington: Indiana UP, 2001.

PABST, Eckhard (Ed.): *"A Strange World": Das Universum des David Lynch*. Kiel: Ludwig, 1999.

RODLEY, Chris (Ed.): *Lynch on Lynch*. London: Faber & Faber, 1997.

SEESSLEN, Georg: *David Lynch und seine Filme*. 5th ed. Marburg: Schüren/Arte Edition, 2003.

SHEEN, Erica & Annette DAVISON (Eds.): *The Cinema of David Lynch. American Dreams, Nightmare Visions*. London/New York: Wallflower Press, 2004.

STAM, Robert & Toby MILLER (Eds.): *Film and Theory. An Anthology*. Malden, MA & Oxford: Blackwell, 2000.

STREET, Sarah: *British National Cinema*, London: Routledge, 1997.

STREET, Sarah: *Costume and Cinema. Dress Codes in Popular Film*, London: Wallflower, 2001.

THOMPSON, Kristin: *Storytelling in Film and Television*. Cambridge MA/London: Harvard UP, 2003.

THOMPSON, Kristin: *Breaking the Glass Armor. Neoformalist Film Analysis*. Princeton: Princeton UP, 1988.

5. Television

ALLEN, Robert C. (Ed.): *Channels of Discourse, Reassembled: Television and Contemporary Criticism*. London/New York: Routledge, 1992.

ALLRATH, Gaby & Marion GYMNICH (Eds.): *Narrative Strategies in Television Series*. Basingstoke: Palgrave Macmillan, 2005.

ANG, Ien: *Watching "Dallas": Soap Opera and the Melodramatic Imagination*. London: Methuen, 1985 [1982].

BIGNELL, Jonathan, Stephen LACEY & Madeleine MACMURRAUGH-KAVANAGH (Eds.): *British Television Drama. Past, Present and Future*. Basingstoke: Palgrave, 2000.

BIGNELL, Jonathan: *An Introduction to Television Studies*. London: Routledge, 2004.

BORSTNAR, Nils, Eckhard PABST & Hans-Jürgen WULFF: *Einführung in die Film- und Fernsehwissenschaft*. Konstanz: UVK, 2002.

BOURDIEU, Pierre: *On Television and Journalism.* London: Pluto Press, 1998. [1996].

BRANDT, George W. (Ed.): *British Television Drama in the 1980s.* Cambridge: Cambridge UP, 1993.

BRANDT, George W. (Ed.): *British Television Drama,* Cambridge: Cambridge UP, 1980.

BRENTON, Sam & Reuben COHEN: *Shooting People. Adventures in Reality TV.* London/New York: Verso, 2003.

BRIGGS, Asa: *The History of Broadcasting in the United Kingdom.* 5 Vols. Oxford/New York: Oxford UP, 1961–1995.

BUSCOMBE, Edward (Ed.): *British Television. A Reader.* Oxford: Oxford UP, 2000.

CALDWELL, John Thornton: *Televisuality. Style, Crisis, and Authority in American Television.* New Brunswick NJ: Rutgers UP, 1995.

CARPENTER, Humphrey: *Dennis Potter.* London: Faber & Faber, 1998.

CASEY, Bernadette et al.: *Television Studies: The Key Concepts.* London/New York: Routledge, 2002.

CAUGHIE, John: *Television Drama. Realism, Modernism and British Culture.* Oxford: Oxford UP, 2000.

CLARK, Vivienne: "It's O.K. to Laugh: Gender and Television Sitcom." Workshop BFI A-Level Conference, 2–4 July 2002. OCR Virtual Media Studies Community Support Site. <http://ital-dev.ucles-red.cam.ac.uk/listsupport/ocr-mediastudies-a/docs_html.> Accessed January 2004.

COOK, John R.: *Dennis Potter. A Life on Screen.* 2nd ed. Manchester/New York: Manchester UP, 1998.

COOKE, Lez: *British Television Drama. A History.* London: British Film Institute, 2003.

CORNER, John: *Critical Ideas in Television Structure.* Oxford: Clarendon, 1999.

COWARD, Rosalind: "Dennis Potter and the Question of the TV Author." *Critical Quarterly* 29 (1987), pp. 79–87.

CREEBER, Glen (Ed.): *The Television Genre Book.* London: British Film Institute, 2001.

CREEBER, Glen: *Dennis Potter – Between Two Worlds: A Critical Reassessment.* Basingstoke & New York: Macmillan/St. Martin's Press, 1998.

CURRY, Ramona: "Madonna from Marylin to Marlene: Pastiche and/or Parody?" *Journal of Film and Video* 42.2 (1990), pp. 15–30.

DAYAN, Daniel & Elihu KATZ: "Political Ceremony and Instant History." In: SMITH 1995, pp. 169–188.

ELDRIDGE, John, Jenny KITZINGER & Kevin WILLIAMS: *The Mass Media Power in Modern Britain.* Oxford: Oxford UP, 1997.

ELLIS, John: *Visible Fictions: Cinema – Television – Video.* London/New York: Routledge, 1982.

FISKE, John: *Television Culture.* London & New York: Routledge, 1987.

FISKE, John & John HARTLEY: *Reading Television.* London: Methuen, 1978.

FRITH, Simon, Andrew GOODWIN & Lawrence GROSSBERG (Eds.): *Sound and Vision. The Music Video Reader.* London/New York: Routledge, 1993.

GIDDINGS, Robert & Keith SELBY: *The Classic Serial on Television and Radio.* Basingstoke: Palgrave, 2001.

GRAS, Vernon & John R. COOK (Eds.): *The Passion of Dennis Potter.* New York/London: St. Martin's Press, 2000.

GURALINCK, Elissa S.: "Stoppard's Radio and Television Plays." In: *The Cambridge Companion to Tom Stoppard.* Ed.: Katherine E. KELLY. Cambridge: Cambridge UP, 2001, pp. 68–83.

HODGSON, Terry: *The Plays of Stoppard for Stage, Radio, TV, and Film.* Basingstoke/New York: Palgrave Macmillan, 2002.

HOOD, Stuart & Thalia TABARY-PETERSSEN: *On Television.* 4th ed. London/Chicago: Pluto, 1997.

LAVERY, David: *Full of Secrets: Critical Approaches to Twin Peaks.* Detroit: Wayne State UP, 1995.

McQUEEN, David: *Television: A Media Student's Guide.* London: Arnold, 1998.

McROBBIE, Angela: "Postmodernism and Popular Culture." In: MARRIS/THORNHAM 2000, pp. 385–392. [1986].

MERCER, Kobena: "Monster Metaphors: Notes on Michael Jackson's Thriller." In: FRITH et al. 1993, pp. 93–108.

MODLESKI, Tania: *Loving with a Vengeance: Mass-Produced Fantasies for Women.* Hamden CT: Archon, 1982.

MORLEY, David: *Family Television. Cultural Power and Domestic Leisure.* London: Comedia, 1986.

MORLEY, David: *The "Nationwide" Audience. Structure and Decoding.* London: British Film Institute, 1980.

NELSON, Robin: *TV Drama in Transition.* London: Macmillan, 1997.

NELSON, Robin: "TV Drama: 'Flexi-Narrative' Form and 'a New Affective Order.'" In: VOIGTS-VIRCHOW 2000, pp. 111–118.

NEWCOMBE, Horace (Ed.): *The Encyclopedia of Television*. 2nd ed. 4 Vols. Fitzroy Dearborn/Routledge, 2004.

SAMPSON, Anthony: *Who Runs the Place? The Anatomy of Britain in the 21st Century*. London: John Murray/Hodder, 2004.

SCHLAEGER, Jürgen (Ed.): *The Media Debate. Die Mediendebatte. Britische und deutsche Perspektiven*. Trier: WVT, 1996.

SCHNEIDER, Cynthia & Brian WALLIS (Eds.): *Global Television*. Wedge Press/MIT Press: New York etc., 1988.

SMITH, Anthony (Ed.): *Television. An International History*. Oxford: Oxford UP, 1995.

TICHI, Cecilia: *The Electronic Hearth: Creating an American Television Culture*. New York/ Oxford: Oxford UP, 1991.

THALER, Engelbert: *Musikvideos im Englischunterricht. Phänomenologie, Legitimität, Didaktik und Methodik eines neuen Mediums*. Munich: Langenscheidt-Longman, 1999.

VOIGTS-VIRCHOW, Eckart: *Männerphantasien: Introspektion und gebrochene Wirklichkeitsillusion im Drama von Dennis Potter*. Trier: WVT, 1995.

WASKO, Janet (Ed.): *A Companion to Television*. Oxford: Blackwell, 2004.

6. Orality, Literacy, Memory

ASSMANN, Aleida & Jan: "Das Gestern im Heute. Medien und soziales Gedächtnis." In: MERTEN, SCHMIDT & WEISCHENBERG 1994, pp. 114–140.

ASSMANN, Jan: *Das kulturelle Gedächtnis: Schrift, Erinnerung und politische Identität in frühen Hochkulturen*. Munich: Beck, 1992.

ASSMANN, Aleida: "Zur Mediengeschichte des kulturellen Gedächtnisses." In: ERLL/NÜNNING 2004, pp. 45–60.

DEFRANCIS, John: *The Chinese Language: Fact and Fantasy*. Honolulu: University of Hawai'i Press, 1984.

DE KERCKHOVE, Derrick: *Schriftgeburten. Vom Alphabet zum Computer*. Munich: Fink, 1995. [*La civilisation video-chretienne*, 1990].

EASTHOPE, Antony: *Englishness and National Culture*. London, NY: Routledge, 1999.

ERLL, Astrid: "Medium des kollektiven Gedächtnisses – ein (erinnerungs-)kulturwissenschaftlicher Kompaktbegriff." In: ERLL/NÜNNING 2004, pp. 3–22.

ERLL, Astrid & Ansgar NÜNNING: *Medien des kollektiven Gedächtnisses. Konstruktivität, Historizität, Kulturspezifizität*. Berlin, New York: De Gruyter, 2004.

GOODY, Jack (Ed.): *Literacy in Traditional Societies*. Cambridge: Cambridge UP, 1968.

GOODY, Jack & Ian WATT: "Consequences of Literacy." In: GOODY 1968, pp. 27–68. [1963].

MOULTHROP, Stuart: "You Say You Want a Revolution? Hypertext and the Laws of Media." In: WARDRIP-FRUIN/MONTFORT 2003, pp. 691–704. [1993].

ONG, Walter: *Orality and Literacy*. London: Methuen, 1982.

PLATO: *Phaedrus* [355–360? B.C.], transl. Benjamin Jowett, <http://ccat.sas.upenn.edu/jod/texts/phaedrus.html> Accessed January 2004.

RUCHATZ, Jens: "Fotografische Gedächtnisse. Ein Panorama medienwissenschaftlicher Fragestellungen." In: ERLL/NÜNNING 2004, pp. 125–158.

7. New Media, Digital Media, Hypermedia, Cybercultures

AARSETH, Espen J.: *Cybertext. Perspectives on Ergodic Literature*. Baltimore: Johns Hopkins UP, 1997.

BELL, David & Barbara KENNEDY (Eds.): *The Cybercultures Reader*. London/New York: Routledge, 2000.

BELL, David: *An Introduction to Cybercultures*. London/New York: Routledge, 2001.

BÖHLER, Michael & Beat SUTER (Eds.): *Hyperfiction. Hyperliterarisches Lesebuch*. Frankfurt/Basel: Stroemfeld, 1999.

BOLTER, Jay David & Walter GRUSIN: *Remediation. Understanding New Media*. Cambridge MA: MIT Press, 1999.

BROWN, Paul: "The Ethics and Aesthetics of Image Interface." <http://www.paulbrown.com/WORDS/ETHICS.HTM> Accessed December 2004. [1994].

BUSH, Vannevar: "As We May Think." In: WARDRIP-FRUIN/MONTFORT 2003, pp. 37–47. [1945].

CHARTIER, Roger: *The Order of Books: Readers, Authors, and Libraries in Europe Between the Fourteenth and Eighteenth Centuries*.

Trans. Lydia G. Cochrane. Stanford CA: Stanford University Press, 1994.

COOVER, Robert: "Abschied vom goldenen Zeitalter." *dichtung digital – journal für digitale ästhetik.* Ed. Roberto SIMANOWSKI (2001) <http://www.dichtung-digital.com/2001/Coover-01–Feb/index.htm> Accessed January 2004.

COOVER, Robert: "The End of Books." *New York Times Book Review,* June 21 (1992), sec. 7, pp. 1, 19–21.

DINKLA, Söke: *Pioniere interaktiver Medienkunst.* Edition ZKM/Cantz: Ostfildern, 1997.

DOELKER, Christian: *Ein Bild ist mehr als ein Bild. Visuelle Kompetenz in der Multimedia-Gesellschaft.* Stuttgart 1997.

DOUGLAS, J. Yellowlees: *The End of Books – Or Books Without End? Reading Interactive Narratives.* Ann Arbor: University of Michigan Press, 2001.

FURTWÄNGLER, Frank: "'A crossword at war with a narrative'. Narrativität vs. Interaktivität in Computerspielen." In: GENDOLLA et al. 2001, pp. 369–400.

GAUNTLETT, David & Ross HORSLEY (Eds.): *Web.Studies.* 2nd ed. London: Arnold/Oxford UP, 2004.

GENDOLLA, Peter, Norbert M. SCHMITZ, Irmela SCHNEIDER, Peter M. SPANGENBERG (Eds.): *Formen interaktiver Medienkunst.* Frankfurt/Main: Suhrkamp, 2001.

GOERTZ, Lutz: "Wie interaktiv sind die Medien?" In: LEGGEWIE/BIEBER 2004, pp. 97–117. [1995].

GRAU, Oliver: *Virtuelle Kunst in Geschichte und Gegenwart. Visuelle Strategien.* Berlin: Reimer, 2001.

HAYLES, N. Katherine: *How We Became Posthuman. Virtual Bodies in Cybernetics, Literature, and Informatics.* Chicago: University of Chicago Press, 1999.

HEIBACH, Christiane: *Literatur im elektronischen Raum.* Frankfurt/Main: Suhrkamp, 2003.

LANDOW, George P.: *Hypertext. the Convergence of Contemporary Literary Theory and Technology.* London/Baltimore: Johns Hopkins UP, 1992.

LAUREL, Brenda: *Computers as Theatre.* Reading MA: Addison-Wesley, 1991.

LEGGEWIE, Claus & Christoph BIEBER (Eds.): *Interaktivität. Ein transdisziplinärer Schlüsselbegriff.* Frankfurt/Main: Campus, 2004.

MANOVICH, Lev: "New Media from Borges to HTML." In: WARDRIP-FRUIN/MONTFORT 2003, pp. 13–25.

MANOVICH, Lev: *The Language of New Media.* Cambridge MA: MIT Press, 2001.

MARESCH, Rudolf & Florian Rötzer: *Cyberhypes. Möglichkeiten und Grenzen des Internet.* Frankfurt/Main: Suhrkamp, 2001.

MERTENS, Matthias: "Computerspiele sind nicht interaktiv." In: LEGGEWIE/BIEBER 2004, pp. 272–288.

MIALL, David S.: "Trivializing or Liberating? The Limitations of Hypertext Theorizing." *Mosaic* 32.2 (1999), pp. 157–171.

MORKES, John & Jakob NIELSEN: *Concise, Scannable, and Objective: How to Write for the Web* (1997). <http://www.useit.com/papers/webwriting/writing.html.> Accessed January 2005.

MORSE, Margaret: *Virtualities: Television, Media Art, and Cyberculture.* Bloomington/Indianapolis: Indiana UP, 1998.

MURRAY, Janet H.: *Hamlet on the Holodeck. The Future of Narrative in Cyberspace.* New York: Free Press, 1997.

NAKAMURA, Lisa: "Race in/for Cyberspace: Identity Tourism and Racial Passing on the Internet." In: BELL/KENNEDY 2000, pp. 712–720.

NELSON, Theodor: "A File Structure for the Complex, the Changing, and the Indeterminate." In: WARDRIP-FRUIN/MONTFORT 2003, pp. 134–145. [1965].

PLANT, Sadie: "On the Matrix: Cyberfeminist Simulations." In: BELL/KENNEDY 2000, pp. 325–336. [1996].

POROMBKA, Stephan: *Hypertext. Zur Kritik eines digitalen Mythos.* München: Fink, 2001.

RECK, Hans Ulrich: *Mythos Medienkunst.* Köln: Walter König, 2002.

RHEINGOLD, Howard: *Smart Mobs.* Cambridge MA: Perseus Books, 2002.

RHEINGOLD, Howard: *The Virtual Community: Homesteading on the Electronic Frontier.* New York: Harper, 1993.

RYAN, Marie-Laure: *Narrative as Virtual Reality. Immersion and Interactivity in Literature and Electronic Media.* Baltimore/London: Johns Hopkins UP, 2001.

SCHWARZ, Hans Peter & Jeffrey SHAW: *Perspektiven der Medienkunst.* Edition ZKM/Cantz: Ostfildern, 1996.

SIMANOWSKI, Roberto: *Interfictions. Vom Schreiben im Netz.* Frankfurt/Main: Suhrkamp, 2002.

SNYDER, Ilana: *Page to Screen. Taking Literacy into the Electronic Era.* London & New York: Routledge, 1998.

TURKLE, Sherry: *Life on the Screen. Identity in the Age of the Internet.* New York: Simon & Schuster, 1995.

WAKEFORD, Nina: "Networking Women and Grrrls with Information/Communication Technology: Surfing Tales of the World Wide Web." In: BELL/KENNEDY 2000, pp. 350–359. [1997].

WARDRIP-FRUIN, Noah & Nick MONTFORT (Eds.): *The New Media Reader.* London/Cambridge MA: MIT Press, 2003.

WEINSTEIN, Deena & Michael: "Net Game Cameo." In: BELL/KENNEDY 2000, pp. 210–215. [1997].

WIENER, Norbert: *Cybernetics: or Control and Communications in the Animal and the Machine.* Cambridge, MA: MIT Press, 1948.

WILSON, Stephen: *Information Arts. Interactions of Art, Science, and Technology.* Cambridge MA/London: MIT Press, 2002.

WINNER, Langdon: *The Whale and the Reactor: A Search for Limits in an Age of High Technology.* Chicago: University of Chicago Press, 1986.

8. Radio, Telephone, Sound, Voice

BARNARD, Stephen: *Studying Radio.* London: Edward Arnold, 2000.

BRÄUNLEIN, Jürgen: *Ästhetik des Telefonierens.* Berlin: Wiss. Verlag Spiess, 1997.

BRÄUNLEIN, Jürgen & Bernd FLESSNER (Eds.): *Der sprechende Knochen. Perspektiven von Telefonkulturen.* Würzburg: Königshausen & Neumann, 2000.

BROOKS, John: *Telephone. The First Hundred Years.* New York: Harper & Row, 1976.

CRISELL, Andrew: *Understanding Radio.* 2nd ed. London/New York: Routledge, 1994.

CRISELL, Andrew: *Understanding Radio.* London: Methuen, 1986.

CROOK, Timothy: *Radio Drama: Theory and Practice.* London/New York: Routledge, 1999.

DE SOLA POOL, Ithiel (Ed.): *The Social Impact of the Telephone.* Cambridge, MA: MIT Press, 1977.

DRAKAKIS, John (Ed.): *British Radio Drama.* Cambridge: Cambridge UP, 1981.

FAULSTICH, Werner: *Radiotheorie: eine Studie zum Hörspiel 'The War of the Worlds' (1938) von Orson Welles.* Tübingen: Narr, 1981.

Forschungsgruppe Telefonkommunikation (Eds.): *Telefon und Gesellschaft.* 2 Vols. Berlin: Spiess, 1989.

FRANK, Armin Paul: *Das englische und amerikanische Hörspiel.* Munich: Fink, 1981.

HUTCHBY, Ian: *Conversation and Technology. From the Telephone to the Internet.* Cambridge: Polity Press, 2001.

MÜNKER, Stefan & Alexander RÖSLER (Eds.): *Telefonbuch. Beiträge zu einer Kulturgeschichte des Telefons.* Frankfurt: Suhrkamp, 2000.

PRIESSNITZ, Horst (Ed.): *Das englische Hörspiel.* Düsseldorf: Bagel, 1977.

PRIESSNITZ, Horst: *Das englische "radio play" seit 1945: Typen, themen und Formen.* Berlin: Schmidt, 1978.

RONELL, Avital: *The Telephone Book. Technology – Schizophrenia – Electric Speech.* Lincoln: University of Nebraska Press, 1989.

ZELGER, Sabine: *'Das Pferd frißt keinen Gurkensalat'. Kulturgeschichte des Telefonierens.* Wien etc.: Böhlau, 1997.

9. Visual Studies

ALLOULA, Malek: *The Colonial Harem.* Minneapolis: Minnesota University Press, 1986.

ARNHEIM, Rudolf: *Art and Visual Perception: The Psychology of the Creative Eye.* New Version. Berkely: University of California Press, 1974.

BALSAMO, Anne: "On the Cutting Edge: Cosmetic Surgery and the Technical Production of the Gendered Body." In: MIRZOEFF 2002, pp. 685–695. [1992].

BAUDELAIRE, Charles: "On Photography [Salon de 1859: Le public moderne et la photographie.]" In: *Charles Baudelaire. The Mirror of Art.* Ed. & transl.: Jonathan MAYNE. London: Phaidon, 1955. [1859].

BERGER, John: *Ways of Seeing.* Harmondsworth/London: Penguin/BBC, 1972.

BLOOM, Lisa: "Gender, Race and Nation in Japanese Contemporary Art and Criticism." In: MIRZOEFF 2002, pp. 215–226.

BOEHM, Gottfried (Ed.): *Was ist ein Bild?* Munich: Fink, 1994.

BROSCH, Renate: *Krisen des Sehens. Henry James und die Veränderung der Wahrnehmung im 19. Jahrhundert*. Tübingen: Stauffenburg, 2000.

CARTWRIGHT, Lisa: "Film and the Digital in Visual Studies: Film Studies in the Era of Convergence." In: MIRZOEFF 2002, pp. 417–432.

CHANDLER, Daniel: "Visual Perception" [1997] <http://www.aber.ac.uk/media/Modules/MC10220/visindex.html> Accessed September 2004.

CUBITT, Sean: *Videography. Video Media as Art and Culture*. Basingstoke/London: Macmillan, 1993.

FASSLER, Manfred: *Bildlichkeit. Navigationen durch das Repertoire der Sichtbarkeit*. Wien, Köln, Weimar: Böhlau/UTB, 2002.

FOSTER, Hal (Ed.): *Vision and Visuality*. Seattle: Bay, 1988.

FOUCAULT, Michel: "Of Other Spaces." In: MIRZOEFF 2002, pp. 229–236.

FUSCO, Coco: "The Other History of Intercultural Performance." In: MIRZOEFF 2002: pp. 556–564. [1995].

GEIER, Manfred: *Fake: Ein Leben in künstlichen Welten. Mythos, Literatur, Wissenschaft*. Reinbek/Hamburg: Rowohlt, 1999.

GOMBRICH, Ernst: *Art and Illusion. A Study in the Psychology of Pictorial Representation*. London: Phaidon, 1972. [1960].

GREEN-LEWIS, Jennifer: *Framing the Victorians: Photography and the Culture of Realism*. Ithaca NY/London: Cornell UP, 1996.

GREGORY, Richard L.: *Eye and Brain: The Psychology of Seeing*. 4th ed. Oxford: Oxford University Press, 1998.

HANHARDT, John G. (Ed.): *Video Culture. A Critical Investigation*. Visual Studies Workshop Press, 1986.

HARAWAY, Donna: "A Cyborg Manifesto: Science, Technology, and Socialist-Feminism in the Late 20th Century." In: WARDRIP-FRUIN/MONTFORT 2003, pp. 516–551. [1985].

HARAWAY, Donna: "The Persistence of Vision." In: MIRZOEFF 2002, pp. 677–684. [1991].

HÜTTER, Hans Walter: *Bilder, die Lügen*. Bonn: Bouvier, 2000.

JAY, Martin: *Downcast Eyes: The Denigration of Vision in Twentieth-Century French Thought*. Berkeley, CA: University of California Press, 1993.

JAY, Martin: "Scopic Regimes of Modernity." In: *Vision and Visuality: Discussions in Contemporary Culture*. Ed.: Hal FOSTER. Seattle: Bay Press, 1988, pp. 3–23.

JONES, Amelia: "Dispersed Subjects and the Demise of the 'Individual': 1990s Bodies in/as Art." In: MIRZOEFF 2002, pp. 696–710. [1998].

KLARER, Mario: *Ekphrasis: Bildbeschreibung als Repräsentationstheorie bei Spenser, Sidney, Lyly und Shakespeare*. Buchreihe der Anglia 35. Tübingen: Niemeyer, 2001.

LEWIS, Reina: "Looking Good: The Lesbian Gaze and Fashion Imagery." In: MIRZOEFF 2002, pp. 654–668. [1997].

McCLINTOCK, Anne: "Soft-Soaping Empire: Commodity Racism and Imperial Advertising." In: MIRZOEFF 2002, pp. 506–518. [1994].

MIRZOEFF, Nicholas (Ed.): *The Visual Culture Reader*. 2nd ed. London/New York: Routledge, 2002.

MIRZOEFF, Nicholas: *Introduction to Visual Culture*. London/New York: Routledge, 1999.

MITCHELL, J. W. T.: "Showing Seeing: A Critique of Visual Culture." In: MIRZOEFF, 2002, pp. 86–101.

MITCHELL, J. W. T.: *Picture Theory. Essays on Verbal and Visual Representation*. Chicago: University of Chicago Press, 1994.

MITCHELL, J. W. T.: *Iconology. Image, Text, Ideology*. Chicago/London: University of Chicago Press, 1986.

MULVEY, Laura: "Visual Pleasure and Narrative Cinema." In: *Screen* 16.3 (1975), pp. 6–18.

NEGRA, Diane (Ed.): *The Irish in Us: Irishness, Performativity, and Popular Culture*. Durham NC: Duke UP, 2005.

OGUIBE, Olu: "Photography and the Substance of the Image." In: MIRZOEFF 2002, pp. 565–583. [1996].

RÖMER, Stefan: *Künstlerische Strategien des Fake: Kritik von Original und Fälschung*. Köln: DuMont, 2001.

ROSCOE, Jane & Craig HIGHT: *Faking It: Mock-Documentary and the Subversion of Factuality*. Manchester: MUB, 2001.

RUTHVEN, Kenneth K.: *Faking Literature*. Cambridge: Cambridge UP, 2001.

SMITH, Terry: "Visual Regimes of Colonization." In: MIRZOEFF 2002, pp. 483–494.

SONTAG, Susan: *On Photography*. New York: Picador, 2001 [1976].

STACEY, Jackie: *Star Gazing: Hollywood Cinema and Female Spectatorship*. London: Routledge, 1994.

STURKEN, Marita & Lisa CARTWRIGHT: *Practices of Looking. An Introduction to Visual Culture*. Oxford: Oxford UP, 2001.

TURNER, John S.: "Collapsing the Interior/ Exterior Distinction: Surveillance, Spectacle, and Suspense in Popular Cinema." *Wide Angle* 20.4 (1998), pp. 93–123.

WAUGH, Thomas: "The Third Body: Patterns in the Construction of the Subject in the Gay Male Narrative Film." In: MIRZOEFF 2002, pp. 636–653. [1993].

10. Study and Career Guides

GAVIN-KRAMER, Karin: *Studienführer Journalistik, Kommunikations- und Medienwissenschaften*. 4th ed. Würzburg: Krick/Lexika, 2003.

NAUMANN, Christiane: *Sprung in die Zukunft: Mit Medien- und Kommunikationsberufen zum Erfolg*. Stuttgart: DVA, 1999.

NÜNNING, Ansgar & Andreas H. JUCKER: *Orientierung Anglistik/Amerikanistik – Was sie kann, was sie will*. Reinbek: Rowohlt, 1999.

SCHMIDT, Siegfried J. & Guido ZURSTIEGE: *Orientierung Kommunikationswissenschaft: Was sie kann, was sie will*. Reinbek b. Hamburg: Rowohlt, 2000.

11. Web Resources

(Cautionary note: information in this section – correct as of this book's going to print – is, however, subject to rapid change)

An accurate, detailed and comprehensive overview is supplied by Mick UNDERWOOD's Communication, Cultural and Media Studies Infobase (University of Queensland): http://www.ccms-infobase.com/

Another recommendation is Daniel CHANDLER's site at the University of Wales, Aberystwyth: http://www.aber.ac.uk/media/index.html

The *Media Guardian* provides reliable up-to-date information on the media and communications scene in the UK: http://media.guardian.co.uk/

An introductory overview on communication studies, based on E.M. GRIFFIN: *A First Look at Communication Theory*. Fifth Edition. McGraw Hill, 2000: http://www.ucalgary.ca/~dhoward/COMS201/

The Chicago School of Media Theory is currently building its Media HyperAtlas – the site includes a media studies web glossary completed by students: http://chicagoschoolmediatheory.net/projectsglossary.htm

Useful jump pages are maintained in various departments of communication studies, such as: http://www.uiowa.edu/~commstud/resources/ http://www.trinity.edu/mkearl/commun.html

David FISHER *(Screen Digest)* has compiled a comprehensive media timeline available at: http://www.terramedia.co.uk

Lively site maintained by David GAUNTLETT (University of Bournemouth), which sports the famous Theory Trading Cards: http://theoryhead.com/

A good jump page, particularly for German sites, is maintained by the *Deutsche Gesellschaft für Publizistik und Kommunikationswissenschaft*: http://www.dgpuk.de

KOLOSS, a DFG-sponsored German overview on communication studies (a companion to KRALLMANN/ZIEMANN's introduction) is located at Essen University: http://www.kowi.uni-essen.de/koloss/

Wolfgang BOCK provides an image gallery to accompany his *Bild – Schrift – Cyberspace* (Aisthesis): www.aisthesis.de/wbock/medien.html

The British Film Institute, good links on sources on British film and TV: http://www.bfi.org.uk

The BFI also supports the UK Media Education website can be found at: http://www.mediaed.org.uk/

A US site which monitors worldwide media: http://www.mediachannel.org

Manfred JAHN's excellent site on film narratology, English Department, University of Cologne: http://www.uni-koeln.de/~ame02/pppf.htm

Media History Project (including timeline), from the School of Journalism & Mass

Communication, University of Minnesota:
http://www.mediahistory.umn.edu/index2.html

A promising online journal of television and media studies is *Flow,* hosted by the University of Texas at Austin:
http://idg.communication.utexas.edu/flow/

Statistics

Statistics only provide a temporary glimpse of changing media habits, they go out of date the moment they are released, and they do not tell us what exactly people do with the media. If anything, constructivism teaches us to automatically distrust the heuristic function of models and empirical data. Up-to-date statistics may be available from the Net. Useful sites include:

Lippincott Library Research Guides at the University of Pennsylvania. They provide good jump pages for media and telecommunications information:
http://gethelp.library.upenn.edu/guides/business/

The US Census Bureau provides annual statistics for communications:
http://www.census.gov/svsd/www/ascs.html

For the UK communications industry and other data:
http://www.statistics.gov.uk/

ITU (International Telecommunication Union): A UN organisation with online statistics
http://www.itu.int/home/

Veronis Suhler Stevenson: Media Merchant Bank, publishes the annual Communication Industry Forecast (USA)
http://www.veronissuhler.com/